MUSIC NOTATION IN THE TWENTIETH CENTURY

A Practical Guidebook

Music Notation in the Twentieth Century

A Practical Guidebook
by **KURT STONE**

W. W. NORTON & COMPANY
New York   London

Music typography by Melvin Wildberger

Layout by Edwina Gluck

Copyright © 1980 by W. W. Norton & Company, Inc.
Published simultaneously in Canada by George J. McLeod Limited, Toronto.
Printed in the United States of America.
All Rights Reserved
First Edition
ISBN 0 393 95053

Library of Congress Cataloging in Publication Data
Stone, Kurt.
  Music notation in the twentieth century.
  Includes index.
  1. Musical notation. I. Title.
MT35.S87   781′.24′0904   79-23093

1 2 3 4 5 6 7 8 9 0

To my wife

Contents

Preface   *xiii*

Introduction   *xv*

Acknowledgments   *xxi*

Part One: Basic Procedures   *1*

I. *General Conventions*   2

ABBREVIATIONS AND SYMBOLS   *3*

ARPEGGIO   *3*

ARTICULATION   *4*

BARLINES   *6*

BEAMS   *9*

DYNAMICS   *16*

GLISSANDOS   *19*

GRACE NOTES   *21*

HORIZONTAL LINES   *22*

INSTRUCTIONS   *26*

IRREGULAR NOTE DIVISIONS:

   GRAPHIC CONSIDERATIONS   *26*

LEGER LINES   *30*

NOTE-HEADS   *30*

PLACEMENT OF DYNAMICS AND OTHER

   VERBAL INDICATIONS   *31*

REPEATS   *33*

RUNNING-HEADS   *35*

SLURS AND TIES:

   PHRASING/BOWING/BREATHING   *35*

SPACINGS, POSITIONS, AND SIZES

   (MISCELLANEOUS)   *44*

STEMS   *47*

II. *Pitch*   52

ACCIDENTALS   *53*

CLEFS   *56*

CLUSTERS   *57*

GLISSANDOS   *63*

HARMONICS   *65*

HIGHEST/LOWEST NOTE(S)   *65*

INDETERMINATE OR APPROXIMATE

   PITCHES   *66*

MICROTONES   *67*

TRANSPOSITIONS   *71*

TRILL/TREMOLO/VIBRATO   *74*

TRILLS AND TRILL TREMOLOS   *75*

UNISONS   *78*

UNPITCHED NOTES: PLACEMENT   *79*

VIBRATO/NON VIBRATO   *80*

III. *Duration and Rhythm: Preliminary Survey* 81

PREFATORY NOTE *81*

RHYTHMIC TRENDS IN
TWENTIETH-CENTURY MUSIC AND THEIR
NOTATIONAL CONSEQUENCES *82*

BEAMING *110*

PRACTICAL EXAMPLES *115*

IV. *Duration and Rhythm: Individual Items* 123

BEAMED ACCELERANDO AND
RITARDANDO *124*

DOTTED NOTES *125*

DURATIONAL EQUIVALENTS *127*

FERMATAS, COMMAS, AND DOUBLE
STROKES *128*

HEMIOLA *129*

IRREGULAR NOTE DIVISIONS *129*

RESTS *133*

SPATIAL OR PROPORTIONAL
NOTATION *136*

TEMPO INDICATIONS *145*

TIES *146*

TIME SIGNATURES (METER) *146*

TREMOLOS *147*

V. *Indeterminate Events* 152

ALTERNATIVE EVENTS *152*

CHOICES *153*

INDETERMINATE REPEATS *154*

VI. *Scores and Parts* 158

CONDUCTOR'S SIGNS *158*

CUES *160*

GROUP STEMS *162*

PARTS: MISCELLANEOUS DETAILS *162*

PARTS: DIVISI (TWO OR MORE PARTS ON A
SINGLE STAFF) *164*

REHEARSAL LETTERS/REHEARSAL
NUMBERS/MEASURE NUMBERS *168*

SCORE SETUPS *170*

SOLO/TUTTI INDICATIONS *175*

TIME SIGNATURES: PLACEMENT *177*

Part Two: Specific Notation 185

VII. *Wind Instruments: General Topics* 186

AIR SOUND OR BREATHY SOUND *186*

BENDING THE PITCH *187*

FLUTTER TONGUE *188*

HUMMING WHILE PLAYING *188*

TONGUING *188*

UNPITCHED SOUNDS *190*

VIII. *Woodwinds*   *191*

AIR PRESSURE   *191*

EMBOUCHURES (LIP POSITIONS)   *192*

HARMONICS   *192*

KEY SLAPS   *192*

MULTIPHONICS   *193*

MUTED   *195*

OCTAVE SIGN   *195*

SMACKING SOUND OR ''KISS''   *195*

SUB TONE (CLARINETS)   *195*

TRILLS (OTHER THAN CONVENTIONAL)   *196*

IX. *Brasses*   *197*

''CRACKED'' TONE   *197*

FINGERING   *198*

FINGERNAILS   *198*

GROWL   *199*

HALF VALVE   *199*

HORN TRANSPOSITIONS   *199*

MOUTHPIECE POP (HAND POP)   *200*

MUTES   *200*

RIP   *202*

SMACKING SOUND OR ''KISS''   *203*

TIMBRAL TRILL   *203*

TONGUE POSITIONS (FOR CHANGES IN TIMBRE)   *204*

VALVE CLICK   *204*

X. *Percussion*   *205*

INSTRUMENT ABBREVIATIONS AND PICTOGRAMS   *205*

STICK, MALLET, AND BEATER PICTOGRAMS   *210*

RANGES OF PERCUSSION INSTRUMENTS WITH DEFINITE PITCH   *213*

SCORE ORDER FOR INSTRUMENT FAMILIES AND MIXED ENSEMBLES   *215*

GENERAL PRACTICES   *219*

EFFECTS AND TECHNIQUES   *221*

XI. *Harp*   *226*

PRELIMINARY REMARKS   *228*

ARPEGGIO/NON ARPEGGIO   *228*

BENDING THE PITCH   *229*

BISBIGLIANDO (WHISPERING)   *229*

CLUSTERS   *231*

DAMPING/MUFFLING (ÉTOUFFER)   *231*

FINGERNAIL BUZZ   *235*

FINGERNAIL PLUCKING   *235*

GLISSANDOS   *236*

HALF PEDAL   *239*

HARMONICS   *239*

LAISSER VIBRER (L.V.): LET VIBRATE   *240*

MUTING   *240*

PEDAL NOISE   *242*

PEDAL SLIDE   *243*

PEDAL TRILL   *243*

PEDALS   *244*

PLACEMENT OF PLAYING INDICATIONS   *246*

PLECTRUM   *246*

RANGE   *246*

SCORDATURA (ABNORMAL TUNING)   *246*

SLAP PIZZICATO   *247*

SOUNDING BOARD   *248*

STRIKING THE BODY OR THE SOUNDING
  BOARD *248*
STRIKING THE STRINGS *249*
STRUMMING *250*
TOP (UPPER ENDS OF STRINGS) *250*
TREMOLOS *250*
TRILLS *251*
TRILLING (VIBRATING) BETWEEN TWO
  STRINGS *251*

TUNING-KEY SLIDES *251*
VERTICAL LOCATIONS ON THE
  STRINGS *252*
VIBRATO *253*
WHISTLING SOUNDS: FINGERNAIL
  SCRAPES *253*
WHISTLING SOUNDS: HAND SLIDES *255*

XII. *Piano*   *257*

BRACES AND BARLINES *257*
CLUSTERS *259*
CROSSING OF HANDS *260*
HARMONICS *261*
INSIDE THE PIANO *262*

PEDALS *269*
SILENT DEPRESSION OF KEYS *272*
STACCATO REVERBERATIONS *272*
TIED NOTES FROM ONE HAND TO THE
  OTHER *273*

XIII. *Organ*   *274*

BRACES AND BARLINES *274*
CLUSTERS *274*
KEYS (HELD AND RELEASED) *274*
MANUALS *277*

PEDALS *278*
REGISTRATION *278*
STOPS *279*

XIV. *Keyboard Reductions*   *281*

CHORAL SCORES *281*

ORCHESTRA SCORES *289*

XV. *Voice*   *292*

ASPIRATION *292*
BEAMS VERSUS FLAGS *293*
FALSETTO *293*
FLUTTER TONGUE *293*
HIGHEST NOTE/LOWEST NOTE *294*
INHALE/EXHALE *295*
INTERPRETIVE MARKINGS (ARTICULATION,
  DYNAMICS, EXPRESSION MARKS) *295*

MOUTH POSITIONS *295*
NASAL VOICE *296*
PHONETICS *296*
PORTAMENTO *296*
SLURS *296*
SPRECHGESANG, SPRECHSTIMME,
  SPOKEN *297*
TEXT PLACEMENT UNDER THE MUSIC *299*

TEXT PRESENTATION *300*
TREMOLOS *301*
UNVOICED VOCAL EFFECTS *303*

VIBRATO/NON VIBRATO *304*
WHISPERING *304*

XVI. *Bowed String Instruments*   *306*

PRELIMINARY NOTE *306*
ABBREVIATIONS *307*
BODY OF INSTRUMENT *307*
BRIDGE *308*
CHORDS *309*
DAMPING (ÉTOUFFER) *310*
DOUBLE STOPS *310*

FINGERING WITHOUT BOWING *311*
FINGERNAIL FLICK *311*
HARMONICS *311*
MUFFLING *312*
PIZZICATO *312*
SLAPPING THE STRINGS *315*
TAILPIECE *315*

XVII. *Taped (Prerecorded) Sound*   *316*

ELECTRONIC NOTATION *316*
CUING OF TAPED SOUNDS *317*

CONTINUOUS VERSUS INTERRUPTED
TAPE *320*

Appendix I: Neumatic Notation (Plainchant or Gregorian Chant)
and Later Developments   *321*

Appendix II: The History and Operation of the Index of New
Musical Notation and the International Conference on New
Musical Notation   *332*

Appendix III: Facsimile Reproductions   *341*

Bibliography   *343*

Index   *345*

Preface

When composers of serious music, in the early 1950s, began to explore areas far beyond all traditional concepts, conventional notation soon proved insufficient for dealing adequately with the new musical techniques and philosophies. The invention of new notational signs and procedures thus became imperative.

As the musical experiments and innovations continued and spread, new notational devices proliferated. Moreover, experiments conducted simultaneously in different parts of the world often brought forth identical signs for different effects, and vice versa.

After two decades of this disconcerting and ever-increasing deluge of new notation, invariably accompanied by endless explanations and more or less idiosyncratic instructions, communications from composer to performer had become seriously impaired. It seemed the right time to take stock, examine the new inventions for clarity and efficiency in practical use, select the devices that appeared most universally satisfactory, eliminate duplications, and codify the results in a practical guidebook.

In 1970, I proposed this plan to a number of individuals and organizations. As a result, the *Index of New Musical Notation* was established, under my direction, in the Music Division of the Library of the Performing Arts at Lincoln Center, New York. (For details, see the Introduction and Appendix 2.)

The Index project was funded by the Rockefeller Foundation (with the New York Public Library as sponsoring organization) and later also by the Ford Foundation (with the Music Library Association as sponsor).

The resulting efforts culminated in an International Conference on New Musical Notation, organized jointly by the Index project and the University of Ghent, Belgium. At the conference, which was held in Ghent in 1974, eighty professional musicians, composers, music editors, and musicologists from seventeen countries scrutinized and discussed close to 400 selected notational signs and procedures presented by the Index project, and then voted on them. The present book contains, as its nucleus, all those devices endorsed or recommended at that conference, along with a comprehensive, integrated presentation of traditional notation, based on more than thirty years of editorial experience in the field. Thus, virtually the entire arsenal of notation, old and new, of serious music in the twentieth century is covered by this guidebook.

Introduction

New Music and New Notation

New notation has never been generated exclusively by new musical ideas. New ideas are an integral part of composed music, at least in Western civilization, and notational procedures have generally been sufficiently adaptable to cope with them.

Only a fundamental break with established musical aesthetics and philosophies can bring about a commensurate notational change, and such profound upheavals have occurred extremely rarely. In fact, there have been only three in all of Western music history.

The first of these basic reorientations was the momentous shift from monody to polyphony around A.D. 900. The notational consequences were epochal: the vagueness of neumatic pitch notation was rendered obsolete and was replaced with the intervallic precision of staff notation. And perhaps even more important, the specificity of durations was introduced: mensural notation. Both of these innovations have remained indispensable elements of music notation ever since.

Centuries went by during which the linear predominance of early polyphony gradually saw itself challenged by emerging vertical phenomena: chords and chord progressions. During the fifteenth and sixteenth centuries, a perfect balance of the horizontal and vertical forces was achieved; but around the year 1600, chordal harmony took on a life of its own by becoming an independent functional force capable of dominating the linear elements that had previously reigned supreme.

Now the traditional partbooks, being purely linear, were no longer appropriate, since they failed to capture the essence of the new music, the harmonic functions. Thus the second major notational change came about: partbooks were superseded by score notation because a score, showing all parts underneath each other, enables the reader to follow not only the horizontal (melodic, linear) aspects of a given composition, but also the vertical (harmonic) ones.

In the 1950s the third stylistic upheaval began to erupt, an upheaval which developed in two sharply contrasting directions. One of these was characterized by an unprecedented increase in precision of every conceivable component of a musical texture, with particular emphasis on formerly subsidiary elements such as dynamics, timbre, pitch inflections (microtones), location of sound sources, and so forth. This trend also went far beyond the traditional note values, often superseding the conventional geometric progression of 1, 2, 4, 8, 16, 32 . . . with the arithmetical 1, 2, 3, 4, 5. . . . Needless to say, traditional notation could not cope with these new demands, and a host of new symbols and procedures had to be devised to accommodate the new musical concepts.

The other stylistic trend rejected precision. Instead, it introduced deliberate ambiguity, varying degrees of indeterminacy, choices between alternatives, improvisation, and the utilization of extraneous, unpredictable sounds and circumstances. All these required radically new notation, even to the abandonment of conventional symbols and procedures altogether, in favor of "implicit graphics," because such graphics assure the greatest possible interpretive freedom by drawing heavily on the performers' contributive imagination and ingenuity. Naturally, this trend not only called for new notational signs, but for an entirely new attitude toward notation as such.

Considering that composers throughout Europe and America, as well as in several countries of Asia, embraced the new musical trends and aesthetics, it is not surprising that new notation, too, was invented everywhere with great abandon. As a result, musicians were soon engulfed in a chaotic deluge of notational duplications, contradictions, and general confusion.

After about a decade of this anarchic proliferation, attempts were made to unravel the notational maze by collecting, describing, and categorizing the new signs.*

The most comprehensive of these efforts was Erhard Karkoschka's *Das Schriftbild der neuen Musik* (Celle, 1966; English translation—*Notation in New Music*—London and New York, 1972). Here we find the first major attempt to classify not only the new signs, but also the underlying aesthetic approaches. In addition there are evaluations of the various signs as to appropriateness, clarity (or deliberate vagueness), and efficiency, and each sign is meticulously documented as to its source of origin.

Other collections followed. The most extensive American one is Howard Risatti's *New Music Vocabulary* (1975, University of Illinois Press) and the monumental, as yet unpublished, *20th Century Notation* by Gardner Read.

All of these collections differ from one another in many ways, but they all have one thing in common: whatever recommendations they contain represent the personal opinions of their respective authors.

The present book—*Music Notation in the Twentieth Century*—is unique in three crucial ways:

1. it is not a collection, but a compendium of selections;

2. these selections do not represent one person's preferences, but are the results of research done by the Index of New Musical Notation (a four-year

---

* One such early treatise was the author's own "Problems and Methods of Notation," written in 1962 (see Bibliography).

project) followed by the deliberations and decisions of the International Conference on New Musical Notation (Ghent, Belgium, 1974);

3. it does not treat new notation as a phenomenon apart from traditional procedures, but integrates it into the total notational vocabulary of all serious music written in the twentieth century.

The Index of New Musical Notation and the International Conference on New Musical Notation

In the early 1950s, when the first published examples of new musical notation arrived from Europe, the author was chief editor of Associated Music Publishers, Inc., New York, then the foremost American importer of European music. The names of the new composers were still quite unfamiliar, but soon they were to dominate the field: for example, Luciano Berio, Pierre Boulez, Sylvano Bussotti, Roman Haubenstock-Ramati, Karlheinz Stockhausen. Shortly thereafter, similar American efforts appeared, mainly in the works of Earle Brown* and John Cage.

The author became interested in these unprecedented manifestations, studied and compared them, attended countless rehearsals and performances to find out how they worked in actual practice, and eventually began to lecture and write about new notational developments.

Writing and lecturing, however, were only one side of the coin. A much less entertaining aspect was that the new notational deluge proved to be a serious hindrance to good performances. Many musicians who had been greatly interested in new music began to resent the ever increasing profusion of notational ambiguities, identical notation for different effects in different compositions, and totally unexplained signs and procedures. Rehearsal time, being expensive, was limited, and performances were (and still are) all too often under-rehearsed and far from what they should have been. Something had to be done.

In the author's view, the most appropriate position in the musical spectrum from which to effect practical improvements is that of the music editor. An editor serves as the mediator between the composer who invents new notation and the performer who must interpret it properly. A conscientious editor, one who involves himself in the musical aspects of the scores under his care, can bring the performers' need for greater notational clarity to the attention of the composer and collaborate with him toward this goal. Conversely, he can elucidate to the performer some of the composer's intentions and visions which may not be fully realized in the notation. Musical notation, after all, is not an ideal method of communication, utilizing, as it does, visual devices to express aural concepts. But it is all we have.

---

* Actually, Earle Brown's efforts in this direction preceded Stockhausen's, even though the latter generally is credited with being the originator of new notational procedures.

An editor's scope, however, is limited, since he deals primarily with the works of composers who happen to be in the catalogue of his particular publishing house. To overcome this proscription, the author initiated the Index of New Musical Notation and located it in the Music Division of the Library of the Performing Arts at New York's Lincoln Center, a context independent of any publishing interests. This enabled the staff of the Index project to examine *any* score considered pertinent.

After conducting detailed notational analyses of a large variety of music containing graphic innovations, and after categorizing and otherwise ordering the findings, about 400 signs and procedures, chosen by statistical and evaluative methods, were submitted for discussion to the active participants of an International Conference on New Musical Notation, organized jointly by the Index project and the Belgian State University at Ghent, and held there in October of 1974.*

All new notational devices and procedures endorsed or recommended by the Ghent Conference are included in the present volume, along with many others which could not be discussed in Ghent, but were dealt with subsequently in consultation with professional musicians in the U.S.

On the Inclusion of Traditional Notation

In spite of the new notational signs generated since the early 1950s, a major part of our era's music, whether "serious" or not, has been, still is, and probably will continue to be written either entirely by means of traditional notation or with a mixture of old and new signs and procedures. It is for this reason that traditional notation has been included in this guidebook.

Elementary rules and practices, however, will not be found here. It is assumed that those who wish to use this book are familiar with the rudiments of traditional notation. What has been admitted are the less obvious features: matters of proper beaming, stemming, and spacing, irregular durational divisions, the proper position of marks of articulation, dynamics, and phrasing, the correct note values for tremolos, and even a few purely graphic fine points. In the past, such details were rarely if ever taught, but in the music of our era they have become increasingly important for two quite separate reasons.

First, since music during the last few decades has grown to unprecedented complexity, in addition to operating according to many new and radically unconventional aesthetic concepts, notation—old and new—has been strained to its utmost capability to meet these challenges. Consequently, each and every notational symbol must be drawn with greater precision and consistency than used to be necessary, because in present-day music any graphic deviation from convention may constitute not simply an accidental flaw, but a deliberate and meaning-

---

* For details of the operation of the Index project and the International Conference, see Appendix 2.

ful variant! In other words, awkward or amateurish imperfections—irregularities which were hardly noticed in former times—have become serious impediments to a clear and proper interpretation of new compositions. One should never forget that notation is the composer's only means of conveying his ideas to the performers: it must be as explicit as possible. (Even if ambiguity or total freedom is intended, the signal for it must be explicit.)

Second, music publishers, for economic reasons, are increasingly given to issuing facsimile reproductions of the composer's manuscript, rather than engraved (or equivalent) editions. It is not at all infrequent, therefore, that a publisher, in determining whether to publish a work or not, will be influenced by the graphic quality and notational professionalism of a manuscript, rather than exclusively by its musical content.*

Performers, too, look more closely now at composers' ways with notation, since any unconventionality is likely to divert a performer's attention from instant perception and interpretation of the notation he sees before him. Even if he is not actually aware of what is wrong with the notation he sees—what the irregularities and flaws really consist of—he will react subconsciously to any visual difference from the standards which have conditioned his reflexes throughout his musical life. He is forced to make adjustments and corrections in his mind during the minute interval between perceiving the symbol and producing the desired effect. It can make him hesitate, even a little, and can slow down the process of learning a piece, thus quite possibly leading to a poorer performance than needs be.

To sum up, then, the meticulous observance of the rules and conventions of traditional notation (rules often ignored by, or not even known to many composers and performers) will increase the effectiveness of a composer's entire notational repertory, old and new. And thus it will improve his ability to communicate his intentions to the performer, which will most certainly result in better, more accurate, and more enjoyable performances.

The traditional rules and conventions included here have not been treated separately from the new notational signs and procedures. Most of them, however, appear within the first section of the book, which covers general categories of notation, and only occasionally in the second section, which deals with notation for specific instrument families, the voice, and electronic sounds.

---

* See Facsimile Reproductions, Appendix 3.

Acknowledgments

Most of what is contained in the present book cannot be credited to any particular individual, being the result of the efforts of everyone who worked at the Index project, all the active participants in the Ghent Conference, and the countless composers, arrangers, performers, engravers, autographers, copyists, and fellow editors whom the author has encountered in the course of his long career as a music editor.

A few people, however, who were not connected with the Index, but who helped greatly with the shaping of the present book and with many of its details, must not be overlooked. From among these I would like to single out the following, listed in the order in which their particular specialties appear in the book:

Woodwinds: Nora Post, New York oboist, for her meticulous scrutiny of many technical details.

Percussion: Frank L. McCarty, percussionist, electronicist, and composer, who helped prepare the Index's percussion and electronics proposals for the Ghent Conference, and who, beyond this, gave the author eminently helpful advice whenever called upon.

Harp: Thanks go to three harpists: Shirley Blankenship, of the University of Illinois at Urbana, for a thorough preliminary discussion of modern harp techniques and harp literature (a field, by the way, which had not been included in the Ghent discussions); Alyssa N. Hess, New York harpist and composer, for her invaluable assistance with every detail of the entire harp chapter (it is largely due to her recommendations that this chapter became as comprehensive as it has turned out to be); Patricia John, harpist from Houston, Texas, for reading through the completed harp chapter and making many valuable additional suggestions.

Organ: Martha Folz, specialist in recitals of contemporary organ music, for generously sharing her experiences with the notational puzzles of many scores of new organ music.

Strings: Clifford G. Richter, violist/violinist, and his violinist wife, Lynne (both long-time editorial colleagues of the author) for contributing to the string chapter the badly needed practical realism so often ignored in more soloist-oriented treatments.

Taped (Prerecorded) Sound: Barbara English Maris, who specializes in recitals of piano music with electronic sounds and sound generators—many of them lecture recitals—for discussing with the author the cuing practices in such music, and for later reading the finished chapter and suggesting many additional practical details based on her uncommon familiarity with this elusive branch of new music.

General Assistance: Sincere thanks and appreciation to Alyssa N. Hess, the harpist mentioned above, for going through the entire book at the final stage, unfailingly spotting remaining flaws, as well as linguistic awkwardnesses; to Professor Leo Kraft (Queens College, New York) for his knowledgeable musical advice, and to Claire Brook and Hinda Keller Farber of W. W. Norton for their unusually perceptive and understanding editorial work; and last but far from least to my wife, Else, for checking the manuscript from the important vantage point of a nonprofessional music lover who insists that things must make sense no matter who the readers might be.

Musical Examples: Melvin Wildberger must be commended not only for his resourceful work, combining music typewriter, transfer type, regular type, and many additional tricks of the trade, but also for his numerous practical suggestions, many of which have been incorporated in this book.

Thanks, finally, are due to the John Simon Guggenheim Memorial Foundation for its generous fellowship grant, without which this book might never have been written.

Part One: Basic Procedures

N.B.: For looking up specific notation, the Index should be used, since some of the items are dealt with in more than one chapter.

I. *General Conventions*

Abbreviations and Symbols	3	Glissandos	19
		A. *Note-to-Note and Note-to-Rest*	
Arpeggio	3	*Glissandos*	19
A. *Arpeggio Sign*	3	B. *Open-Ended Glissandos*	20
B. *Direction*	4	C. *Curved or Undulating Glissandos*	20
C. *Rhythm*	4	D. *Quick, Short Slides (Portamento)*	20
D. *Speed*	4	E. *Compound Durations of*	
E. *Non Arpeggio*	4	*Glissandos*	21
Articulation	4	Grace Notes	21
Barlines	6	Horizontal Lines	22
A. *In Music for Individual*		A. *Staff-Lines*	22
Instruments	6	B. *Grids*	23
B. *In Chamber and Choral Scores*	7	C. *Solid Lines, Brackets, and Arrows*	23
C. *In Orchestra and Band Scores*	7	D. *Dotted or Broken Lines*	25
D. *Vertical Alignment of Barlines*	8	E. *Wavy Lines*	25
E. *Dotted Barlines*	8		
F. *Double Barlines*	8	Instructions	26
G. *Final Barlines*	9		
Repeat Bars, see page 34		Irregular Note Divisions:	
		Graphic Characteristics	26
Beams	9	A. *Brackets versus Slurs in Unbeamed*	
A. *Beam Thickness*	9	*and Partially Beamed Groups*	26
B. *Space between Beams*	9	B. *Beamed Groups*	27
C. *Beam Positions in the Staff*	9	C. *Irregular Note Divisions within*	
D. *Beams in Two-Staff Notation*	12	*Regular Groups of Notes*	28
E. *Extended and Bridging Beams*	15	D. *Irregular Note Divisions within*	
		Irregular Groups of Notes	28
Durational Equivalences		E. *Horizontal Locations of Numerals*	
see page 127		*and Brackets*	29
Dynamics	16	Leger Lines	30
A. *Dynamic Balance/Dynamic Levels*	16		
B. *Fluctuating Dynamics*	17	Note-Heads	30
C. *Levels of Prominence of Musical*		A. *Shapes*	30
Materials	17	B. *Uses of Different Shapes*	31
D. *Niente*	18		
E. *Note-Size Dynamics*	18	Placement of Dynamics and	
F. *Subito Changes of Dynamic Levels*	19	Other Verbal Indications	31

A. *Dynamics*   *31*
B. *Tempo Indications*   *32*
C. *Playing Instructions*   *32*

Placement of Rests
  see page 133

Repeats   *33*
A. *Repeated Articulation* (Simile)   *33*
B. *Repeated Chords*   *33*
C. *Repeated Measures*   *33*
D. *Repeated Pairs of Measures*   *34*
E. *Repeated Sections*   *34*

Running Heads   *35*

Slurs and Ties:
Phrasing/Bowing/Breathing   *35*

A. *The Different Meanings of Slurs*   *35*
B. *The Notation of Slurs and Ties*   *36*

Spacings, Positions, and Sizes
(Miscellaneous)   *44*
A. *Opening Measures* (*in Traditional*
   Notation)   *44*
B. *Clef Changes*   *46*
C. *Time Signature Changes*   *46*
D. *The End of a Line*   *46*
E. *Accidentals*   *46*
F. *Notes and Rests*   *46*

Stems   *47*
A. *Stem Lengths*   *47*
B. *Stem Directions*   *49*

Abbreviations and Symbols

All abbreviations included in this book appear in the pertinent sections. For other abbreviations, current music dictionaries should be consulted (see Bibliography).

Most abbreviations suggested in this guide were chosen according to the following criteria:

If possible, the abbreviation should be applicable to several major languages, such as *n.* = *niente* (Italian), *nothing* (English), or *nichts* (German).

The abbreviation must not be misleading from language to language. For example, the abbreviation of an English term must not be similar to the abbreviation of a word with a different meaning in another major language. Thus, the abbreviations *Tromb.* or *Trb.* for Trombone might confuse Italian musicians because they could mean *Tromba.* Less ambiguous choices, therefore, are *Tbn.* and *Trbn.,* which also serve (though perhaps not ideally) to convey the Italian and French terms. Similarly, *Cor.* for Cornet is too close to the French *Cor* and the Italian *Corno.* As a result, *Ct.* was chosen for the English term Cornet, and while it may not immediately convey *Kornett* to a German, it will not indicate a different instrument either.

Arpeggio

A. Arpeggio Sign

An ordinary arpeggio sign is generally taken to mean that the notes are to be rolled upward, and that the arpeggio begins before the beat, with its last note falling on the beat:

If the arpeggio is to begin on the beat, this must be indicated verbally, or the arpeggio must be written out.

B. Direction

If precise directional indications are desired, arrowheads should be added at the top or bottom, respectively, of the arpeggio sign:

If rapid successions of up and down rolls are wanted (for example, in guitar or harp music), the following arpeggio sign should be used:

C. Rhythm

Slow arpeggios and arpeggios in rhythmic patterns must be written out.

D. Speed

Arpeggios with increasing or decreasing speed are best notated with accelerando or ritardando beams:

E. Non Arpeggio

If individual arpeggio signs are replaced by the instruction *sempre arpeggio,* a vertical square bracket or the instruction *non arpeggio* must be used when the chords or intervals are to be played together again:

Articulation

The traditional signs of articulation are imprecise and progress abruptly, whether from slight to heavy accents or from staccatissimo to molto tenuto. Yet none of the numerous proposals for improvement have found wide enough acceptance so far to warrant endorsement. Traditional signs remain the most frequently employed and most universally understood, except for a few additions from Schoenberg's *Suite for Piano,* Op. 25, and other sources, intended to fill the gaps in the traditional succession:

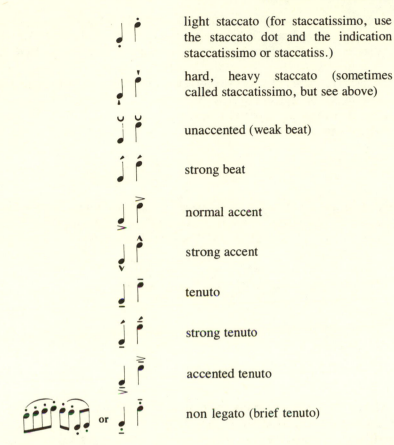

light staccato (for staccatissimo, use the staccato dot and the indication staccatissimo or staccatiss.)

hard, heavy staccato (sometimes called staccatissimo, but see above)

unaccented (weak beat)

strong beat

normal accent

strong accent

tenuto

strong tenuto

accented tenuto

non legato (brief tenuto)

The proper positions of these signs inside or outside the staff are governed by certain conventions.

The following signs should always appear outside the staff (except the tenuto lines):

The following signs depend on the note-heads or stem-ends for their positions inside or outside the staff:

*This accent almost always appears outside the staff.

Staccato dots are one or 1½ spaces from the center of the note-head, depending on whether the note-head is in a space or on a line. For note-heads outside the staff, the staccato dots should never be closer than one full staff-space from the center of the note-head.

Tenuto lines are spaced like staccato dots, and in combinations of tenuto lines and staccato dots (non legato) the distance between the dot (which is closest to the note-head) and the line is one staff-space.

In double-stemmed notation, staccato dots and tenuto lines should appear as shown:

Although accents are usually placed outside the staff, there are situations when it is necessary or desirable to place an accent inside the staff, in which case it should appear in a space rather than on a line and should never be closer to the note-head than a fourth:

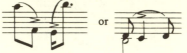 or

Articulation signs on whole notes are centered above or below the note(s), as if the notes had stems:

Articulation signs in combination with slurs and ties: see Slurs and Ties in Combination with Articulation Signs, page 42 ff.

Embouchure and tonguing indications: see Woodwinds and Brasses, pages 192 and 204.

Phrasing: see Slurs and Ties: Phrasing/Bowing/Breathing, page 35 ff.

See also the listings of the various instruments and voice for specific effects and their notation.

Barlines

A. In Music for Individual Instruments

Harp: the barlines connect both staves.

Organ: the barlines connect only the manual staves; the pedal staff is barred separately, except at the beginning of each line; there, the curved brace covers the two manual staves only, while the straight line that follows must always connect all three. (See also page 274.)

Piano: the barlines connect both staves. If more than two staves are needed, it may be advantageous to bar the right- and left-hand staves separately, the musical texture permitting. (This does not, however, affect the brace at the beginning of each line: while each of the two hands might have its own curved brace, the straight line that follows must always connect all staves.) (See also page 257 ff.)

One-staff instruments and voice: added staff-lines for unpitched or unvoiced effects should have short barlines not connected to the barlines of the pitched staff, except at the beginning of the line.

Percussion: Most individual percussion instruments, from snare drum to marimba, will fit one or another of the situations listed above.

B. In Chamber and Choral Scores

One solo (instrument or voice) with accompaniment: the solo staff should be barred separately.

More than one solo with accompaniment: each solo staff should be barred separately.

Duos, trios, quartets, etc., consisting of instruments notated on single staves (such as string quartets or woodwind quintets): all staves should be barred together. In cases of a single nonfamily member (clarinet quintets, for example), the nonmember generally is barred separately. If a piano or other two-staff instrument is included (e.g., a piano trio), it must be barred separately. In such cases the other instruments are often barred separately too.

Vocal or choral ensembles: each staff must be barred separately, although choral music is occasionally barred together when condensed onto two staff-lines (see ** below).

Percussion: since percussion groups change from piece to piece, the only general suggestion one can advance is to keep in mind the procedures listed above when deciding how to handle single-line, single-staff, and two-staff instruments, whether singly or in groups. It is generally not advisable to bar different kinds of percussion instruments, notated on separate lines, together. (For a more detailed discussion, see Percussion, page 215 ff.)

C. In Orchestra and Band Scores

Instrumental families should be barred together as follows:

Orchestra scores: woodwinds; brasses; percussion;* harp(s); keyboard(s) (each harp and/or keyboard instrument separately); instrumental solo(s);** vocal solo(s); chorus;** strings (see sample score on page 171).

Band scores: flutes and double reeds; clarinets; saxophones; brasses (sometimes subdivided); string bass; percussion* (see sample score on page 174).

---

* If there is a great deal of percussion, it should be subdivided into pitched (staff-notated) instruments and unpitched ones (those generally notated on single lines), and the barlines should show such groupings. (See also Percussion, Score Order, page 215 ff.)

** Vocal parts and instrumental solos are barred separately. If the full score includes a chorus, it is best (the musical texture permitting) to condense it onto two staves and to bar the two staves together, regardless of the barlines' possible interference with the text. Such an arrangement makes the total picture clearer for the conductor.

N.B.: Some contemporary scores contain relatively large numbers of unconventional instruments or are structured according to principles that ignore or contradict conventional concepts. These must, of course, be barred according to such unconventional instrumentations or ideas, but in general it is best, if for none other than practical reasons, to adhere to conventional setups.

D. Vertical Alignment of Barlines

An exact vertical alignment of the barlines in single-line parts and, to a lesser degree, in double- and triple-staff music (piano, harp, organ, etc.) can be confusing to performers, especially in relatively uniform-looking music. It is therefore advisable to create, if necessary, very slight irregularities in the horizontal spacing of the music so that the barlines will not fall directly above or below one another:

Poor alignment—barlines coincide

Correct alignment—barlines do not coincide

E. Dotted Barlines

Dotted barlines, ⦙ or ⦙, are used for subdividing complicated meters, such as:

and in new editions of old music to distinguish between the original barlines (solid lines) and those added by the editor (dotted lines).

F. Double Barlines (two regular barlines)

1. AT METER CHANGES

In the past, meter changes occurred so rarely that double barlines were placed before each new time signature to alert the performer. With the increase in meter changes in more recent music, this practice has largely been abandoned, and double barlines should no longer be used at meter changes.

2. AT TEMPO CHANGES

Double barlines should be used at tempo changes unless such changes occur very frequently, in which case double barlines should be used only at structurally significant divisions.

3. OTHER USES

Double barlines should be used chiefly between major sections of a movement, i.e., before and after a trio section, between variations, etc.

G. Final Barlines (one regular and one heavy barline)

These appear at the end of a composition or movement.

H. Repeat Bars (final barlines with repeat dots)

See Repeated Sections, page 34 f.

Beams

A. Beam Thickness

The thickness of a beam should be equal to half a staff-space. This is important because a musician's eye is so accustomed to this thickness (due to more than 100 years of standardized engravers' tools) that the slightest variation can inhibit perception. (Most musicians are not even aware of these minute variations; they react subconsciously.) There can be circumstances, however, which make it desirable or even necessary to reduce (never increase!) the thickness of the beams, as explained in the following paragraph.

B. Space between Beams

When two or more beams are used, the engravers' rule is that the space between beams should be a quarter of a staff-space (see the first example below). In hand-drawn (autographed) music, there is always a danger that such narrow spaces may fill in. Some autographers therefore widen the space to half a staff-space, but this is not a good solution because the beams then take up too much vertical space, especially in groups of three or more (see the second example). The best compromise is to reduce the thickness of the beams slightly (see third example) and adhere to the engravers' rule:

Good	*Poor*	*Acceptable compromise*

C. Beam Positions in the Staff

1. HORIZONTAL BEAMS

a. SINGLE BEAMS

In upstemmed groups, the beam either hangs from a line or straddles it, except when the notes are in the second space, in which case the beam lies on the top line (see *):

In downstemmed groups, the beam either lies on top of a line or straddles it, except when the notes are in the third space, in which case the beam hangs from the bottom line (see *):

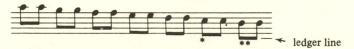

In the last pair of notes (**), the beam straddles an imaginary leger line.

N.B.: Beams should never be centered between two staff-lines, since the very narrow spaces remaining between the beam and the staff-lines are almost sure to fill in:

Incorrect

b. TWO OR MORE BEAMS

The rules for single-beam positions given above also apply to double and multiple beams: the outside (primary) beam either hangs from a staff-line (up-stems), lies on a line (downstems), or straddles a line (either stem direction). The inner (secondary) beam(s) are governed by the position of the primary beam:

Concerning the lengths of stems, see page 47 f.

2. SLANTING BEAMS
a. SINGLE BEAMS

The engravers' rules for the proper slanting angles of beams are too complex to permit inclusion in this list of general guidelines.† A widely followed compromise is to use horizontal beams most of the time, and to slant the beams only for wide skips, broken chords, and similar extreme cases. Even in these latter situations, however, the beams should slant as little as possible—not more than one staff-space—and they should slant around a staff-line

---

† For detailed information (including, for example, charts with close to 300 different two-note single-beam slants alone!) see *The Art of Music Engraving and Processing* by Ted Ross, pages 104 ff.

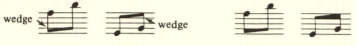, rather than from one line to another . The reason for avoiding line-to-line slants is that they form narrow triangles or wedges between the beam and the staff-lines (see left example below), which are likely to fill in (see example below, right):

Line-to-line slants   **The wedges filled in**

Note also the differences between manuscript and engravers' slants:

Manuscript slants

¼-space
slant   no slant   ½-space slant   whole-space slant

Engravers' slants

When the notes move along an irregular path, the beam should slant according to the general trend of the notes (but at a shallower angle) or not slant at all:

   or

b. DOUBLE BEAMS (TWO BEAMS)

The above also applies to double beams, especially the caveat that the space between the two slanting beams should not cross a staff-line:

Correct   *Incorrect*

c. THREE OR MORE BEAMS

Unlike the situation for horizontal beams, the spaces between three or more slanting beams are generally widened to half a staff-space to avoid wedges:

Correct   *Incorrect*

If such slanting beams occur outside the staff, normal spacing (i.e., one quarter of a staff-space between beams) is used:

3. FRACTIONAL BEAMS

Fractional beams are used for the individual shorter notes within a beamed group. They should be as long as the note-head is wide and must point toward the note of which they are a fraction, usually a dotted note:

Fractional beams also occur without complementary dotted notes:

In cases of syncopation, fractional beams must point in the direction of the syncopated note:

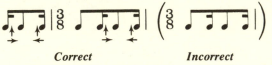

This last parenthetical notation is wrong in $\frac{3}{8}$ because the incorrectly placed first fractional beam suggests that the sixteenth is rhythmically grouped with the preceding eighth, whereas it is not. It would be correct if the time signature were binary ($\frac{6}{16}$):

For details of proper rhythmic beaming, see Duration and Rhythm, page 110 ff. For stem directions in beamed groups, see Stems, page 50.

D. Beams in Two-Staff Notation

In two-staff notation the notes of a beamed group may be placed in the upper *and* lower staff, with the beam between the staves.

1. IDENTICAL TIME-VALUES THROUGHOUT THE BEAMED GROUP

There seems to be no rule concerning the horizontal spacing of the note-heads versus that of the stems. The best procedure is to arrive by eye at a judicious compromise or disregard stem spacing altogether.

2. DIFFERENT TIME-VALUES

Shorter time-values naturally necessitate additional beams. These should be placed above or below the basic beam(s), depending on whether the note-head of the first shorter time-value points up or down. Since this notation is sometimes rather complex, the following step-by-step procedure is suggested:

The rhythm to be notated is ♩♫ , i.e., a long note followed by shorter ones (in this case two).

Step 1: write the notes and draw only the basic or primary beam:

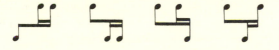

Step 2: add the additional beam above or below the basic beam on the note-head side of the first shorter value:

If Step 2 is not followed, beam corners (see circles) result, which should be avoided.

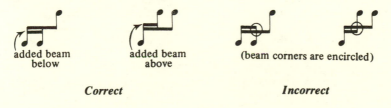

Incorrect

If a beamed group begins with short notes which are followed by longer ones, the rules become more elusive,* but one consideration persists—if possible, beam corners should be avoided, as follows:

added beam below   added beam above   (beam corners are encircled)

Correct   *Incorrect*

---

* Unlike the complex rules of beam slants, one finds practically no directions on these beaming problems in English-language manuals.

If beam corners cannot be avoided, they should appear at the end, rather than at the beginning of the faster notes:

| **Correct** | **Incorrect** |

(The arrows show the beam corners.)

Mixtures

To repeat: the rule is to avoid beam corners.

3. METRIC DIVISIONS OR BEAT-UNITS IN GROUPS OF SIXTEENTH NOTES

These are indicated by interrupting the second beam wherever the metric division occurs. When the second beam returns, the note-head position of the first note determines whether the beam should be drawn above or below the basic beam (i.e., the one which continues throughout the group):

4. METRIC DIVISIONS OR BEAT-UNITS IN GROUPS OF THREE OR MORE BEAMS

The basic beam(s) must be either on the top or bottom, rather than in the middle, in order to avoid beam corners:

| no division | connecting double beam | connecting single beam | *wrong* (beam corners are encircled) |

(For beaming in vocal music, see Voice, Beams versus Flags, page 293.) A more detailed discussion of metric/rhythmic beaming will be found in Duration and Rhythm, Beaming, page 110 ff.

E. Extended and Bridging Beams

1. SIMPLE BEAM EXTENSIONS AND BRIDGES

In music of metric/rhythmic complexity it is helpful to notate syncopated entrances (phrases beginning off the beat, or notes in off-beat position) by extending the beam(s) leftward to the nearest beat:

Similarly, if the beat-unit ends with one or more rests, the beam(s) should be extended to the right:

Finally, the beam(s) should bridge rests appearing within a beat-unit:

N.B.: The rests as well as the beams may have to be adjusted slightly up or down to prevent them from touching each other.

2. BEAM EXTENSIONS AND BRIDGES WITH STEMLETS

Everything suggested above can be notated even more clearly by adding very short stems (stemlets) to the beam extensions or bridges wherever they cover rests.

Note that rests or beams may have to be raised or lowered even more than in notation without stemlets, to assure sufficient space between rests and stemlets.

Note also that the first group of the second measure of this example can not be notated without stemlets, because this would result in unattached second beams, which is not considered proper notation:

(The following notation, all too often employed, should not be used, since it robs the beam of its proper function of indicating time-values: ⁊ ♩ ⁊ .)

The positioning of rests and the shortness of the stemlets are of particular importance in eighth rests, because their "buttons," especially if hand-drawn and slightly enlarged, may at first glance look like note-heads if they touch the stemlets:

(eighth-rest "button" too large and stemlet too long)

Correct   **Incorrect**

Stemlets in two-staff notation

3. SINGLE NOTES

A single note, especially if it occurs as the first or last note in a beat-unit, is often written traditionally, i.e., with flag(s), rather than with extended beam(s):

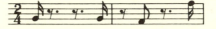

It might be more sensible, however, not to make such exceptions, and to use extended beams in all instances, as shown in the following notation of the above example:

Extended and bridging beams should either be used consistently throughout a composition, or not at all. Mixtures of extended and unextended beaming usually lead to confusion.

For the use of beams in rhythmically complex textures (polymetric, polyrhythmic, and aperiodic music, etc.) see Duration and Rhythm, Beaming, page 110 ff.

Dynamics

A. Dynamic Balance/Dynamic Levels

In the last few decades, composers have striven for greater precision in dynamics. Among the numerous experiments, two major directions are discernible:

1. ABSOLUTE DYNAMICS

Numerals indicating precise decibel levels replace the vague traditional indications. Often these numerals denote twelve different, equidistant levels.

2. INDIVIDUAL DYNAMICS

Each instrument or voice is marked according to its actual dynamic intensity, so that a flute's *forte* would equal a trumpet's *mezzo piano,* etc. This procedure has proved impractical and unrealistic in actual performance situations and has largely been abandoned. Only one innovative aspect of this technique has survived: the creation of subdivisions of the traditional levels by placing a plus sign (+) after a dynamic marking:

$$p, \; p+, \; mp, \; mp+, \; mf, \; mf+, \; f, \; f+, \; ff, \; \text{etc.}$$

(A minus sign [−] has proved less practical because it can, in certain contexts, be misread as a tenuto line, or as a hyphen.)

It is advisable, however, to use the plus sign only in the notation of electronic music, where such minute differences in dynamic levels can be achieved mechanically, with dials. Another reason for discouraging its use is that the plus sign can be misleading: a $p+$, for example, may be interpreted as "more piano," i.e., softer!

B. Fluctuating Dynamics

1. NARROW RANGE

A ± is placed after the conventional dynamic to indicate that the desired level should be more or less that of the dynamic marking. The marking should be boxed:

$$\boxed{f \; \pm}$$

It is understood that the indicated fluctuation implies growing louder and softer, rather than remaining on one particular level.

If the boxed marking is followed by crescendo and diminuendo wedges, all dynamic changes indicated by the wedges must remain within the narrow limits of the ± indication:

$$\boxed{f \; \pm} \; \Longleftarrow \Longrightarrow < \; < \; \Longleftarrow \Longrightarrow \; \boxed{p \; \pm} \; \Longleftarrow \Longrightarrow \; > \; > \; \Longleftarrow \Longrightarrow$$

2. WIDE RANGE

If a wider range of fluctuation is desired, a two-headed arrow should be placed between the upper and lower limits:

$$\boxed{pp \longleftrightarrow mf}$$

This indication may also indicate that the performer is to choose one level within the given boundaries. In such cases, the words *ad lib.* or *choice* should be placed above the box on first occurrence.

The boxed dynamics are considered cancelled as soon as an unboxed dynamic marking appears.

See also Indeterminate Events, Choices, page 153 ff.

C. Levels of Prominence of Musical Materials

Prominent or solo material should be indicated with bold angles at the beginning and at the end of the respective passages: ⌐   ¬ .

If different levels of prominence are wanted, the angles should be identified with letters (rather than with numerals, since numerals already have too many functions in musical notation):

A⌐ or ⌐**A**   ⌐ = first in prominence

B⌐ or ⌐**B**   ⌐ = second in prominence

C⌐ or ⌐**C**   ⌐ = third in prominence, etc.

N.B.: The A B C . . . system has the advantage over Schoenberg's **H** (*Hauptstimme*—principal part) and **N** (*Nebenstimme*—secondary part) in that it does not depend on any language and is not limited to two marked levels only.

D. Niente

If abbreviated, an "*n.*" should be used, rather than a zero, since the latter already has a number of other meanings:

$$n. \diagdown\!\!\!\!=== p ===\!\!\!\!\diagup n.$$

E. Note-Size Dynamics

Note-size dynamics are best suited for nontraditional, approximate notation of pitches and/or durations, where they can express a great variety and subtlety of dynamic inflections.

Large notes are louder; small notes are softer; crescendo and diminuendo effects follow the same principle:

In conventionally notated music, note-size dynamics are generally not advisable:

The following, to show but one alternative, is at least as efficient:

Placement of Dynamics: see Placement of Dynamics and Other Verbal Indications, page 31 f.

F. Subito Changes of Dynamic Levels

The rapid changes of dynamic levels, typical of the music of our era, often leave too little space for the abbreviation *sub.* A vertical stroke should be used instead:

If the abbreviation *sub.* is used, it should follow the dynamic indication rather than precede it, so that the new dynamic level will appear precisely where it is to begin:

Glissandos

There is no universal agreement concerning the ''proper'' execution of glissandos on bowed string instruments (smooth slides versus fast chains of individual pitches). If a particular interpretation is wanted it should be explained at its first appearance.

A thin, straight line should be used to indicate a glissando. It is customary to add the abbreviation *gliss.*, but this is not mandatory; the line suffices.

(To facilitate comparison, most of the following examples show the same duration [a half note] within one measure. For glissandos across a barline, see page 21.)

A. Note-to-Note and Note-to-Rest Glissandos

1. GLISSANDO ENDING IN A NOTE
The line leads to the next regular note:

2. GLISSANDO FOLLOWED BY A REST
The line ends with a small, parenthetical note-head. The small note-head is not articulated; it merely ends the glissando:

3. GLISSANDO FOLLOWED BY A SLIGHTLY SEPARATED NOTE

A small comma is placed between the end of the line and the new pitch:

B. Open-Ended Glissandos

1. FINAL PITCH IS APPROXIMATE

The line ends in the vicinity of a final pitch: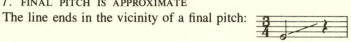

The line ends with an arrowhead when the final pitch lies beyond the arrow:

2. OPENING PITCH IS APPROXIMATE

The duration of the glissando must be indicated with a cue-note and bracket:

3. OPENING AND FINAL PITCHES ARE APPROXIMATE

The durations of glissandos must be indicated with cue-notes and brackets:

C. Curved or Undulating Glissandos

The line traces the approximate course of the glissando:

D. Quick, Short Slides (Portamento)

1. INTO A NOTE

Short slides having no specific opening pitch or duration should be performed like grace notes. Use a short line:

2. OUT OF A NOTE

Same as above, except that it is customary to use short, curved lines:

N.B.: All the glissandos described above may be supplied with dynamic indications, as well as with constant or changing timbral specifications (mutes, bow positions, mouth positions in vocal music, etc.).

E. Compound Durations of Glissandos

Compound durations are those which cannot be expressed by a single note-value within a measure, or which go across a barline. To indicate such durations, stems with or without flags or beams must be attached to the glissando line (but without note-heads) specifying intermediate stages in the total glissando. (Stems without flags or beams should only denote quarter notes in order to avoid ambiguities, since mere stems without note-heads do not differentiate between quarter notes and half notes. An explanatory footnote at first occurrence is recommended.)

1. GLISSANDO ENDING IN A NOTE

Within a measure:

Across a barline:

2. GLISSANDO FOLLOWED BY A REST

Line ends with a small, parenthetical note-head:

3. OPEN-ENDED GLISSANDO

4. UNDULATING GLISSANDO

In this example, a rather long, undulating glissando has a duration cue-line which shows approximately where and when the various pitches are to sound:

Grace Notes

Grace notes are performed as fast as possible and must always be notated before the beat. They should have upstems regardless of their position in the staff unless the staff contains more than one part.

Single grace notes should be notated as eighths; two or more grace notes as sixteenths. Single grace notes must have a thin slanted line through stem and flag; two or more grace notes must have the slanted line through stem and beams.*

It used to be customary to slur grace notes to the main note, but since such slurs are superfluous it is recommended that they be omitted. As a result of this omission, a tied grace note becomes more immediately recognizable. Should it be desired to perform a grace note detached, which is very rare, a staccato dot will serve to indicate this.

It was also customary to begin a full-size legato slur at the first main note of a phrase, regardless of whether or not that note was preceded by one or more grace notes. This practice should be revised to include the grace note(s) in the slurs:

See also Slurs and Ties on Grace Notes, page 42.

Horizontal Lines

A. Staff-lines

Staff-lines may take the form of either five-line staves or single staff-lines.

For alternations of five-line staves and single lines, the middle line of the staff should become the single line:

For combinations of five-line staves and single lines, the single line may be added above or below the staff (see individual instruments); it should be sepa-

---

*If the slanted line is omitted, single grace notes turn into appoggiaturas, which have measured durations depending on the durational context in which they occur:

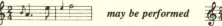

Although appoggiaturas are not often used in twentieth-century music, they are nevertheless part of today's musical vocabulary due to our century's revival of old music. Thus, for example, knowledge of the proper notation and execution of appoggiaturas is essential for editors preparing new editions of Baroque music and for performers presenting that repertory.

rated sufficiently from the five-line staff to prevent mistaking it for part of the full staff:

B. Grids

The lines of a grid must be spaced farther apart than those of a regular five-line staff, for example:

Two-line grid for two cymbals or three tom-toms:

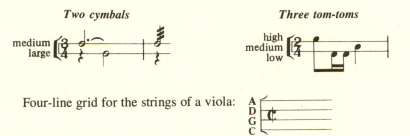

Four-line grid for the strings of a viola:

Practically all horizontal lines not belonging to the staff or grid categories are temporary (occasional) and essentially durational. As a result of music's increasing complexity, however, freedom concerning graphic details has had to give way to greater specificity. Thus the variety of horizontal lines—solid, dotted, broken, wavy, etc.—which used to be employed quite indiscriminately, has become identified more and more with distinct meanings, as itemized below. Unfortunately, there are also occasional mixtures and cross-overs, such as the combination of solid and dotted lines for piano pedaling, or the occasional use of solid lines for timbral phenomena rather than the dotted lines customary for this category.

In spite of these occasional inconsistencies, it is strongly suggested that the procedures listed below be employed wherever possible.

C. Solid Lines, Brackets, and Arrows

These are generally used for purely durational indications and structural groupings.

1. SOLID LINES, ETC., FOR DURATIONAL INDICATIONS

Brackets, solid (⎯) or broken (⌐ ⌐), are used for irregular note divisions and similar groupings:

---

* Broken brackets have the advantage of saving vertical space: ⌐5⌐ versus ⌐5⌐ .

** For the feathered beam, see Duration and Rhythm, Beamed Accelerando and Ritardando, page 124.

Heavy lines and arrows are used for pitch durations in spatial notation:

either

or

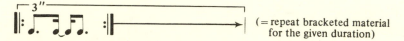 the gaps represent silences.

Brackets denote durational indications in spatial notation, including a heavy continuation line with arrowhead:

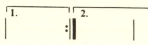 (= repeat bracketed material for the given duration)

Brackets show first and second endings:

Solid lines serve as word extenders in vocal texts:

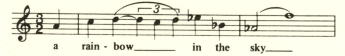

a   rain - bow_____   in   the   sky____

2. SOLID LINES, ETC., FOR TIMBRAL INDICATIONS
Thin arrows are used for gradual transitions of mute positions in brass music:

and for mouth positions in vocal music:

ah _____

Thin lines with several arrowheads in the same direction convey variations in the rates of transitions:

Trumpet: decelerating (from muted to open)

+ →→ → → →o

Voice: accelerating (from nasal to normal)

Δ ⟶ → →→➤ *norm.* (or *nat.* = natural)

3. MIXED SOLID AND BROKEN LINES

Pedaling indications for piano, vibraphone, etc., include a broken line for gradual lifting of the pedal:

℘ed. ⎯⎯⎯⌋   ⌊⎯⎯⎯⎯⎯⋀⌋   ⌊⎯⎯⌋ ⌊⎯⎯⎯ ⸍⸍

D. Dotted or Broken Lines

These are generally used for transpositions and timbres and for the instrument manipulations which produce them:

Octave transpositions:*	8············· ⌐ 15··········⌐
	8 *bassa* ....⌋ or 8.........⌋, etc.
non vibrato:	*n. v.* ·············⌐
half valve:	½v.··········⌐ or ½v.·············⌐
hand tremolo (voice):	hand over mouth
	+ o + o + o *etc.*·············⌐
bocca chiusa (voice):	*b. c.*·············⌐
nasal tone (voice):	Δ ·····················⌐

See also the mixture of broken and solid lines in pedaling indications for piano, etc., above.

E. Wavy Lines

These are generally used for pulsating pitch inflections or quickly alternating pitches.

N.B.: All wavy lines must appear above the note(s) to which they pertain, except in double-stemmed music:

1. SHADED LINES

trill:	*tr* ⟿⟿⟿⟿⊣
double trill:	*tr* ⟿⟿⟿⟿⊣
flutter tongue:	*fl. t.*⟿⟿⊣ or *f. t.*⟿⟿⊣
flutter lips:	*fl.lips* ⟿⟿⟿⊣

---

*The traditional *8ᵛᵃ* and *15ᵐᵃ* are in the process of being replaced by a mere numeral *8* or *15*, resp.

2. UNSHADED LINES, REGULAR

vibrato: *fast* ⋁⋀⋁⋀⋀⋀   *slow* ∿∿∿∿

tremolo (wide, fast vibrato):   ⋃⋀⋀⋀

3. UNSHADED LINES, IRREGULAR

vibrato or tremolo with variations in width and/or speed:

⋀⋀⋀∿∿   or   ⋀⋀⋀∿∿⋀⋀∿∿→ ·*(etc. sim.)*

4. SHADED AND IRREGULAR LINES

the same as above, but with dynamics "built in" (thin = soft; heavy = loud):

⋀⋀∿∿∿⋀   or   ⋀⋁ ⋀⋁ ⋀⋁ ⋁ *(etc. sim.)*

With these last graphic devices, the limits of standardizable wavy lines have been reached. The next step would enter the field of "implicit graphics," which should not be subjected to standardization (see Notation Suited for Standardization, page 336 f).

Instructions
Verbal instructions are best placed where they apply, instead of in footnotes, which require the performer to look down and possibly lose his place.

Irregular Note Divisions: Graphic Characteristics
(For durational aspects see Duration and Rhythm, Irregular Note Divisions, page 129 ff.)

A. Brackets versus Slurs in Unbeamed and Partially Beamed Groups
Square brackets, rather than slurs, should be used for unbeamed triplets, etc., to avoid ambiguities. Slurs will thus only indicate phrasing or refer to other typical slur functions such as bowing.

The numerals and brackets should be placed at the stem-side of the respective groups so that the space at the note-heads will be free for slurs and other articulation marks:

Bracket notation

The same with slurs instead of brackets (incorrect)

N.B.: The difference between non legato (the first, *unslurred* triplet) and legato (the second, *slurred* triplet), which is obvious in the bracket notation, is impossible to indicate in notation with triplet slurs.

If a group contains both upstems and downstems, it is often best to let the majority of stems determine the position of the numeral and bracket, but much depends on the amount of articulation. The less interference with articulation and phrasing, the better. The same applies to groups with an equal number of up- and downstems:

(The versions within vertical brackets are less desirable.)

Phrasing and articulation marks are always placed closer to the note-heads than the numerals and brackets.

B. Beamed Groups

1. FULL-LENGTH BEAMS

No brackets are needed as long as the numeral is placed at the beam side:

If the numeral must appear at the note-head side, as, for example, in down-stemmed groups in vocal music (see Voice, page 297), brackets do become essential:

2. FULL-LENGTH BEAMS WITH SUBDIVISIONS

Multiple beams make it possible to show the individual sub-units of a beamed group through interruptions of the beam closest to the note-heads. No brackets are needed in such beaming:

3. EXTENDED BEAMS

In recent practice, beams are often extended in order to show complete beat-units (see Beams: Extended and Bridging Beams, page 15 f). This style of notation reduces the need for brackets in irregular groups:

4. COMBINATIONS OF BEAMED AND UNBEAMED NOTES (OR RESTS)

These require brackets, because there is no full-length beam to show the total group:

C. Irregular Note Divisions within Regular Groups of Notes

Although it is possible to show such irregular units by interruptions of secondary beams, it is safest to use brackets as well:

Regular and irregular sub-units must not be beamed together if there is only a single beam:

Correct

Incorrect

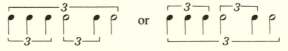

D. Irregular Note Divisions within Irregular Groups of Notes

The numeral for the total group and the numerals for the irregular subunits should be placed at opposite sides of the group:

or

Single-beam groups (eighth notes):

or

Multiple-beam groups (sixteenths and shorter values):

In double-stemmed music (two parts on a staff), all numerals are placed at the stem sides of the respective parts, along with all other signs, and all numerals should be bracketed:

(This would be clearer on two staves.)

E. Horizontal Locations of Numerals and Brackets

Traditionally, the numeral for an irregular group of notes was centered on the total group regardless of whether its graphic center happened to coincide with its durational center. In the first two examples below, the graphic and durational centers coincide (more or less); thereafter, they do not:

In more recent music the numerals of a bracketed group are often placed in the group's durational center, and the bracket extended to the right to show spatially the group's actual, or at least approximate ("horizontal") duration:

In groups with full-length beams and without brackets, the traditional style of placing the numeral in the graphic center is still valid (but see below):

Since the last two methods contradict each other, it is suggested that a compromise system be employed for groups with full-length beams, i.e., groups which normally would not require brackets for the numeral:

If the graphic center of the group coincides reasonably well with its durational center, place the numeral at its durational center without brackets:

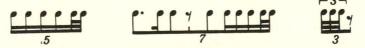

If the two centers are too dissimilar to assure proper execution, add brackets and extend them to the right where necessary:

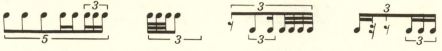

This example is a borderline case and had better be notated with a bracket:

Exception: The following groups are so short that their duration is clear in spite of the off-center position of the numeral and the lack of brackets. It is customary, therefore, to place the numerals for such groups in the "wrong" position:

 *etc.*

Leger Lines

Leger lines must maintain the same vertical spacing as staff-lines, since they represent vertical extensions of the staff.

If intervals of a second are on leger lines, the line(s) between the second(s) and the staff must be twice as wide as ordinary leger lines:

Note-Heads

A. Shapes

1. REGULAR NOTE-HEADS

Black note-heads are slightly oval: . White note-heads: the heads of

whole notes and half notes ( ) must be clearly distinguished by

their different shadings.

2. DIAMOND-SHAPED NOTE-HEADS

These should have slightly inward-curved sides to distinguish them as much as possible from ordinary note-heads:

3. X-SHAPED NOTE-HEADS

These have their stems attached right or left, in the same manner as regular note-heads: (not). For half and whole notes the x is encircled ( ),

although the whole note is often replaced by two tied half notes ( ) because a stemless, encircled x might not be recognized as a note.

Traditionally, x and diamond-shaped note-heads were combined: x for quarter notes and shorter values; diamonds for half and whole notes ( ).

They continue to be used this way, especially for cymbals in simple percussion contexts (see page 219), but it is preferable to keep them separate, thus providing two sets of note-heads (and   ) instead of only one.

Less frequently used note-heads are included below.

B. Uses of Different Shapes

Whenever possible, the following broad rules for correct note-head usage should be observed:

regular note-heads	for exact pitches
diamond note-heads	for special playing modes or tone production, such as half-valve (brass), tablature for string harmonics, falsetto voice, silent depression of keys (piano), held (mechanically secured) keys (organ), etc.
x-shaped note-heads	for indeterminate pitches, noises, speaking voice and unvoiced sounds, release of certain held notes (organ)
round note-heads pierced by stems	for sounds of air blown through an instrument
arrow-shaped note-heads	for highest and lowest notes possible on a given instrument
triangular note-heads	for triangles (see page 217)

Placement of Dynamics and Other Verbal Indications

It is important to observe the customary placement of dynamics and other instructions because performers expect them to appear in specific locations. Exceptions to these routines tend to slow down rehearsals.

A. Dynamics

1. INSTRUMENTAL MUSIC (SCORES AND/OR PARTS)

Single staves (scores): below the music.

Single staves (parts): below the music.

Single staves with two or more polyphonic parts: at the stem side of the up- and downstemmed parts.

Double staves (piano, etc.): centered between staves unless polyphonic texture makes it necessary to position dynamics close to the respective voices.

Three staves (organ): manual staves as in other double-staff notation; pedal staff below, to avoid confusion with dynamics appearing below the lower manual staff.

Full score, group dynamics: if an entire choir (e.g., all woodwinds or all strings), or an entire ensemble (e.g., a string quartet), have the same dynamic level, a large dynamic marking may be placed below the group or ensemble instead of under each line. If the group is large (e.g., an entire orchestra), the marking should be repeated higher up. (Separate parts extracted from such a score must of course contain all dynamics pertaining to them.)

2. VOCAL AND CHORAL MUSIC (OPEN SCORES, PARTS, REDUCTIONS)

Single staves: above the music, so as not to interfere with the text, which is always placed below the staff.

Single staves with two polyphonic parts should be avoided, but single staves with two parts having the same rhythm, text, and dynamics are common. Although the two parts should be notated with double stems, the dynamics should always be placed above, with only the text below.

Two-staff reductions (choral): above and below the staves (text between the staves). Polyphonic textures do not lend themselves easily to reductions, and it is impossible to generalize solutions.

(N.B.: For a discussion of keyboard reductions for rehearsal—i.e., reductions without text and with a minimum of explicit voice leading—see page 281 ff.)

B. Tempo Indications

1. MAIN TEMPOS (ALLEGRO, LARGO, ETC.)

These are placed above the music.

In orchestra scores repeat tempo indications above the string section; in large scores repeat additionally wherever it may seem helpful (above brasses, harp(s), chorus, etc.).

In band scores, repeat tempo indications above the brasses.

In open choral scores, place tempo indications above the top staff and above the keyboard (if any).

In music with frequent tempo changes, it is helpful to repeat the prevailing tempo and/or metronome speed in parentheses at the beginning of all left-hand pages.

(See also page 143 and top of page 164.)

2. MODIFICATIONS (RIT., ACCEL., ETC.)

Single staves (parts): preferably above.

Double staves (piano, etc.): preferably centered between the staves; if too crowded, above.

Three staves (organ): centered between the upper two staves or, if too crowded, above the top staff.

Choral scores (open): above each staff.

C. Playing Instructions

1. EXPRESSIVE

Directly related to a dynamic degree (*p subito; sempre mf; ff marc.;* etc.): below the staff along with the dynamic indication.

Not directly related to the dynamics (*grazioso, marcato,* heavy, *scorrevole, mit Humor,* etc.): preferably above the staff.

2. TECHNICAL

Indications such as pizz., arco, a2, *bocca chiusa,* mute, take Picc., div., solo, tutti, etc.: above the staff.

N.B.: In vocal and choral music, all such instructions must be placed above the staff or staves.

Repeats

N.B.: Signs discussed in sections **B, C,** and **D** below are chiefly used in parts rather than in scores.

A. Repeated Articulation (Simile)

The indication *simile* must always be preceded by at least one written-out measure, and each new line of music must also begin with one written-out measure.

B. Repeated Chords

If the chords coincide with beats, they are indicated with heavy slanted strokes. Otherwise, they are indicated with headless stems. (This notation is rarely used for single notes.)

Note that, as with *simile,* each new line must begin with the written-out chord. It is not necessary, however, to write out an entire measure, as shown in both examples. Dynamic indications may be added without repeating the chord.

C. Repeated Measures

These are shown by a heavy slanted stroke centered and flanked by two dots:

If more than four measures are repeated in succession, a small numeral in parentheses should be placed above the repeat sign in every fourth measure, as shown in the example above.

D. Repeated Pairs of Measures

These are indicated by a slanted double stroke flanked by two dots, straddling the barline between two-measure units:

If more than four pairs of measures are repeated in succession, a small number in parentheses should be placed above the repeat sign in every fourth pair of measures, as shown in the example above.

E. Repeated Sections

1. REPEAT BARS

Repeated sections should be indicated according to traditional procedure:

*There is no uniformity. :‖: and :‖: are found equally often.

Note that no repeat sign is needed at the beginning of a movement. (See also Indeterminate Repeats, page 154 ff.) However, repeats might be indicated verbally: *Da Capo al Fine,* meaning "From the beginning to the end" (i.e., to the word *Fine*).

2. REPEAT SIGNS

Instead of repeat bars, the sign 𝄋 may be used as follows:

Dal Segno al Fine = From the sign 𝄋 to the word *Fine;*
Da Capo al Segno = From the beginning to the sign 𝄋;

Da Capo al Segno e poi la Coda = From the beginning to the sign 𝄋 followed by the coda.

The word *Segno* may be followed by the sign itself, as in the English translations above (for example, *Dal Segno* 𝄋 *al Fine*), or omitted altogether (as in *Dal* 𝄋 *al Fine*).

If two signs are needed, ⊕ is used for the second one:

Dal Segno 𝄋 *al* ⊕ *e poi la Coda* = From the sign 𝄋 to ⊕ and from there to the coda;
Da Capo al Segno 𝄋 *e poi al* ⊕, or *Da Capo al* 𝄋 *e poi al* ⊕.

The second *Segno* (⊕) is also used if two different repeats are marked by signs; 𝄋 for the first *"Dal Segno . . ."* and ⊕ for the second.

Running-Heads

In most published books, headings at the top of each page indicate the respective chapter headings or subject matter. These are called running-heads. Unfortunately, they are almost unknown in music. Only instrumental parts contain them, and there they do not identify either the composition or its movements, but the instrument in question.

It is recommended that running-heads be used more often in scores, parts, and vocal scores of works having several movements, acts, scenes, or "numbers," etc., such as ballets, operas, oratorios, cantatas, and so on.*

Slurs and Ties: Phrasing/Bowing/Breathing

A. The Different Meanings of Slurs

It is important to realize that slurs differ in specific functions. In music for bowed string instruments, slurs indicate bowing, not phrasing. In music for wind instruments, slurs indicate the notes to be played with one breath, again not phrasing.

In vocal music, slurs show the notes to be sung on a single syllable. Only in keyboard instruments and pitched percussion capable of sustained sounds do they indicate actual phrasing.

1. SUPERIMPOSED DOTTED PHRASING SLURS

If it is found desirable to indicate phrasing in music for winds, bowed strings, or voice, an additional set of slurs must be superimposed upon those fulfilling

---

* See, for example, the vocal score of Bach's *St. John Passion* in the edition by Arthur Mendel (New York: G. Schirmer, Inc., 1951), in which each page shows the respective movement number at the top center, or the score of Elliott Carter's song cycle *A Mirror on Which to Dwell* (New York: Associated Music Publishers, Inc., 1977), in which each page shows the relevant song title in the top center.

other functions. This can lead to certain ambiguities. To avoid them, dotted slurs are often used for phrasing. Dotted phrasing slurs may also be used in non-legato music which nevertheless requires some unambiguous phrasing indication.

All such dotted slurs should be placed above the music to prevent interference with dynamics and vocal texts. Only if differently phrased parts appear on the same staff should dotted slurs be placed above and below. If both parts are phrased similarly, one dotted slur above suffices.

Examples of dotted phrasing slurs:

The practice often employed by Wagner, Mahler, and Webern, among others, of indicating only the phrasing (with regular slurs) and leaving the details of bowing and breathing to the performers, is no longer considered adequate.

B. The Notation of Slurs and Ties

1. POSITION

The placement of slurs and ties above, below, or within the staff is governed by the positions of the note-heads: if they point up, the slurs or ties must be above the notes; if the note-heads point down, so must the slurs and ties:

In mixtures of up and down note-heads, the slurs must be placed above the notes, even if only one single note-head points up in the group to be slurred:

Slurs and ties on whole notes are treated as if the notes had stems:

2. COMBINATIONS OF SLURS AND TIES

The curve of a tie is governed by the up or down positions of the two tied note-heads. If both tied note-heads point down, the tie also curves downward, regardless of the position of the slur, which is governed by the total phrase:

If one or both of the tied note-heads point up, the tie curves upward:

If the stem directions change in the course of a series of tied notes, the directions of the ties' curvatures must change accordingly:

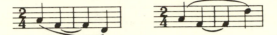

(In the last example, the first and third ties curve upward because one of the two note-heads points up; the second tie curves downward because both note-heads point down.)

As already demonstrated, tied notes ought to be included under the slur, since the slur should always embrace the entire passage in question:

In the following example, the same melody is notated with chains of slurs and ties: the slurs, instead of covering an entire phrase, are interrupted for the duration of each tie. This style of notation is not recommended, because it often makes the phrasing difficult to recognize:

3. SLURS AND TIES FROM LINE TO LINE: LENGTH

a. END OF LINE

At the end of a line, neither slurs nor ties should extend beyond the barline:

If the line ends with a change of time signature, the slurs and ties still extend only to the barline and not beyond: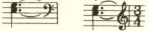

If the line ends with a change of clef, the slurs and ties should stop just before the new clef: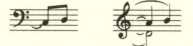

b. BEGINNING OF NEXT LINE

At the beginning of the next line, the slurs or ties begin just after the clef: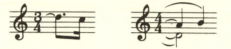

If there is a new time signature, the slurs and ties begin just after it:

If there is a key signature, the slurs and ties begin just after it:

4. SLURS AND TIES FROM LINE TO LINE: POSITION

The up or down positions of ties and slurs going from one line to the next are governed by the complete phrase, regardless of the break from line to line. This will occasionally result in wrong-looking slur and/or tie positions:

COMPLETE PHRASES	THE SAME PHRASES: END OF LINE	NEXT LINE

Slurs only:

With ties:

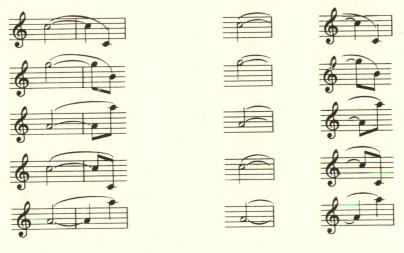

5. SLUR-TO-SLUR NOTATION

This kind of chain slurring (slur to slur on the same note) is used when a phrase ends on a note which also represents the beginning of the next phrase:

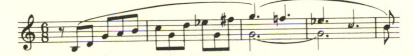

6. SLURS AND TIES IN DOUBLE-STEMMED NOTATION

In such cases, all rules given so far are suspended, since in double stemming, all slurs must be at the stem-ends of the upstemmed and downstemmed parts, respectively, and all ties, although close to the notes, must curve in the direction of the respective stems:

See also Score and Parts, Divisi Parts: Slurs and Ties, page 167.

7. SLURRED AND TIED INTERVALS AND CHORDS

If intervals or chords on single stems are to be slurred, only one slur should be used:

(The rule given on page 36 f that slur positions are governed by the positions of the note-heads also applies here.)

If intervals or chords are to be tied, all notes must be tied (unlike the single slur for slurred intervals or chords). The curvature of the ties is governed by two factors:

a. The top and bottom ties must curve in opposite directions:

b. The ties between the top and bottom notes (in chords of three or more notes on a single stem) must curve according to their position in the staff:

for notes on the center staff-line and above, the curve is upward;
for notes below the center staff-line, the curve is downward:

If a chord includes the interval of a second, the rule above is often modified as follows: since the notes of a second are very close together, it is clearer to curve the two ties in opposite rather than in the same direction, which may affect the up or down curve of one or more adjacent inside ties. (Only the top and bottom notes of a chord keep their up- and down-ties under all circumstances.)

In the following example, the F and A would normally have had down-ties, but since the F is the upper note of a second and should therefore have an up-tie, the next higher inside note of the chord (A) must also have an up-tie, or the ties would run together:

(without the second)

If a chord includes more than one second, the ties from second to second usually have to curve in the same direction, because there would not be enough space to have them curve in opposite directions. Care must be taken that each tie stays in its own staff space:

8. COMBINATIONS OF SLUR AND TIE(S)

If at all possible, double stemming should be used:

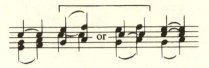

(Note that the rule for double stemming—that all slurs and ties follow the directions of the respective stems—must also be followed when it comes to intervals and chords.)

If it is impossible to use double stemming, the above examples would look as follows:

N.B.: Similar problems are discussed in a different context in Keyboard Reductions, Choral Scores, page 281 ff.

9. SLURS ON TRIPLETS AND OTHER IRREGULAR NOTE DIVISIONS

a. INSTRUMENTAL MUSIC

The tradition of placing slurs on triplets, etc., regardless of the desired articulation, should be abandoned in favor of square brackets or, if the entire group of notes is beamed together, of numerals at the beam side with no slurs or brackets:

Basic principle

A few slightly more complex examples

Correct with articulation slurs on the quintuplet

Incorrect*

If a group includes mixtures of beamed and unbeamed notes, or if the beam(s) are interrupted, brackets, rather than slurs, must be used:

*This form may, however, be used in vocal music (see Vocal Music, below).

b. VOCAL MUSIC

In vocal music, all numerals and brackets should be placed above the notes so as not to interfere with the text, but slurs and ties must be in their normal positions:

If an entire group of notes is beamed together with the beam(s) pointing down, the numeral is placed at the note-side (up) with brackets, not slurs:

For general information concerning irregular note divisions, see page 26 ff and Duration and Rhythm, Irregular Note Divisions, page 129 ff.

10. SLURS AND TIES ON GRACE NOTES

See separate entry, Grace Notes (page 21 f), where it is recommended that the customary small slurs from the grace note(s) to the main note be omitted and that full-size slurs begin at the grace note(s) rather than at the main note.

If, in spite of these recommendations, grace notes are to be treated in the more traditional way, the following rules should be observed:

The small slurs or ties should curve downward (the stems always point up) and full-size slurs begin at the main note.

In double-stemmed passages, grace notes are treated like the other notes: up-stems and upward-curving slurs or ties for the upper voice, the opposite for the lower voice:

11. SLURS AND TIES IN COMBINATION WITH ARTICULATION SIGNS

In slurred passages with accents and other articulation signs, the slur should begin and end between the note-head (or stem-end) and the accent. All other accents, etc., should be covered by the slur:

An exception to this rule should be made in cases of very wide, slurred intervals, where the first or last accent should be placed between the note-head and the slur:

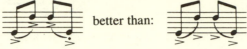

better than:

Staccato dots and tenuto lines in slurred passages, unlike accents, should all appear between the note-heads (or stem-ends) and the slur (this applies equally to the first and last notes):

Ties must always be placed as close to the note-heads as possible, regardless of any accents or staccato dots, etc.:

The following slurred combinations occur frequently:

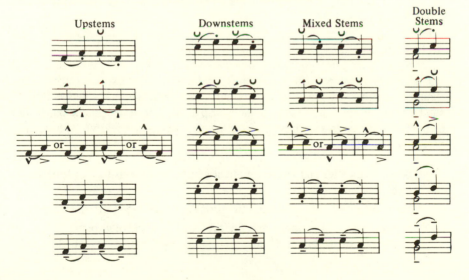

Fermatas in slurred passages are treated like accents:

8va signs should always be outside the slur:

In vocal music all accents should appear above the music, while staccato dots and tenuto lines generally appear at the note-heads even if they point down. This makes for certain irregularities, since accents may appear above the music while slurs appear below. The following example demonstrates the most common occurrences:

See also Articulation, page 4 ff.

For slurs in vocal music, see Voice, page 296 f.

For proper use of ties within a measure, see Duration and Rhythm, Ties, page 146.

Spacings, Positions, and Sizes (Miscellaneous)

The proper horizontal spacing of notes and accidentals, etc., is too complex to be included in these rather general guidelines.* A few basic rules, however, should prove helpful.

A. Opening Measures (in Traditional Notation**)

At the beginning of a composition or movement, always indent the first line.

Clefs, key signatures, time signatures, and notes with or without accidentals should be neither too far apart nor too close together. The gaps between them can best be measured by cutting a short strip of staff from the music paper and using its cutting edge as a measuring device (see examples below). The spacing should be as follows:

> between the clef and any subsequent symbol (key signature or time signature): one staff-space or a little less;
>
> between the key signature and the time signature: one staff-space;
>
> between any of the above and the first note or accidental or rest (with the exception of whole rests and measure-filling whole notes): 1½ staff-spaces.

---

* For details, see engravers' manuals such as *The Art of Music Engraving and Processing* by Ted Ross.

** For new approaches, see pages 158 ff and 177 ff.

(With cutting edges of staff to show how to measure the gaps)

clef, key signature, time signature, accidental, note

clef, key signature, accidental, note

clef, time signature, accidental, note

clef, accidental, note

clef, note

Whole-measure whole notes and whole rests:

See also Notes and Rests, page 46 f.

In music requiring two or more staves, the notes having accidentals (if any) are spaced according to the rules above, and the notes without accidentals must be aligned vertically with the notes having the accidentals, not with the accidentals:

B. Clef Changes

At changes of clefs between measures, the new clef is placed about one staff-line space before the barline:

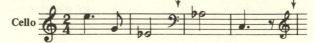

There are no specific rules for clef changes within a measure.

C. Time Signature Changes

Changes of time signatures must be placed one staff-line space after the barline, whether within a line or at the end of it:

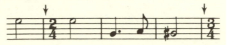

D. The End of a Line

In the past, composers did not plan the length of their lines too carefully, but in view of the current prevalence of facsimile publication it is advisable to devote greater care to the planning of each line so that all lines end flush right with a barline. The only exceptions are (1) music without barlines or with measures that are too long and must be broken; and (2) changes of time signature, which necessitate placing the last barline before the end of the line (see arrow) to make room for the new time signature. (The new time signature must always be placed inside the staff.)

It is of great importance to strive for practical page turns. Only conductors' scores and vocal music do not require them; all other music does.

See also Facsimile Reproductions, page 341 f.

E. Accidentals

Accidentals are often drawn too small in manuscripts, which makes for poor legibility. Their proper width and height depend on the width of the staves. This proportion must be maintained when writing on staves of different widths. Correctly proportioned accidentals should look like the following:

F. Notes and Rests

All notes in multistaff music must be in proper vertical (rhythmic) alignment. The same is true for rests (see arrows "1" in example below), with the following exceptions:

(1) Full-measure rests (usually represented by whole rests regardless of the

prevailing meter) must be centered, no matter what other note- or rest-values occur in the same measure (see arrows "2").

(2) Full-measure notes are placed a little to the left of center, but only when all other notes and rests in the same measure are also full-measure values (see arrows "3"). If this requirement is not met, all notes in such measures must be in their proper rhythmic positions, including those filling an entire measure (see arrows "4").

N.B.: The convention of almost centering notes and centering rests filling an entire measure, and of using whole rests in all full-measure silences irrespective of the actual duration of the measure, has begun to break down as rhythm in contemporary music has increased in complexity. It is suggested, therefore, to replace the traditionally centered whole rests shown above (arrows "2") with rests representing the actual duration of the measure in question, and to place these rests in their proper rhythmic positions (see next example, mm. 1, 2, and 4 of the cello and m. 3 of the violin):

For durational spacing in spatial (proportionate) notation, see Spatial Notation, page 136 ff.

Stems

A. Stem Lengths

1. SINGLE NOTES (UNBEAMED)
Stems on single notes should be one octave long unless the note is farther than

one octave from the middle line of the staff, in which case the stem is lengthened to reach the middle line:

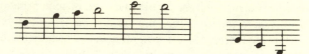

In other words, all stems must either cross the middle line or reach it (except, of course, in double stemming—see below).

2. INTERVALS AND CHORDS (UNBEAMED)

Stems on intervals and chords should be one octave long, or a little shorter, measured from the end of the stem to the nearest note. If that note is farther than one octave from the middle line of the staff, the stem is lengthened to reach the middle line. (In the example, small arrows point to the notes governing stem lengths.)

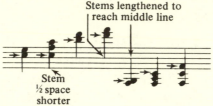

3. BEAMED GROUPS OF NOTES

a. SINGLE BEAM (IDENTICAL PITCHES THROUGHOUT THE BEAMED GROUP)

The basic rule for unbeamed notes, that stems should be 3½ spaces (one octave) long, also applies to notes with one beam, provided the notes are all in a space. (The stems are measured from the center of the note to the outside of the beam.) For notes on a line, the stem is a quarter of a staff-space shorter because the beam straddles a staff-line, i.e., the outside of such a beam does not reach all the way to the center of the staff-space:

See also Beams, page 9 ff.

b. SINGLE BEAM (DIFFERENT PITCHES)

Here the stem lengths cannot be regulated, except that the stem of the note(s) closest to the beam should not be shorter than the interval of a sixth:

With minimum slant

With greater slants (used by engravers)

c. DOUBLE AND MULTIPLE BEAMS

Stems are usually lengthened by half a space for each additional beam, but when three or more beams are used, no rigid rule is followed and a balance is attempted between lengthening the stems just enough to prevent the note(s) nearest the beams from being too close:

Regular lengths   *Compromise lengths*

4. FLAGGED NOTES

For eighth notes and sixteenth notes the length of the stems should remain the same as for unflagged stems. From three flags on, however, the stem must be lengthened to accommodate the additional flag(s):  *etc.*

5. IN DOUBLE-STEMMED NOTATION

In double stemming, the stems are usually shortened by ½ to 1 space, i.e., from an octave to a seventh or sixth, except in multiple beaming, where such reductions would bring the secondary beam(s) too close to the notes. There also are other situations that do not permit shortening of the stems, such as when tremolo bars are drawn through the stem: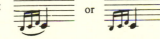

6. GRACE NOTES

Stems usually take up about 2½ spaces: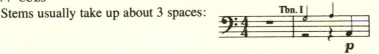

7. CUES

Stems usually take up about 3 spaces: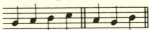

B. Stem Directions

1. SINGLE NOTES (UNBEAMED)

Notes below the middle line of the staff are stemmed up; notes above and on the middle line of the staff are stemmed down:

N.B.: The old rule that the stem direction for notes on the middle line of the staff is governed by the majority of the other stems in the measure (see example below) is rarely if ever followed any longer, at least not by today's professional engravers and autographers.

Not recommended

2. INTERVALS AND CHORDS (UNBEAMED)

If there are multiple notes on a single stem, the stem direction is determined by the note farthest from the middle line of the staff. (Arrows point to the notes governing stem direction.)

If the outside notes of an interval or chord are equally far from the middle line of the staff, the stem goes down:

3. BEAMED GROUPS OF NOTES

The rules governing stem directions of unbeamed notes, intervals, and chords generally apply to beamed groups also:

The note(s) farthest from the middle line of the staff determine(s) the direction of all the stems in a beamed group.

If the outside notes of a beamed group are equally far from the middle line of the staff, the group is stemmed down. (The governing notes in the following examples are marked with small arrows.)

N.B.: Both of these rules may be broken if the avalaible space makes their rigid application awkward or even impossible. The most common such "violation" is to let the majority of the notes govern the stem direction, in which case the second example above would have upstems:

4. GRACE NOTES

Grace notes should always have upstems except in double-stemmed contexts, where their stems generally follow the part to which they belong, i.e., point away from the staff:

In single-stemmed notation   *In double-stemmed notation*

See also Slurs and Ties, page 35 ff, and Grace Notes, page 21 f.

5. CUES

Cues generally are stemmed opposite to normal, except that the stem direction should not be changed within any one cue, even if this means that some of the cue notes will have "correct" stems:

For group stems, see page 162 f.

II. *Pitch*

Accidentals   53
  A. *Size*   53
  B. *Cancellation (Naturals)*   54
  C. *Double Sharps and Double Flats* 54
  D. *At Clef Changes*   54
  E. *Tied Accidentals*   54
  F. *Cautionary Accidentals*   55
  G. *In Scores*   55
  H. *Note-for-Note Accidentals*   55

Clefs   56
  Clef Changes   57

Clusters   57
  A. *Cluster Notation*   58
  B. *Clusters in Ensemble Music*   58

Glissandos   63
  A. *Note-to-Note Glissando*   63
  B. *Open-Ended Glissando*   64
  C. *Curved or Undulating Glissando* 64
  D. *Slides into a Note*   64
  E. *Dynamics and Timbral Indications* 64

Harmonics   65

Highest/Lowest Note(s)   65

*Indeterminate or Approximate
Pitches*   66
  A. *On a Five-Line Staff*   66
  B. *On a Grid*   66

Microtones   67
  A. *Exact Pitches: Quarter Tones*   67
  B. *Exact Pitches: Other Microtones* 70
  C. *Approximate Pitches*   70

Random and Choice Pitches
  see page 155

Slides
  see page 64

Transpositions   71
  A. *In C-Scores*   71
  B. *In Performance Scores*   71
  C. *In Individual Parts*   71
  D. *Clefs Used in Scores and Parts*   72

Tremolo
  see pages 76, 141, and 147

Trill/Tremolo/Vibrato   74
  A. *Vibrato*   74
  B. *Trill*   74
  C. *Tremolo*   74

Trills and Trill Tremolos   75
  A. *Single-Step Trills*   75
  B. *Wide Trills (Trill Tremolos)*   76
  C. *Microtonal Trills*   76
  D. *Nonroutine Trill Openings*   77
  E. *Ending a Trill*   77
  F. *Afterbeats*   77
  G. *Trill Continuing from One Line
    to the Next*   77
  H. *Timbral Trills*   77

Unisons   78

Unpitched Notes: Placement   79
  A. *Occasional Unpitched Notes*   79
  B. *Extended Passages*   79

Vibrato/Non Vibrato   80
  A. *Marked Vibrato*   80
  B. *Vibrato of Varying Width
    and/or Speed*   80

Accidentals

Basic procedures concerning accidentals are assumed to be known to the reader. The following are specific suggestions. (For microtonal accidentals, see page 67 ff.)

A. Size

Care should be taken to adapt the size of the accidentals to that of the staff. Disproportionately large or small accidentals seriously impair quick perception (see Spacings, Positions, and Sizes, page 44 ff).

B. Cancellation (Naturals)

Although traditionally the barline at the end of a measure automatically cancels all non–key-signature accidentals (except for tied notes), in more recent music, accidentals not canceled in their own measure are usually canceled in the measure following:

(The B-natural in the last measure does not need a natural because it occurs more than one measure after the preceding B-flat.)

Accidentals should not only be canceled for notes on identical pitch levels, but for the entire pitch class (i.e., at any octave level):

In multistaff notation for a single player, such as in keyboard and harp music, the staves should not be treated separately, as was formerly customary. Accidentals should be canceled regardless of the staff in which they occur:

If an accidental is canceled within the same measure, but in a different octave, it must be canceled again if the note subsequently recurs in the original octave:

(In the example above, the F-sharp is canceled when an F occurs in the upper octave. When at the end of the measure an F occurs in the original octave, it is canceled again.)

The following example contains the same notes as above, but the meter has been changed from $\frac{9}{8}$ to $\frac{6}{8}$, causing the last F to fall into the *next* measure, i.e., after the barline. In this case there is no need for another natural; the natural on the preceding F suffices:

If the last F is to be an F-sharp, another sharp must be placed in front of it even though no natural has occurred on the same pitch level. The new sharp has become necessary because the F in the upper octave had a natural sign. In other words, if any pitch has been canceled at a different level and then recurs uncanceled on its original level, its accidental should be repeated:

(In $\frac{6}{8}$ it would have become necessary to repeat the sharp, because accidentals do not carry from one measure to the next unless tied, and then only for the duration of the tie.)

C. Double Sharps and Double Flats

A single natural suffices to cancel a double accidental. If a double sharp or flat is to be reduced to a single sharp or flat, no natural is needed, only the single accidental:

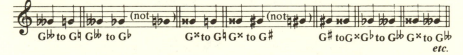

G♭♭ to G♮ G♭♭ to G♭　　　G×to G♮　G×to G♯　　　G♯ toG×G♭ to G♭♭　G×to G♭♭

etc.

D. At Clef Changes

If a clef changes within a measure and the same note occurs before and after the clef change, the accidental must be repeated:

E. Tied Accidentals

If notes with accidentals are tied from one line to the next, the accidental(s) should be repeated at the beginning of the new line. No parentheses should be used, because they crowd the image. (There is no need to repeat accidentals on notes tied from measure to measure within the same line.)

End of line   **Beginning of new line**

♭ need not be repeated

♯ must be repeated

repeated
tied ♭

♯ need not be repeated
(within the line)

Here is the same example with the break from line to line one measure later:

End of line   **Beginning of new line**

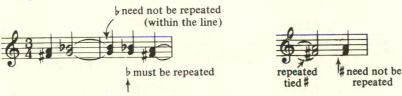

♭ need not be repeated
(within the line)

♭ must be repeated

repeated
tied ♯

♯ need not be
repeated

F. Cautionary Accidentals

Accidentals and naturals which have no primary function but serve only to clarify possible ambiguities are the only ones to be placed in parentheses. Although theoretically superfluous, they are often of crucial value to the performer. The simplest rule as to whether to add a cautionary accidental or not is: When in doubt, add it:

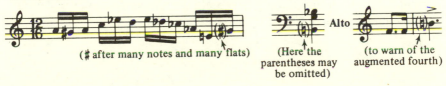

(♯ after many notes and many flats)

(Here the
parentheses may
be omitted)

(to warn of the
augmented fourth)

G. In Scores

In general, the use of cautionary accidentals should depend only on what goes on within each instrument, but once in a while situations arise which are greatly clarified by cautionary accidentals. For example, if there is a unison on G-sharp, except for a sforzato G-natural in the trombones, the trombones should definitely have parenthetical naturals. In vocal and choral music, it is advisable to add cautionary accidentals in case of augmented fourths, when clashes occur with other voices, or when there are prominent conflicting pitches in the accompaniment. (These situations are less important in instrumental music because it is easier to operate a key, valve, or string than to form a pitch vocally.)

H. Note-for-Note Accidentals

The discussion of accidentals should not be concluded without mentioning one radically different trend which is gaining prominence and may eventually win out over the system explained above. This trend reduces accidentals to a minimum. Its basic rules are:

1. Accidentals affect only those notes which they immediately precede.

2. Accidentals are not repeated on tied notes unless the tie goes from line to line or page to page.

3. Accidentals are not repeated for repeated notes unless one or more different pitches intervene.

4. If a sharp or flat pitch is followed directly by its natural form, a natural is used (A♯–A♮; E♭–E♮).

5. Cautionary accidentals or naturals (in parentheses) may be used to clarify ambiguities, but should be held to a minimum.

versus traditional:

Clefs

Although many clefs and clef positions were used at various times in the past, only the following survive in twentieth-century music:

G-clef   **Bass clef**

C-clefs;
Alto clef
(viola)   **Tenor clef**
                (bassoon, trombone, cello, but only
                for notes too high for the bass clef)

No-pitch clef
(such as in unpitched percussion)

Certain transpositions are indicated with a small numeral:

Tenor-voice clef
(also used for tenor recorder)

Piccolo clef in C-scores
(also used for descant recorder)

Double-bass clef in C-scores
(also used for contrabassoon
and other very low instruments)

Horn bass clef in traditional (transposed) scores and parts (Horn in F):

Sounds a fifth lower than notated   *Sounds a fourth higher than notated*

N.B.: In popular music (jazz, rock, show music, etc.), clefs are usually omitted in the parts after the first line, since they are (rightly) considered "understood." This practice is very rarely found in "serious" music, except in random compositions with deliberately indefinite pitches.

Clef Changes

1. AT A BARLINE

If a clef change takes place at a barline, the new clef, which should be of a slightly smaller size, is placed before the barline:

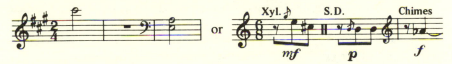

2. FROM LINE TO LINE

If a clef changes from one line to the next, a warning clef, of a slightly smaller size, is placed at the end of the line before the barline to signal that the next line begins with a new (full-size) clef:

End of line   **Beginning of next line**

See also Spacings, Positions, and Sizes at Clef Changes, page 46, and Clefs used in Scores and Parts, page 72 f.

Clusters

A tone cluster may be defined as a combination of three or more pitches too close to each other to form a chord in the traditional sense. The degree of closeness, or density, may range from adjacent whole tones to the immeasurable density of electronic white noise.

Certain instruments have relatively unalterable densities: white-key or black-key clusters on keyboard instruments consist mostly of whole tones. Slightly greater density, at least in narrow clusters, is possible on harps. Black and white keys together produce chromatic clusters.

Single-tone instruments can produce clusters only if combined in groups. Of these, most wind instruments are limited in cluster density because their pitches depend largely on fixed keys or valves. On the other hand, string instruments, especially in large groups and pitched only microtones apart, can produce the densest clusters short of electronic devices.

Choruses, at least theoretically, can perform clusters as dense as string clusters, except that their total range is of course narrower. There is, however, an additional drawback: it is much more difficult to sing and sustain a controlled microtone or even a half tone than to play it on an instrument, especially if surrounded by the other pitches of the cluster.

Clusters are used in two contrasting ways: as very short sounds for percussive effects, and as sustained sounds. The latter may be constant or changing in width and/or density, or they may move up or down, either maintaining their width or changing it.

A. Cluster Notation

The notation of clusters differs depending on whether they are to be performed by a single player (keyboard or harp) or by a group of single-tone instruments or bowed strings. For keyboard and harp clusters, see the entries under piano (page 259) and harp (page 231). Group clusters are dealt with below.

B. Clusters in Ensemble Music

(Examples follow the sections *a* and *b* below.)

1. SUSTAINED CLUSTERS

a. PITCH NOTATION

In scores, filled-in horizontal bands of constant or varying width and/or position (pitch level) are the most effective form of cluster notation.*

In parts, such bands are not recommended, since they do not indicate to the individual player where he fits into the total pitch spectrum of the cluster. Instead, parts should be notated with more traditional means: constant clusters should be notated with ordinary notes and their chromatic or microtonal accidentals, one part for each player (see example below); varying clusters should begin like constant clusters, with a specified pitch for each player, followed by glissando lines wherever gradual changes of pitch are called for.

---

*This does not apply to instruments whose sound is of relatively short duration—see, for example, Piano Clusters, page 259 f.

b. DURATIONAL NOTATION

In scores, to insure proper synchronization, notes of appropriate duration should be placed above the cluster band (which, unfortunately, is rarely done). In spatial notation, beat signs should be used (see pages 102 and 159 f.)

In parts, in constant clusters, ordinary note-values should be used, while the glissandos of changing clusters may benefit from the same kind of small notes above the music recommended for the score. (In spatial notation, the method suggested for the score should also be followed in the parts.)

c. EXAMPLE: A CLUSTER OF CONSTANT WIDTH AND PITCH, FOR SIXTEEN VIOLINS

Score (*cluster-band notation*)

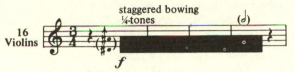

Parts (*ordinary notes*)

* ¾ sharps ⎫
⎬ see Microtones, page 67 ff.
** ¼ sharps ⎭

N.B.: The sixteen pitches may be indicated more precisely as follows:

d. EXAMPLE: A CLUSTER OF 36 VIOLINS AND 12 DOUBLE BASSES

Both begin with specified outer pitches (with a footnote saying that the individual pitches should be quarter tones apart). The clusters remain constant for a while, after which the violins have a very slow glissando upward with a simultaneous gradual reduction in width, ending on the highest pitches of the G, D, and A strings. The basses have a glissando downward, also with reduction of cluster width, ending on a unison G. (Excerpted from *Riff 62* for orchestra, by Wojciech Kilar.)

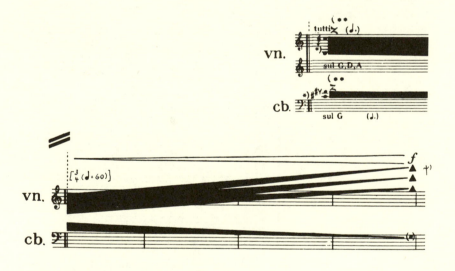

Copyright 1963 by PWP, Warsaw, Poland. Used by permission.

* All the quarter tones within the indicated range.

** ⤬ is the Polish publisher's symbol for tremolo.

† ▲ is the Polish publisher's symbol for the highest note possible. In the reproduced passage the upper cluster is to be played by twelve violins on the three lower strings (see ''sul G, D, A'' at the beginning of the cluster). The slow upward glissando ends on the highest possible note of each of the respective strings.

e. EXAMPLE: A CLUSTER, VARYING IN WIDTH AND PITCH, FOR AN ENTIRE STRING SECTION

Cluster-band notation in the score

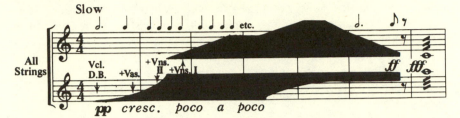

Traditional notation in the parts

N.B.: In clusters such as the one above, it is impossible to indicate specific pitches in the score. Note also that even though all the examples given here consist of unspecified or quarter-tone intervals, this is not necessarily the case for all clusters. Many consist of half-tone steps only.

In notation with indeterminate (approximate) pitches, it is generally preferable to use either a single staff-line to mark the pitch center:

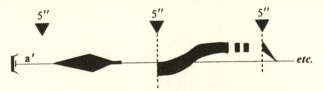

or two staff-lines, fairly far apart, to show the upper and lower pitch limits:

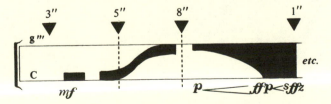

As is clear from the examples, the staff-lines are marked with the pitches they represent (unless the composer prefers to leave the choice to the performers).

Since such clusters usually appear in rather free music in which everyone plays from the score, the question of how to transcribe them for individual parts rarely arises. And since the number of players in such music often varies from performance to performance, it would be inconsistent with the style of the music to be very specific. The players have to work out among themselves how to interpret the notated cluster bands—their density, possible doublings of certain pitches, gradual additions or subtractions of instruments, etc. If, on the other hand, greater specificity is desired, the guidelines given above should be able to solve most problems.

2. FAST, RHYTHMIC CLUSTERS
a. SPECIFIED PITCHES
In scores, clusters with specified pitches and note-values should be notated according to the recommended system described in Piano: Clusters (page 259 f), namely:

> The note-heads of the outside pitches of a cluster are connected in the center with a heavy, solid line;
>
> The stem (if any) is attached to the top or bottom note, according to the regular rules of stem directions;
>
> Ties connect only the top and bottom notes. (See examples below.)

A cluster notated in this way is assumed to have half-tone density. If a different density or doublings, etc., are wanted, the parts will show what is intended, but the score should also include a footnote or other indication to this effect.

In parts, the same procedure shown under Sustained Clusters earlier in this section should also be used for fast clusters, i.e., an indication of the appropriate specific pitch(es) must be shown for each performer. The spacing from pitch to pitch and the number of pitch doublings (if any) will vary depending on the width of the cluster, the size of the ensemble, and/or the composer's special requests for unequal density or for emphasis of one or more pitches through doubling(s), etc.

Score

Parts (sampling)
Highest

Middle

Lowest

* ¾ sharps (see Microtones, page 67 ff.)

b. INDETERMINATE BOUNDARY NOTES; APPROXIMATE PITCHES

Narrow vertical boxes replace the boundary note-heads; the length of the boxes indicates the approximate width of the clusters. Since the clusters are indeterminate, the players must work out their individual pitches. Chromatic density is assumed unless marked otherwise.

Glissandos

A thin, straight line should be used to indicate a glissando. It is customary to add the abbreviation *gliss.*, but this is not mandatory; the line suffices.

A. Note-to-Note Glissando

From one note to another:

From a note to a small note-head:

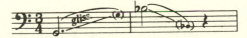

The small, parenthetical note-heads are not articulated; they merely mark the final pitches.

B. Open-Ended Glissando

The free end of the glissando line implies an approximate final pitch:

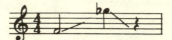

The arrowhead shows that the final pitch lies beyond the end of the glissando line:

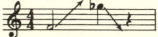

C. Curved or Undulating Glissando

A glissando in which the degree and direction varies, as traced by the glissando line:

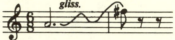

D. Slides into a Note

1. QUICK SLIDES

These have neither specific opening pitches nor specific durations, and are to be performed in the manner of grace notes:

(No rests should be used.)

2. SLOW SLIDES

These are glissandos with indefinite opening pitches:

Straight slide   *Curved slide*

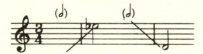
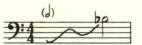

(Parenthetical notes should be used to show the duration of the slide.)

E. Dynamics and Timbral Indications

All the glissandos described above may be supplied with dynamic indications, as well as with constant or changing timbral specifications (mutes, bow positions, mouth positions in vocal music, etc.).

See also Glissando, page 19 ff.

Harmonics

Be sure that the small circle (o) which indicates harmonics is not shaded like a zero (0), which would mean "open string," nor that it is too large, which would mean "open" in brass instruments, or "hand tremolo" in vocal notation. Given our present profusion of symbols, proper sizes and other details have become much more important than ever before.

For details of harmonics notation, see the entries for specific instruments or instrument groups.

Highest/Lowest Note(s)

In general, only the highest notes are written without specified pitch, because they may differ from instrument to instrument (even of the same kind) and from player to player.

Lowest notes, on the other hand, are generally not variable and should therefore be notated as specific pitches according to the instrument(s) involved. Exceptions: the voice, woodwinds with attachments, pedal tones of brasses, "mistuned" strings (scordatura).

Highest note

Lowest note

*tied half-notes should be used in lieu of a whole-note.

For string instruments, two or more triangular notes may be used to indicate the highest notes of two or more strings, played simultaneously. If only one triangular note is used, it always means the highest pitch of the instrument, and thus of the highest string.

Two strings

(See also the Kilar excerpt on page 60.)

Note that the stems go to the center of the notes.

In free notation, no staff-lines are required: ↑ ⇑

Quick slide to the highest note:

Ordinary (measured) glissando to the highest note:

(For a general discussion of glissandos, see pages 19 ff and 63 ff.)

Indeterminate or Approximate Pitches

A. On a Five-Line Staff

If the ordinary five-line staff is used, note-heads should be omitted. The stem-ends show the approximate pitches.

N.B.: Only eighth notes and shorter values are suitable for this kind of notation. In quarter notes and half notes—notes without flags or beams—it is impossible to determine which end of the noteless stem represents the pitch end.

Symbolic durational notation   *Spatial durational notation*

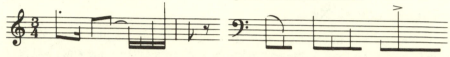

B. On a Grid

If a register grid is used instead of the five-line staff, there is no need for omitting the note-heads. As a result, the note-values need not be restricted, as suggested above.

Three-line grid, symbolic durational notation   *Three-line grid, spatial notation*

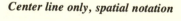

Center line only, symbolic durational notation   *Center line only, spatial notation*

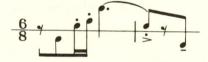

Whenever three-line grids or center lines are used within a five-line staff context, they should always replace that staff, and not be placed above or below it:

Microtones

A. Exact Pitches: Quarter Tones

1. PRELIMINARY REMARKS

Quarter tones are used in different ways. They may be

> ornamental inflections of a given pitch;
>
> part of a quarter-tone scale or other set of pitches that includes quarter tones;
>
> one of a number of microtonal divisions, such as sixth, quarter, and third tones.

Because of this diversity, some quarter-tone notations may be more appropriate than others, depending on the musical and notational contexts in which they occur.

2. ARROWED ACCIDENTALS FOR ORNAMENTAL INFLECTIONS, SCALES, AND OTHER SETS OF PITCHES

The notation of quarter-tone sharps and flats is shown here in the context of scale formations:

Quarter-tone naturals:

This system shows that there are two or more ways in which a quarter-tone pitch can be notated:

similar to the enharmonics of traditional notation:

The choice of the most appropriate accidentals depends on the kind of music in question and the harmonic context (if any) in which the pitches occur. Thus, in music based on any kind of tonal relationships, the up and down directions from tone to tone—the tonal gravity—should be reflected in the "grammar" of the notation:

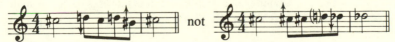

In atonal music, choices of this kind are generally irrelevant, especially if the sound source has ready-made pitches, such as quarter-tone keyboard instruments or xylophones with quarter-tone bars. Even in nontonal music, however, the notation of quarter tones should be chosen with care, since faster and more accurate results will be achieved in rehearsal if the quarter-tone sharps, flats, and naturals are not jumbled too randomly.* Moreover, it must be remembered that string players tend to differentiate between sharps and flats (F-sharp versus G-flat, for example) and that wind players, too, often use different fingerings for similar differentiations, even in atonal music.

The following examples show the same music in three different notations:

No flats

No sharps

Mixed

3. OTHER QUARTER-TONE ACCIDENTALS

Among the many quarter-tone accidentals invented over the years there is none with identical alterations for both sharps and flats except the arrow system shown above. Nor is any system quite as self-explanatory. But since the approach to the use of microtones—whether as structural components (scale steps) with or without tonal implications, or as ornamental ''bendings''—is still in flux, it seems somewhat premature to propose notational standard procedures at this time without at least providing a glance at a few alternatives for structural quarter tones. (The ornamental ones present less of a problem.**)

Thus, among the signs for quarter-tone sharps, the oldest and actually most convincing are those first proposed in 1756 by Giuseppe Tartini: ‡ ♯ ♯♯
(¼) (¾)

Strictly atonal music, i.e., music in which the pitches have no tonal implications (leading tones, etc.) could be notated with the three Tartini sharps and no quarter or three-quarter flats at all. All pitches originally thought of as quarter or three-quarter flats would then have to be ''translated'' enharmonically into equivalent sharps. The advantage of such notation is that it is easier to write and read than the arrowed accidentals. Its disadvantage is that it lacks quarter and three-quarter flats.

---

* But see the system presented at the end of the next section, page 69.
** See Approximate Pitches, page 70, and Microtonal Trills, page 76.

The following example shows the same music as above, notated with Tartini sharps:

As for quarter-tone flats, no method comparable in practicality and explicitness to either the arrows or the Tartini system has evolved so far, although there is no dearth of inventions.

The most frequently encountered flat adaptations are: ↓ ↘ ♭ and ♩ ⦚ ◖

None of these flats conveys as clearly as the Tartini sharps whether it lowers the pitch by one or by three quarters. Besides, the first three flats can easily be mistaken for carelessly written regular ones, and the other three are equally ambiguous except that they are clearly backward.

There is, however, one practical quarter-tone flat—a regular flat written backward (◖)—which is not likely to be mistaken. It has not been included above because it is part of a system which functions well and which, in fact, has already attained near standard status in atonal music for woodwinds. This system uses Tartini's one-quarter sharp (‡) and the backward one-quarter flat just mentioned.

Unfortunately, it does not include three-quarter sharps or flats because its quarter-tone accidentals can be used only on natural pitches (white keys). Thus a certain amount of enharmonic manipulating is necessary. Nevertheless, the system is highly recommended where appropriate, i.e., in a strictly nontonal context.

The enharmonics function as follows:

a ¾-sharp C must be notated as a ¼-flat D;

a ¾-flat D must be notated as a ¼-sharp C;

A quarter-tone scale, notated in this system, would read as follows:

Upward

Downward

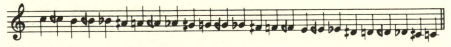

and the example quoted above would read:

B. Exact Pitches: Other Microtones

1. MICROTONE NUMERALS

A microtonal pitch other than a quarter tone should. be notated with small numerals, with arrows at the top or bottom to show the direction of the microtone from the written pitch:

$\uparrow\!\!3$ = one-third tone higher than the written pitch;

$6\!\!\downarrow$ = one-sixth tone lower than the written pitch; etc.

The numerals should be placed above rather than in front of the notes. If double or triple stops occur, such as in string instruments, one numeral applies to both or all three notes. If, however, different microtonal alterations are desired for such simultaneous notes, the respective numerals should be placed above one another in corresponding order:

In cases where altered and unaltered notes are mixed, double stemming should be employed and the numerals placed at the stem-end of the note(s) to be altered:

2. QUARTER-TONE NUMERALS

If quarter tones occur along with other microtones in a given composition, it is essential to notate all micro alterations according to the same system, i.e., to use the microtonal numerals for the quarter tones also: $\uparrow\!\!4$ or $4\!\!\uparrow$ and $4\!\!\downarrow$

N.B.: Never use more than one system of notation in any one composition, or, at least, in any one movement. Also, no matter which system is used, it must be explained at the beginning of the composition or movement, and not only in the score, but in the parts (if any) as well.

C. Approximate Pitches

1. CONSTANT PITCHES

Slightly higher or lower than the note

N.B.: The arrows must be quite small and thin so that they will not be confused with the larger, heavier arrows used for other purposes (highest or lowest notes, conductor's signs, synchronization arrows from part to part, etc.).

2. GRADUALLY CHANGING PITCHES

Slow pitch inflections

Transpositions

A. In C-Scores

All instruments are notated according to their actual sound (concert pitch), except the following because of their extreme ranges:

piccolo: a small *8* should be placed at the top of the G-clef to show that the sound is one octave higher than notated: ;

contrabass clarinet, contrabassoon, and double bass: a small *8* should be placed at the bottom of the bass clef to show that the sound is one octave lower than notated: ;

tenor voice: unlike the instruments listed above, the tenor voice does not have an extreme range. There is, however, a strong tradition of notating the tenor in the G-clef, one octave above its sound. This notation should be retained, though with a small *8* below the G-clef ( ) to indicate the actual pitch.

B. In Performance Scores

All transposing instruments in performance scores, i.e., scores actually played from, must be notated in their customary transpositions, not in their actual sound.

C. In Individual Parts

All transposing instruments must be notated in their customary transpositions, regardless of whether the score is in C or transposed.

Cues must be transposed (where applicable) to match the part(s) in which they occur. (For details, see Cues, page 160 f.)

N.B.: In former days there was much less variety of notation: it was understood that the piccolo, double bass, and tenor voice, etc., were notated in octave transposition, rendering the small *8* at the clefs superfluous. Today, with some scores notated in C and some in transpositions, and with some of the C scores having piccolos and double basses at actual pitch, while others have them in their customary octave transpositions, the small *8* has become necessary to avoid ambiguity.

Note further that all scores must carry an explanatory note in a prominent location, such as the upper left corner of the first page of music, saying "Score in C" or "Transposed Score," whichever applies. If, in a C score, no *8*s appear above or below the clefs of instruments which customarily were written in octave transposition (chiefly piccolo and double bass), the information should read "Score in C (actual sound; no octave transpositions)," or more explicitly,

"Score written at actual pitch with the exception of the following instruments:

(a) piccolo, xylophone, and harp harmonics sound one octave higher than written;

(b) glockenspiel sounds two octaves higher than written;

(c) contrabass clarinet, contrabassoon, and double bass sound one octave lower than written."

D. Clefs Used in Scores and Parts

Most instruments are notated in one clef only, regardless of the many leger lines required for very high or very low notes. Only a few instruments, such as horns or cellos, permit the use of more than one clef to make such extreme pitches easier to read.

In the following chart, the third column shows the clefs customarily used in transposed scores and parts. In C-scores one may be slightly more liberal with clef changes, though only in C-notation of transposing instruments.

Table of Transposing and Nontransposing Instruments: Notation, Actual Sound (Concert Pitch), and Clefs Used (in Score Order)

For the notation of pitched percussion instruments, see page 213 ff.

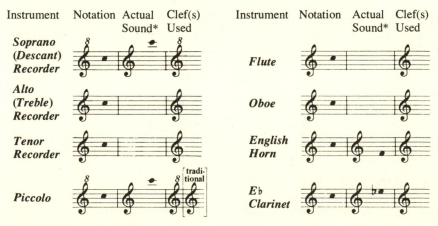

*Transposing instruments only.

** Notation preferred by players.

† Scores (in C) should be notated in C (bass clef); parts should be in C and in B♭ (G-clef).

Trill/Tremolo/Vibrato

Throughout music history there have been numerous interpretations of tremolo and vibrato, while trills have been comparatively stable in their meaning. At the present time the following interpretations are the most widely accepted:

A. Vibrato

Vibrato is a slight fluctuation of pitch, which should always be less than one half tone from the main note (but see N.B. below). It can be modified in width (*molto* or *un poco vibrato*) and in speed (fast or slow vibrato). It may also be canceled altogether (*non vibrato*).

Singers and performers on wind and string instruments normally produce a rather narrow, moderately fast vibrato, so that if any of the modifications mentioned above is wanted, this must be indicated and subsequently canceled with the abbreviation *ord.*, or the entire modified passage must be indicated by a broken-line bracket placed above it and ended with a downstroke.

A vibrato is never written out in actual notation, but in recent music, wavy lines have come to be used to indicate its approximate width and speed and gradual changes (see page 80).

B. Trill

The trill is essentially a half- or whole-tone vibrato, except that while the pitches of a vibrato usually are vague, those of a trill must be exact. As for the speed of a trill, it used to be as fast as possible, but in more recent music it is occasionally modified (''slow trill''). Also unlike a vibrato, trills are always indicated in the notation. (For details, see Trills, below.)

C. Tremolo

The term applies to several quite different techniques:

1. a fast repetition of one or more tones (e.g., a violin tremolo or a drum roll);

2. a fast alternation of two or more different pitches (e.g., a piano tremolo). This is related to the trill, except that the smallest tremolo interval must be larger than a second. (In certain contexts, this rule is occasionally broken; see Wide Trills, page 76.)

Perhaps the most versatile sound source for trills, tremolos, and vibratos is the voice (see detailed discussion in the Voice section).

For details of durational notation, see page 147 ff; see also individual listings.

N.B.: In recent music, gradual changes of the width of a vibrato have gone beyond the intervallic limit of less than one half tone. This has injected renewed confusion into the terminology, since vibratos of such great widths should either be called trills or tremolos. It would, however, be most impractical to change the nomenclature in midstream. Therefore, for those who wish to be very meticulous, a pitch fluctuation that begins narrow might be called a vibrato regardless of how wide it becomes later, while a pitch fluctuation that begins with a wide interval might be called a tremolo regardless of how narrow it becomes later.

Trills and Trill Tremolos

Trills are notated with the abbreviation *tr* in Italic type, followed by a wavy line. A short stroke at the end of the wavy line may be used to indicate whether the trill leads directly into the subsequent note or rest, or ends before it (see page 77).

On single trilled notes the wavy line may be omitted, especially if the notes occur in succession and there are no ties:

If, on the other hand, passages like the one above are to be performed molto legato, a single trill sign followed by a long wavy line may be used:

A. Single-Step Trills

It is understood that one trills with the note above the written pitch or main note, modified, if needed, by a small accidental just to the right of the *r* of the trill sign or by a small, stemless note-head in parentheses, following the main note:

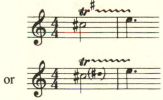

or

See also Ending a Trill, page 77.

If a trill is to begin with the note above the main note, a grace note (the upper pitch) should precede the main note:

If a trill is to begin with two or more opening notes, small sixteenth notes with a slash should precede the trill note:

Trills with the note below the main note are only rarely notated with a small, parenthetical note showing the lower pitch. Instead, the main note is lowered, preceded by a grace note showing that the trill begins with the upper pitch, or, if this obscures the true (harmonically primary) main note, it is notated as a tremolo:

Customary

Rare
(not recommended)

B. Wide Trills (Trill Tremolos)

Any trill wider than one whole step is a "wide" trill and requires a parenthetical note-head following the main note:

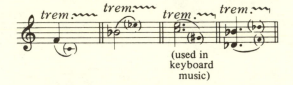

(used in
keyboard
music)

Since wide trills are the same as tremolos, they may also be notated as the latter.

If the music alternates between trills and tremolos it is often advisable to notate everything according to the same notational method, either all tremolos or all trills. The first example shows the preferred notation:

All tremolos

rather than

Mixed notation

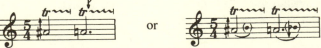

See also page 147 ff, and Voice, Tremolos, page 301 ff.

C. Microtonal Trills

A microtonal accidental must be placed in front of the main note, or above the *r* of the trill sign, or in front of the parenthetical trill note-head, depending on the desired pitches:

See also Microtones, page 70 ff.

D. Nonroutine Trill Openings

If a trill is to begin with a tongue click, scratch bow, cracked tone, etc., verbal instructions should be used:

E. Ending a Trill

The end of a trill should be indicated by a short vertical stroke cutting off the wavy trill line. It is important to show whether the trill is to end just before the next note or on the note. If the former, and if the next note comes after the barline, the wavy line must end at the barline, regardless of the amount of space between the barline and the next note:

F. Afterbeats

If specific pitches are wanted with which to end the trill, they must be indicated with small notes and slurred either to the preceding trill note (the main note) or to the note following the trill, depending on the circumstances:

G. Trill Continuing from One Line to the Next

End of one line   *Beginning of next line*

H. Timbral Trills

1. PRECISE RHYTHM, SPECIFIED FINGERING

2. PRECISE RHYTHM, FREE FINGERING

(A.F. = Alternate Fingering)

See also individual instruments where applicable, such as Brass, Percussion, etc.

Unisons

Unisons are most common in reductions and in parts with two voices or instruments on a single staff. Whole-note unisons require two notes written close to each other:

Stemmed notes do not require double-note notation as long as the unison consists of either two black or two white notes (but see dotted notes, below):

Unisons consisting of two different types of note-heads require two note-heads, with their up- and down-stems as close as possible as above:

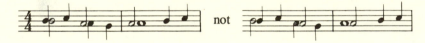

Dotted notes follow the rules given above, as long as both notes of the unison are dotted:

Unisons consisting of a dotted and an undotted note require two note-heads, with the undotted note preceding the dotted one, regardless of the position of the stems:

Double-dotted notes are treated the same as dotted notes.

For further details on dotted-note unisons, see Duration and Rhythm, Dotted Notes, page 125 f.

Unpitched Notes: Placement

A. Occasional Unpitched Notes

These should be written on an extra line added to the full staff. This extra line must not be so close that it will be mistaken for part of the regular staff. The extra line is placed either above the staff, between two staves (such as in piano music), or below the staff. If it appears above or below a single staff, the stems should point toward the staff.

1. INSTRUMENTAL MUSIC NOTATED ON A SINGLE STAFF
Here the extra line should, as a rule, be placed above the staff:

2. INSTRUMENTAL MUSIC NOTATED ON TWO STAVES
Here the extra line should be placed between the staves:

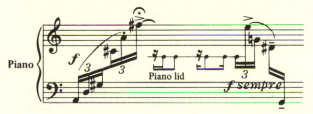

3. VOCAL MUSIC
The extra line should be placed below the staff so that the note-heads are close to the vocal text:

But see also Voice, pages 298 and 303 ff.

B. Extended Passages of Unpitched Notes in a One-Staff Part

This warrants temporary interruption of the full staff in favor of a single line, which should be the continuation of the middle line of the full staff (see Horizontal Lines, page 22).

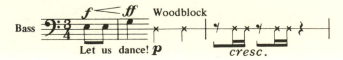

Vibrato/Non Vibrato

A slight vibrato is normal for the voice and most instruments. It should not be marked unless contrasted with molto vibrato or non vibrato (*n.v.**), in which cases the resumption of normal vibrato should be marked *ord.* or *norm.:*

A. Marked Vibrato

If a vibrato indication is used to call for a slight increase above normal vibrato, an unshaded wavy line should be placed above the music. The *vib.* at the beginning of the wavy line is optional:

B. Vibrato of Varying Width and/or Speed

If a vibrato of varying width and/or speed is wanted, the wavy line should outline the desired fluctuations:

1. ONLY THE SPEED VARIES

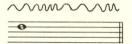

2. ONLY THE WIDTH VARIES
a. VIBRATO ABOVE THE PITCH
(Accidentals are optional.)

b. VIBRATO AROUND THE PITCH

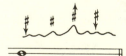

3. SPEED AND WIDTH VARY
a. WITH OPTIONAL ACCIDENTALS

b. WITH GUIDELINE

See also page 74 f, and Voice, Vibrato/Non Vibrato, page 304.

***n.v.* is preferable to *s.v.* (*senza vibrato*) because *n* is less likely to be misinterpreted.

III. *Duration and Rhythm: Preliminary Survey*

Prefatory Note   81

Rhythmic Trends in Twentieth-Century Music and Their Notational Consequences: A Brief Historical Survey   82

A. *Irregular Meters: Changing Time Signatures*   82
B. *Beaming by Rhythms and Phrases; Polymetric Textures*   82
C. *Beaming by Beat-Units*   87
D. *Polymetric Combinations: Notation by Reference Meter*   90
E. *Aperiodic, Nonmetric Durations (Fragmentation)*   94
F. *Spatial (or Proportional) Notation*   96
G. *Nonspecific Notation*   99
H. *Graphic Notation (Implicit Graphics)*   103

I. *Summary*   108
J. *New Music versus Traditional Notation*   108

Beaming   110
A. *Beat-Units*   110
B. *Simple Binary Measures*   110
C. *Irregular Note Divisions*   111
D. *Shorter, Simple Binary Measures*   113
E. *Simple Ternary Measures*   113
F. *Compound Measures*   113
G. *Irregular Metric Divisions within a Measure*   114
H. *Rhythmic versus Metric (Neutral) Beaming*   114

Practical Examples   115
A. *Cross Rhythms*   115
B. *Polymetric Textures*   116
C. *Different Rates of Speed*   119
D. *Spatial (or Proportional) Notation*   122

Prefatory Note

This section differs from all other substantive chapters in this guidebook in two respects:

1. In all other chapters, the notational signs and procedures are presented as isolated phenomena, divorced, with very few exceptions, from any musical context. This cannot be done with rhythm. For rhythm to be perceptible as such, a context is essential. Stated more simply: a sixteenth note by itself is no more than a time-value; it becomes a rhythmic phenomenon only in the context of what happens immediately before and after.

2. Considering the extraordinary complexity and diversity of the rhythmic and durational characteristics of music in our time, and the problems of

dealing with them notationally, it seemed inadvisable to present the various phenomena in alphabetical order. Instead, they appear as follows:

a. a brief historical survey of rhythmic/notational trends in the twentieth century, from Stravinsky's *Sacre du printemps* to the present;

b. a description of the most common rules and practices for the notation of rhythms and durations in present-day music (under the heading "Beaming");

c. a set of extended rhythmic and polyrhythmic phrases in various notational interpretations (under the heading "Practical Applications").

Rhythmic Trends in Twentieth-Century Music and Their Notational Consequences: A Brief Historical Survey

In the music of approximately the last four centuries, rhythmic or durational notation rarely presented any great difficulties, since meter, rhythm, and even phrasing were all bound up with one another. The fact that terms like *syncopation* or *cross rhythm* exist at all only proves that metric/rhythmic kinship was the norm, whether from part to part in a polyphonic texture, or within the individual parts themselves. Occasional irregularities thus could easily be recognized and labeled.

This equilibrium was profoundly upset during the twentieth century. The first major innovative trend was characterized by a gradual emancipation of rhythm and phrasing from the confines of a steady meter. Notation coped with this innovation in a number of ways, depending on the style and structure of the music at hand.

A. Irregular Meters: Changing Time Signatures
Music in which metric irregularities apply equally to the entire texture was usually notated with frequent meter changes which generally followed the rhythmic accents of the music (see facing page).

B. Beaming by Rhythms and Phrases; Polymetric Textures
Music in which the metric irregularities do not apply equally to the entire texture (i.e., music in which different irregularities occur simultaneously in different parts) was often notated with the function of the beams changed from indicators of metric divisions to indicators of rhythmic groupings and even of phrases.

In the excerpt from Béla Bartók's *Fifth String Quartet* (1934) on pages 84–5, the meter at the top of the page is $\frac{4}{4}$. Note that at the end of the first measure of the example, after the *Più mosso*, triplets are introduced in the violins (though without the identifying triplet number *3*). Once the notation of the triplet motion has been

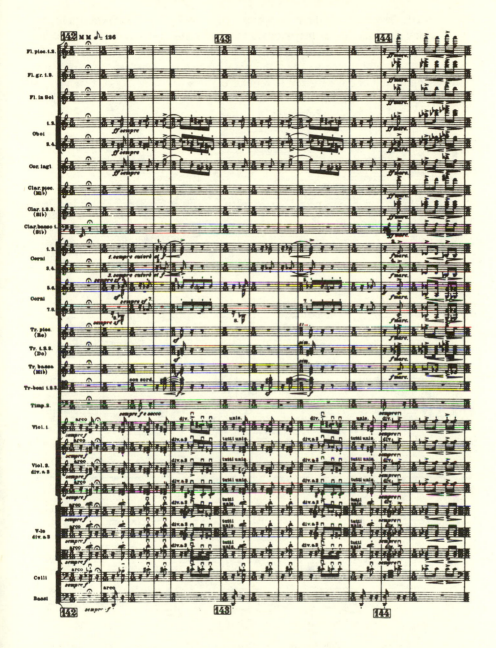

Igor Stravinsky: *Le Sacre du printemps, Danse sacrale* (1913), page 112 of
miniature score. (Copyright 1921 by Edition Russe de Musique. Copyright assigned
1947 to Boosey & Hawkes for all countries of the world. Reprinted by permission.)

established, the customary three-note beaming is discontinued in favor of phrase-beams, and there are no further indications concerning metric divisions until the chord at letter F. Here, since the beams no longer reflect metric divisions, the players are literally forced to count the notes to find out whether the triplet motion is continuing or has reverted to regular eighths—obviously not a very practical solution.

Béla Bartók: *String Quartet No. 5* (1934), first movement, mm. 119–26.
Copyright 1936 by Universal Edition; Renewed 1963. Copyright and renewal assigned to Boosey & Hawkes, Inc. (for the U.S.A.) Reprinted by permission.

Anton Webern's *Second Cantata,* Op. 31 (1943), presents a different problem in that its entire sixth movement is polymetric: the fifteen vocal and instrumental parts move simultaneously in four different, ever-changing meters (see page 86).

Fortunately, these meters have a common beat-unit—the half note—and are thus easy to notate,* but it is virtually impossible for a conductor to give equal attention to the indigenous characteristics of each of the metric progressions.

*for polymetric textures with different beat-units, see page 90 ff.

Anton Webern: *Second Cantata*, Op. 31 (1943), sixth movement.
© Copyright 1965 by Universal Edition A.G., Vienna; used by permission.

All three innovative methods—the frequent meter changes in the Stravinsky example, the beaming by rhythms and phrases in the Bartók excerpt, and the polymetric notation of the Webern movement—proved too inefficient to survive, especially in orchestral and ensemble music. Consequently, more and more composers restored the beams to their former function as metric indicators (beaming by beat-units), reduced meter changes to an essential minimum, largely abandoned conflicting simultaneous time signatures, and instead used accents and occasional rhythmic cue lines to show the different metric stresses.

C. Beaming by Beat-Units

A particularly interesting example of reversion from innovative phrase-beaming to traditional metric divisions may be found in Stravinsky's own 1943 revision of the *Danse sacrale* from the *Sacre du printemps*. He also renotated the entire movement with larger note-values—eighths instead of the original sixteenths as the basic units—for greater visual clarity. Obviously, both changes were made for practical reasons only: to make it easier to perform the piece.

Corresponding rehearsal numbers of the 1943 version:

Igor Stravinsky: *Le Sacre du printemps, Danse sacrale*, page 115 of the original (1921) miniature score. (Copyright 1921 by Edition Russe de Musique. Copyright assigned 1947 to Boosey & Hawkes for all countries of the world. Reprinted by permission.)

Corresponding rehearsal numbers of the 1921 version:

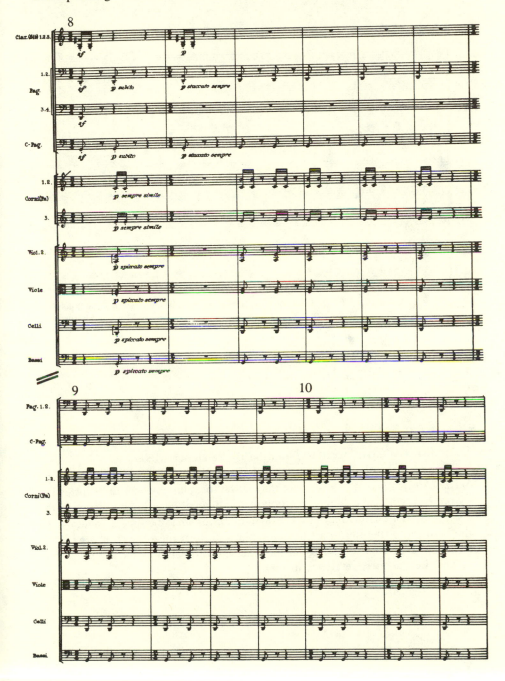

Igor Stravinsky: *Danse sacrale*, revised version of 1943, published separately. (Copyright 1945 by Associated Music Publishers, Inc.)

D. Polymetric Combinations: Notation by Reference Meter

The next example—the opening of the second movement of Elliott Carter's *Second String Quartet* (1959)—not only shows beaming by beat-units instead of by phrases, but also exhibits such polymetric diversity and independence in the four parts—far beyond the Bartók example above—that the time signatures and the barlines for the most part have lost their musical meaning, functioning instead as mere technical devices for the precise coordination of the different note-values, i.e., as mere reference meters:

Presto scherzando

* Alternate rhythmic notation for Violin II indicating how its part should sound, within itself. This alternate notation also indicates the correct length of resonance of each note, regardless of the note-values which appear in the actual part.

Elliott Carter: *String Quartet No. 2* (1959), beginning of second movement.
© 1961 by Associated Music Publishers, Inc. Used by permission.

COMMENTS

A rhythmic analysis of this example reveals the following:

Violin I follows the metric divisions of $\frac{5}{4}$ and $\frac{6}{4}$ with its fairly regular triplet movement until, from the E-flat in m. 175 on, its own pulse speeds up to beats of two triplet eighths, an example of Carter's "metric modulation":

At this point the $\frac{5}{4}$ meter becomes musically irrelevant: it simply turns into a reference meter for keeping the players together.

Violin II barely fits into the given time signatures, which have nothing to do with its own pulse. An added rhythm cue shows that this pulse actually consists of very simple eights and quarters in a $\frac{4}{4}$ meter at the rate of ♩ = 140, as against the ♩ = 175 of the $\frac{5}{4}$ and $\frac{6}{4}$ meters.

The viola progresses without any discernible metric regularity until it intones four beats in a pulse of three sixteenths, beginning on the F-sharp in m. 174, and again beginning on the C-natural in m. 176.

The cello's predominantly regular eighth notes seem to have suggested the $\frac{5}{4}$ and $\frac{6}{4}$ time signatures, since there is no conflict between the musical pulse and that of the notation.

The following example from the same string quartet shows similar features in a slightly more complicated context:

* Viola: in measures 585 to 588, the four accented F's should be played as regular beats of MM-84.

COMMENTS

This entire segment is subject to a carefully controlled accelerando beginning with ♩ = 101 and progressing via 120, 134, and 151 at the respective barlines to 168 at the beginning of m. 588 (not shown). Within this accelerando, the following rhythmic/metric progressions take place:

Violin I, after its septuplets and quintuplets, settles on a pulse of three thirty-seconds (in mm. 586 and 587), a division quite independent of the notated reference meter of $\frac{2}{4}$.

Violin II plays triplets which at first fit into the $\frac{3}{4}$ meter. Beginning with the low A-sharp, however, it performs its own accelerando (within the overall accelerando!), thus deviating musically from the notated metric beats.

The viola's sixteenths seem at first to fit with the cello's eighths, even though the phrasing is quite different. In m. 585, however, slow but regular beats at a metronome speed of 84 (see Carter's footnote) appear, which are not of the overall accelerando.

As in the first example, the cello fits the notated meter and probably determined it, since it is the only instrument in these four measures which does not change its pulse.

E. Aperiodic, Nonmetric Durations (Fragmentation)

1. ENSEMBLE MUSIC: Luigi Nono, *La terra e la compagna*

In the following example, the time signatures and beat-units are completely without musical relevance, since the music has neither pulse nor patterns—only sounding and silent durations. Coherence has given way to fragmentation. Even the text has been split up into individual syllables which are scattered over the divisi choral and solo parts, and at times the vowels are sung separated from their consonants.

The text, at this point, reads:

> *Tu non sai le colline*
> *dove s'è sparso il san[gue].*

Luigi Nono: *La terra e la compagna* (1958) for soprano and tenor solos, 24-part mixed chorus, 4 flutes, 4 trumpets in D, 4 trombones, strings, and percussion. (© 1959 by Ars Viva Verlag (Hermann Scherchen) GmbH.)

NB. Schlaginstrumente: ♪ immer ausklingen lassen.

COMMENTS

Although the durational units in the preceding example do not follow any metric pattern, they are nevertheless made to fit into the coordinating framework of meters ($\frac{2}{4}$ during the excerpt shown) and beat-units (pairs of eighths, rather than quarters, to judge by the rests). This notational procedure causes the majority of the durations to begin on offbeats, as if the music contained a preponderance of syncopations—a complete misrepresentation, since syncopations are possible only as irregularities in a regular metric context, which is quite alien to music of this kind.

2. SOLO MUSIC: Pierre Boulez, *Third Piano Sonata—formant 2—trope*

Realizing the notational incongruity demonstrated in the Nono example, Boulez dispenses with meter and barlines altogether in order to have each duration enter on its own terms, independent of its position even within a mere (meter-related) beat-unit. The only musically irrelevant groupings still in use are triplets and similar sets, which make occasional offbeatlike entrances unavoidable. Boulez is, after all, still dealing with traditional durational notation—a system not designed to serve problems of this nature.

A final observation: this is a work for a single performer, i.e., one that does not involve the coordination of different musicians. Boulez's notational approach could not be applied to the Nono work, which, to be performed accurately, requires the help of some system of coordinating devices.

Pierre Boulez: *Third Piano Sonata—formant 2—trope,* segment from *Commentaire*. (© Copyright 1961 by Universal Edition (London) Ltd.)

F. Spatial (or Proportional) Notation

With works such as those by Nono and Boulez, the culmination of measured durational diversity has been reached, at least within the capabilities of traditional notation. Electronic sound generators can of course be programmed to bring forth still more minute subdivisions, and especially combinations of subdivisions (like 15 against 17), as well as more complex rhythmic patterns which are totally independent of any metric framework. But machines do not perform from scores and parts!

Simultaneous with the tendency toward ever greater complexity, a trend has developed in the opposite direction: less notational precision and ever greater interpretive freedom. It represents a fundamental break with all previous notational systems: the change from symbolic durational notation (quarter notes, eighth notes, etc.) to spatial (or proportional) notation in which durations are indicated through horizontal spacing of sounds and silences. Measures (if any) represent units of time (usually one or more seconds or a certain number of metronome clicks), but not meters.

Note-heads are placed at the approximate horizontal locations within a "measure" at which they are to be performed. Sustained sounds have durational "extenders" to show how long they are to be held. The extenders are either heavy horizontal lines following the (stemless) note-heads at the same vertical level, or they are represented by extended—usually single—beams.

The first of the two following examples shows note-heads with and without extenders. The second example shows beam extensions.

1. NOTE EXTENDERS: Aribert Reimann, *Rondes for String Orchestra*

The duration of each page is about 6 to 7 seconds (according to indications which appear elsewhere in the score). The texture varies between synchronized material (marked with dotted vertical lines), and relatively free successions of notes. Short notes (mostly pizzicato, but also bowed, as in the cellos and basses) have no extenders; sustained notes do.

Aribert Reimann: *Rondes* for String Orchestra (1967), © 1969 by Ars Viva Verlag, Mainz.

(*This example continues on page 98.*)

The composition as a whole alternates between traditional (symbolic) dura-tional notation and spatial sections like the segment shown. There are also mixtures of spatial and traditional notation, primarily where prominent parts must be performed with precision while the spatially notated material provides contrasting, flexible background.

2. DURATION BEAMS: Luciano Berio, *Tempi concertati*

The example on page 100, scored for principal flute and four groups of instruments, shows beam extensions. The short, slightly slanted "beamlets" indicate short notes. The cornered fermatas mean long holds, and the wavy lines between them mean *ad lib.* continuations of the preceding music. The arrows at the beginning and again at the end of the flute part instruct the flutist to motion to the ensemble to enter. (The first arrow is necessary because the flute had been solo until the beginning of the excerpt.)

3. MIXED NOTATION: Elliott Schwartz, *Texture for Strings, Winds, and Brass*

A good example of simultaneous use of symbolic and spatial notion is shown in the excerpt on page 101. It differs from the mixed notation described in connection with the Reimann example in that the ensemble is divided into groups. These groups are notated either symbolically or spatially, i.e., not mixed within any one group, but they interact, alternate, operate simultaneously, and so forth.

Note also that Schwartz, unlike many other composers, has included complete instructions as to which player cues in and cuts off other players. These instructions are in the text, not in prefatory remarks where reference is inconvenient during rehearsals and impossible in performance. The same applies to all other indications for coordinating the various performers and groups of performers, such as the instruction for the woodwinds, "cut off at pizz." (upper right), or subsequently, "Fl. cues" (meaning that the flute gives the cue for the next woodwind entrance). Because of these instructions in the music itself, the piece can easily be performed without conductor. All players perform from the score.

G. Nonspecific Notation

The example on page 102 from the *Impromptu fantasque* (1973) by Kazimierz Serocki, for 6 recorders, 3 (6) mandolins, 3 (6) guitars, piano, and 2 percussion groups, is representative of the large number of compositions that depend chiefly on effects and contain large numbers of new notational signs and symbols. These compositions often differ greatly in appearance, but they all have one feature in common: extensive prefatory explanations of new notational signs. The present case is no exception: before the music begins, there are five pages of instructions and explanations in Polish, German, and English. The following are the instructions needed for the page reproduced here:

"The arrows at the top are conductor's signals, numbered consecutively, like measure numbers. Only those with thin arrowheads (Nos. 2–6) are periodic, indicating beats 2½ seconds apart (or M = 24). The heavier ones are governed by the number of seconds shown at the bottom of the score: arrow 1 initiates a seven-second unit; arrows 8 and 9 subdivide the ten-second unit initiated by arrow 7." *(Text continues on page 102.)*

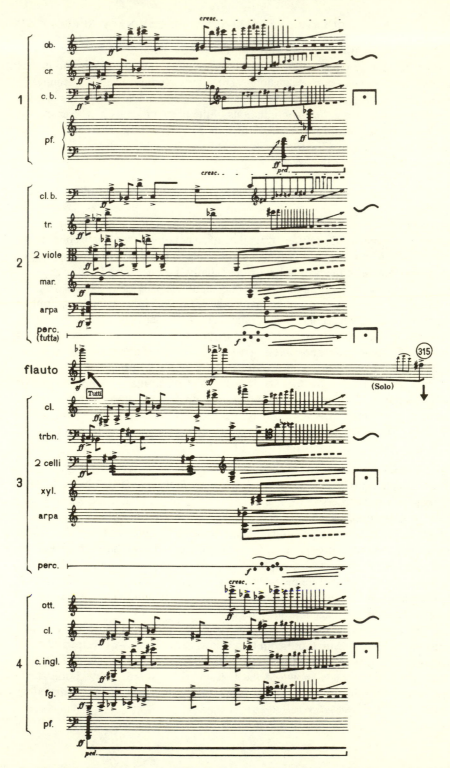

Luciano Berio: *Tempi concertati* (1960). © Copyright 1962 by Universal Edition (London) Ltd.

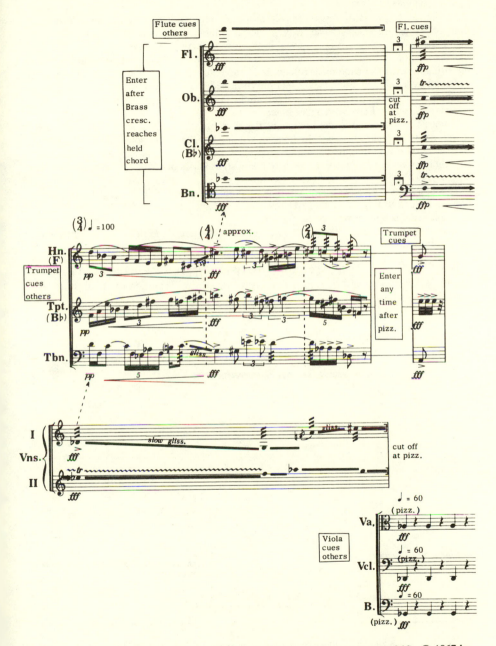

Elliott Schwartz: *Texture for Strings, Winds, and Brass* (1966). © 1967 by Tetra Music Corp. (Alexander Broude, Inc.), New York. Used by permission.

A few explanations of details are needed for the reader to understand the score page here reproduced.

The music begins with a maracas roll *ppp—fff—ppp,* followed by the piano and the gong of percussion group II. The arrow at the bottom of the piano's clef indicates playing inside the piano, on the strings exposed in the lowest section of the metal frame. The *Z*-like sign denotes "rapid, dense tremolo" [with the fingers rubbing back and forth across the strings]; the broad band means "cluster," and below it, the symbol of the right pedal followed by a horizontal line means that the right pedal is to be held down.

The gong is to be struck with a hard felt stick, in time with the signals.

At No. 7, guitar 1 and vibraphone enter.

Guitar: the semicircle at the bottom of the first (thin) vertical line indicates that the strings are to be played between the fingerboard and the pegs. The notes and lines call for free, aperiodic improvisation ("rapid groups of notes"). The subsequent curved and straight lines are not explained but seem to mean short bursts of sound rather than continuous playing.

The vibraphone is played similar to the piano: the tremolo is produced with wire brushes instead of fingers; pitches to be used are indicated on the staff below the cluster; the right pedal is held down.

Guitars 2 and 3 operate like guitar 1, except that the notes and lines suggest different pitch patterns.

Needless to say, each page of the thirty-eight-page score presents different sounds, techniques, and degrees of freedom or control. (Hence the multitude of prefatory instructions.)

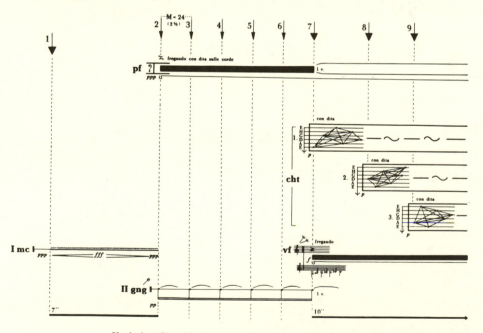

Kazimierz Serocki: *Impromptu Fantasque* (1973) for 6 recorders, 3(6) mandolins, 3(6) guitars, piano, and 2 percussion groups. © 1975 by PWM Edition, Krakow, Poland, and Moeck Verlag, Celle, West Germany. Used by permission of Moeck Verlag, Celle, and Belwin Mills Publishing Corp., Melville, New York.

As for notational standardization, the Polish publishers have brought out such a volume of modern scores that many of the signs used have indeed become standard devices, at least in contemporary Polish music, and quite a number of them have spread to the rest of Europe, as well as to America and Japan.

On the other hand, since many of these works live on unique effects, they require a great deal of new notation in addition to the standard devices. Prefatory explanations of new signs are therefore inevitable just the same.

From this point on in the development of graphic notation, ever greater musical indeterminacy and unpredictability has been paralleled by a proliferation of new notational signs. Most of these have come and gone with the compositions for which they were invented. The few that have survived and become standard procedure, or are well on the way, will be found in the appropriate places throughout the book.

H. Graphic Notation (Implicit Graphics)

For the sake of completeness, a few words must be added concerning graphic notation, i.e., music notated with "implicit graphics," even though such notation does not fit into the present guidebook, being incompatible with any form of standardization. The reason: graphic notation differs fundamentally from all other forms of notation, because it is deliberately not intended to convey any specific instructions whatsoever—no pitches, durations, dynamics, timbres, synchronization, or anything else.

The performers are provided with drawings, usually abstract, which are intended to spark their imagination and inspire them to express in sound their reactions to what they see in front of them. They may react differently from day to day, or from hour to hour; nor are any two musicians expected to derive identical inspiration from the same graphics. No two interpretations should ever be the same.

The "scores" may be in black and white or in color; they may contain clearly differentiated shapes, undefined, cloudlike washes, or blank pages; they may even include an occasional word or musical symbol; and they may include all manner of instructions. But they are never specific, they are never "mere" notation. No other approach permits greater freedom of "composition" or interpretation.

However, notation which deliberately avoids not only all specificity but also all forms of repetition obviously cannot be subjected to any kind of standardization. All that is possible is to show a few manifestations, which may give substance to what has been described above.

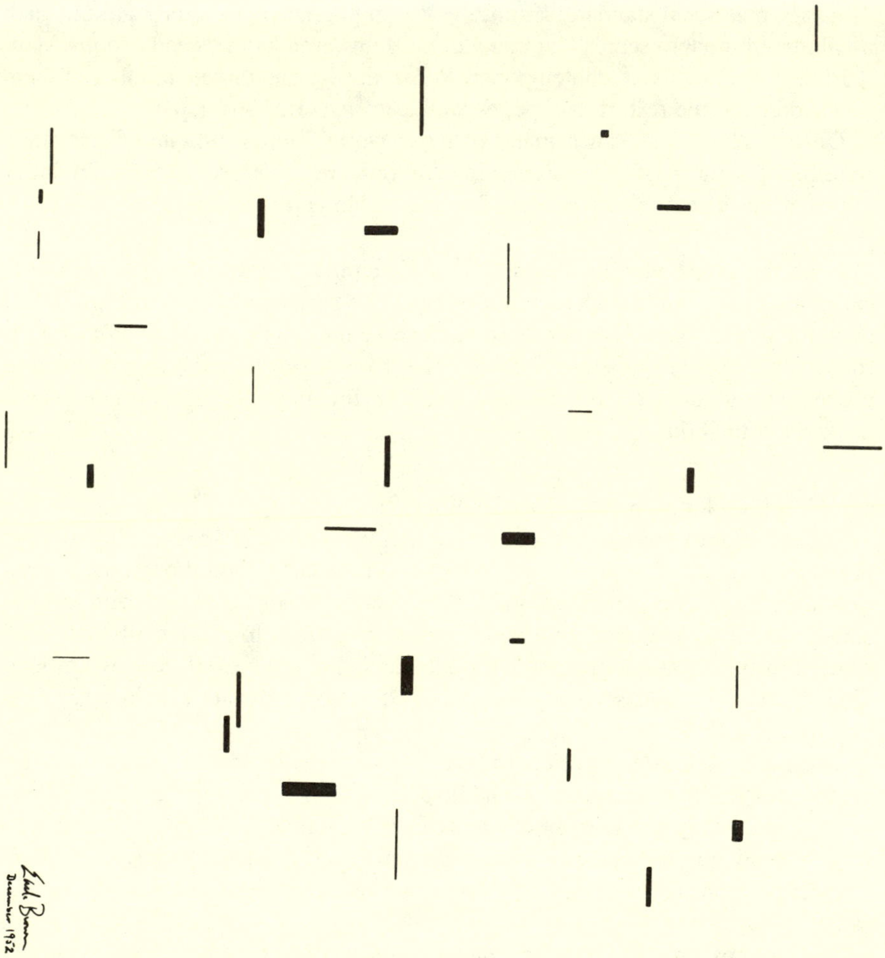

Earle Brown: from *Folio* (1952).
© Copyright 1961 by Associated Music Publishers, Inc., New York. Used by permission.

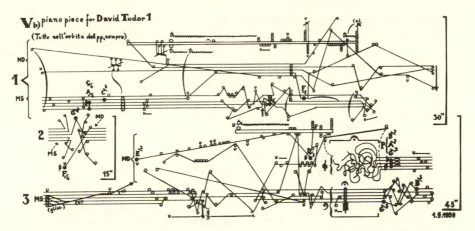

Sylvano Bussotti: *Five Piano Pieces for David Tudor—No. 1.* © 1959 by Universal Edition (London) Ltd.; assigned 1970 to G. Ricordi & C.s.p.a., Milan; reprinted with permission.

Sylvano Bussotti: *Five Piano Pieces for David Tudor—No. 3* © 1959 by Universal Edition (London) Ltd.; assigned 1970 to G. Ricordi & C.s.p.a., Milan; reprinted with permission.

The following is a more recent example in which a certain amount of control has been incorporated:

Adam Walaciński: ALLALOA *(1970).*

Instructions

> The piece should be performed on the whole piano, both on the keyboard and on the inner parts (the strings, soundboard, lid, etc.), using additionally sticks and wire brushes. Division into three registers — high, middle and low — applies only to the sounds produced on the keyboard and strings. Percussive sounds should be produced on the appropriate dynamic level (the high register — the highest dynamic level). The basic graphic symbols are assigned to the respective sound categories, the remainder may be interpreted *ad lib.*, according to the following rule: the more intricate and ambiguous the graphic picture, the more complicated and difficult to identify the sound effect. The piano may be partly prepared, also contact microphones and other electro-acoustic means of transforming sound may be utilized as well. Where the traditional dynamic indications have not been given, the player should follow the graphic suggestions. Duration is optional, but it should by no means exceed 8 min.

Notational details (see opposite page, upper half)

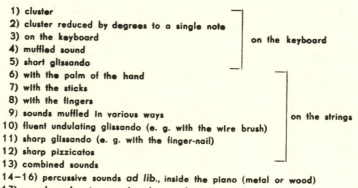

1) cluster
2) cluster reduced by degrees to a single note
3) on the keyboard
4) muffled sound   on the keyboard
5) short glissando
6) with the palm of the hand
7) with the sticks
8) with the fingers
9) sounds muffled in various ways   on the strings
10) fluent undulating glissando (e. g. with the wire brush)
11) sharp glissando (e. g. with the finger-nail)
12) sharp pizzicatos
13) combined sounds
14—16) percussive sounds *ad lib.*, inside the piano (metal or wood)
17) sounds and noises produced away from the piano
18) all categories of sounds (1—16), as differentiated as possible, accelerando and ritardando

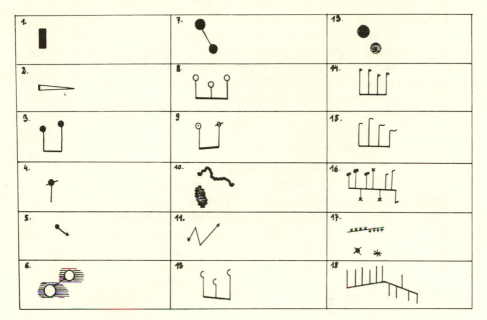

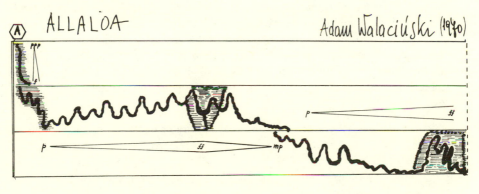

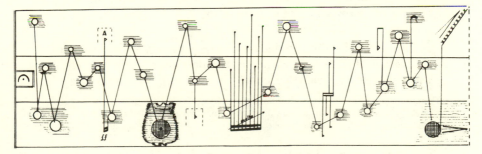

I. Summary

Each new notational approach, each new sign and procedure shown so far in this sampling, is valid under certain circumstances. All of them coexist in our era,* together with traditional notation at one end of the spectrum, and entirely new notational systems (such as Equiton**) at the other. The choice as to which to use depends, or should depend, exclusively on the kind of music and performance situation involved. Notational ingenuity and daring are all very well, but with the possible exception of implicit graphics, notation must never be confused with the musical substance as such.

J. New Music versus Traditional Notation

It is obvious from the examples quoted that unconventional rhythmic and durational phenomena, especially when they occur in polymetric/polyrhythmic combinations, are more fundamentally incompatible with traditional notation than practically anything else. Dodecaphonic pitch successions, for example, can be notated without causing confusion, no matter how unsuited our diatonic staff, accidentals, and nomenclature are to such music.

Even microtones can be indicated quite satisfactorily with the help of a few modified traditional accidentals or with "bent" horizontal lines and the like.

But the durational innovations of the music of our era constitute an as yet unsolved dilemma. Fortunately, the excessively complicated, aperiodic, yet minutely differentiated rhythms typical of the '50s and '60s seem to have passed their greatest flowering, perhaps because of the virtual impossibility of performing or perceiving them accurately. Thus, rhythmically speaking, one might say that from around 1970 onward, the former diversity of trends has come down to three basic nontraditional manifestations with which traditional notation must deal:

1. music involving aperiodic, constantly changing durations of sounds and silences, all governed or coordinated by nonmetric means (mostly serialism);

2. music involving simultaneous motion at different rates of speed, in different meters, with controlled accelerandos and ritardandos, and with complex augmentations and diminutions of rhythmic patterns and similar phenomena;

3. music in which different meters and speeds, etc., as well as nonmetric successions of durations are combined without any fixed or rigid coordination, but, rather, with deliberately flexible organizational instructions

* The fact that most of the examples hail from the 1950–60s shows that those were the years of greatest notational innovation. Since then, the drive toward new notation has calmed considerably, which is why the present book has become possible; it could not have been written while everything was still in flux.

** See Erhard Karkoschka: *"Ich habe mit Equiton komponiert"* (Melos 29, July/August 1962, pp. 233–39).

which usually invite the performer(s) to exercise varying degrees of interpretive freedom.

The notation of aperiodic durations is relatively simple if one omits all metric components, since, being alien to such music, they encumber the notation. Lacking metric coordinators (or equivalents), however, such music lends itself best, if not exclusively, to performance by a single interpreter. The Boulez excerpt above is a good example of how to notate music of this nature.

The durational complexities of simultaneous speeds strain the capabilities of traditional metric/rhythmic notation to their very limits, though not beyond, i.e., such music can (and invariably is) notated by traditional means—symbolic note-values, measures, and time signatures—and it can thus be performed accurately by chamber groups and orchestras as well as by individuals.

The notation combining different meters, etc., is the simplest by far, since such music does not require any precision comparable to the other two approaches. On the other hand, the music's freedom has generated almost as many notational presentations as there are compositions. One very moderate example is that of *Texture* by Elliott Schwartz. But the field is so wide and varied—there is no such thing as a typical example.

In contemplating this compilation of musical/notational trends, one can draw three practical conclusions:

1. SPATIAL AND GRAPHIC NOTATION

The new systems of spatial or graphic notation and the equally novel flexibility of synchronization are actually a good deal easier to work with than traditional notation, because they generally require only approximations, as against the rigid precision demanded by traditional notation.

2. NEW NOTATIONAL SIGNS AND SYMBOLS

The multitude of duplications and/or ambiguities among the new signs and symbols, no matter in which system they occur, is impractical and confusing and should be reduced as much as possible.

3. THE ROLE OF TRADITIONAL NOTATION IN NEW MUSIC

The new ways of utilizing traditional notation for expressing new musical phenomena (such as polymetric textures and controlled gradual speed changes, etc.) necessitate a much more detailed study of notation's capabilities than used to be needed. The following discussion shows in which way this necessity might be dealt with.

As the examples of traditional notation from Stravinsky to Carter have shown, the use of beams is of crucial importance. When rhythmic irregularities first appeared, beams were often used to show at a glance the difference between an irregular rhythmic group of notes and the prevailing (regular) meter. Irregular beaming, however, gradually changed to beaming by beat-units (i.e., from rhythmic to metric beaming) when the musical textures grew so complex that it became more important to focus on the unifying metric beats than on the individual nonmetric rhythms, even though this procedure resulted in visually obscuring most of the contrasting rhythmic groupings and polymetric strands.

In recognition of this, the next section deals with beaming, first methodically, then applied to practical problems.

Beaming

N.B.: For the graphic characteristics of beams (thickness, etc.), see Beams, page 9.

A. Beat-Units

In general, measures should be divided into metric beat-units to help the performers recognize the beats and the metric structure of the measures, whether these metric structures coincide with the rhythm of the music or act as mere coordinating devices. (But see Irregular Metric Divisions, below.)

The best method of identifying beat-units is through beaming (note-values permitting); either single beat-units or pairs of them should be beamed together.

There are two basic types of beat-units: duple units and triple units, depending on the meters (time signatures) in question:

Simple meters ($\frac{4}{4}, \frac{2}{4}, \frac{2}{2}, \frac{3}{4}$, etc.) have duple beat-units:

Compound meters ($\frac{6}{8}, \frac{9}{8}, \frac{12}{8}, \frac{6}{4}, \frac{9}{16}$, etc.) have triple beat-units:

If rests occur, especially in rhythmically complex music, the beams should cover them, so that the beat-units remain clearly recognizable. (For details, see Extended and Bridging Beams, page 15 f.)

B. Simple Binary Measures

If simple binary measures contain four beat-units, such as $\frac{4}{4}$ and $\frac{4}{8}$ measures, the first and last pairs of beat-units may be beamed together, provided that both units of each pair either contain only the same note-values (only eighths or only sixteenths), or certain identical rhythms (see below). Such pairing of beat-units results in only two beamed groups per measure instead of four, thus making the middle of the measure stand out clearly.·

In the following examples, brackets show the two halves of the measures.

Identical note-values

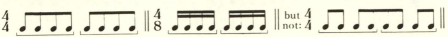

Identical rhythms

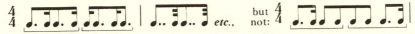

In earlier days, unequal combinations of note-values were often beamed together rather indiscriminately, just as beams often crossed the middle of the measure or even the barline:

This uncontrolled practice has become more regulated over the years, although certain unequal beat-units are still beamed together if the rhythmic texture of the music is fairly simple. Of these, the following are among the most frequently encountered:

The principle of showing the center of the (four-beat) measure also operates if no beat-units are paired, or only the first or second pair is beamed together:

Similarly, if a note-value lasts across the middle of the measure, it must be split up into two notes, with a tie across the middle of the measure:

C. Irregular Note Divisions

1. TRIPLETS AND OTHERS

Triplets and other irregular note divisions are generally not combined into double beat-units, but if they are part of a single beat-unit, they are beamed together.

They must, however, be clearly identified through interruption of the secondary beam(s) or through brackets, or through other appropriate means:

(Needless to say, the last septuplet is a "natural" double beat-unit because it cannot be broken up.)

2. IRREGULAR NOTE DIVISIONS ACROSS A BARLINE

If irregular note divisions extend across a barline, the beam(s) or bracket(s) should also cross the barline, even in cases of beaming by beat-units.

In the following excerpt from Elliott Carter's *Symphony of Three Orchestras* (1976) a quintuplet begins on the last beat of a measure and ends at the end of the subsequent first beat:

The quintuplet could have been notated broken up and tied:

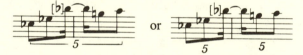

but it is not recommended. A single, continuous beam is clearer.

3. OFFBEAT IRREGULAR NOTE DIVISIONS

If irregular note divisions occur in offbeat positions in the measure, it is recommended to add a rhythm cue to help the performer. The following occurs in Milton Babbitt's *Composition for Twelve Instruments* (1948/54):

D. Shorter, Simple Binary Measures

In shorter, simple binary measures ($\frac{2}{4}, \frac{2}{8}$) the rule that the middle of the measure should always be recognizable is not always adhered to. Such measures are short enough to be grasped as a single unit unless one deals with very short note-values, i.e., with many notes in the measure. Thus $\frac{2}{4}$ ♪♪ ♪♪ | may also be notated: $\frac{2}{4}$ ♪♪♪♪ |, and $\frac{2}{8}$ ♪♪.♪♪ | may be changed to $\frac{2}{8}$ ♪♪♪.♪ |. On the other hand, a measure such as: $\frac{2}{4}$ ♪.♪♪♪♪♪♪♪♪♪ | should definitely not be beamed together, since this would make it too difficult to perceive quickly.

If a two-beat measure is not beamed together, the rule that the middle of the measure must be clearly recognizable must be adhered to:

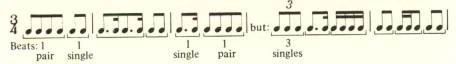

etc., but *not*:

E. Simple Ternary Measures

In simple ternary measures ($\frac{3}{4}, \frac{3}{8}$, etc.) it is customary to combine one pair of equals (if there is one) and leave the remaining beat-unit separate:

Even if the rhythms are more complicated, the principle of beaming by beat-units remains the same:

If all notes are of the same value, or all three beat-units have the same rhythm, the entire measure may be beamed together, but this is recommended chiefly for $\frac{3}{8}$ measures:

F. Compound Measures

In compound measures, unlike simple measures, pairing of beat-units is not permissible; all beat-units must be notated separately:

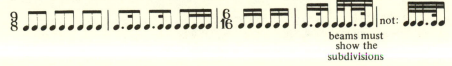

not:

beams must
show the
subdivisions

G. Irregular Metric Divisions within a Measure

Beams may be used to indicate irregular metric divisions:

[musical notation example in $\frac{8}{8}$]

Note that the time signature shows smaller unit durations (in this case, eighths) than the beat-units which would normally divide a measure containing eight eighths ($\frac{4}{4}$, $\frac{2}{2}$, **C**, or **¢**). In other words, the $\frac{8}{8}$ signature indicates that the eighths are grouped into irregular beat-units, and the beaming shows how they are grouped. Such meters are called composite meters (see pages 118 f and 135).

Time signatures of this kind are suitable for binary meters only. In ternary meters, they become misleading, since a change, for instance, from $\frac{3}{4}$ to $\frac{6}{8}$ implies a change from three regular (simple) beats ($\frac{3}{4}$ [notation]) to two regular (compound) beats ($\frac{6}{8}$ [notation]), i.e., not a change from regular to irregular beats. (See further under Time Signatures, page 158 f.)

The problems of regular versus irregular metric divisions do not arise in meters such as $\frac{5}{4}$, $\frac{5}{8}$, $\frac{7}{4}$, and $\frac{7}{8}$, since these are by nature already divided asymmetrically.

[musical notation example in $\frac{5}{8}$]

[musical notation example in $\frac{7}{8}$]

It is unfortunate that notes of longer duration than eighths do not have beams or equivalent devices for the indication of the desired rhythmic/metric divisions and phrases. If a composer plans a work with complex rhythms and is not set on particular basic note-values he would be well advised to use beamed notes, rather than longer values—for example:

[musical notation example in $\frac{5}{8}$] rather than [musical notation example in $\frac{5}{4}$]

H. Rhythmic versus Metric (Neutral) Beaming

As mentioned at the beginning of this chapter, beaming by beat-units is generally preferred in rhythmically complex textures, but there are situations in which irregular beaming (as well as irregular time signatures) may be better suited to indicate the rhythm of the music.

When a composer is confronted with the question of which system of beaming to choose, he should be guided by the following considerations:

1. If the rhythms of a given composition suggest irregular groupings of otherwise regular note-values, it is generally best to follow these groupings with matching time signatures and beams, for example:

$\frac{5}{8}$ ♩. ♪♩♩ | $\frac{8}{8}$ ♩♩♩♩♩. ♩♩ | $\frac{5}{8}$ ♩. ♩♩♩♩ | $\frac{7}{8}$ ♪ ♩ ♩♩♩♩ | *etc.*

2. If the composition contains different irregular groupings in different parts to be performed simultaneously, or if the composition's sounds and silences are ametrical (aperiodic), or if two or more parts proceed at different speeds or at gradual changes of speed, it is best to use a neutral framework of regular meters divided into regular beat-units, and then fit the different irregular durations into it (see the examples by Carter, pages 91, 92–3, and Nono, pages 94–5).

3. In music for a single performer, the notational method is of course less crucial than it is for ensemble music (see the Boulez example, page 96).

4. In all the situations mentioned above, dotted barlines may be helpful for clarifying irregular metric divisions of measures.

Practical Examples

In the following examples, the problems described above are dealt with in somewhat greater detail and applied to a few specific examples.

A. Cross Rhythms
These are rhythms which go against a prevailing meter.

1. CONSTANT METER
The beams show the rhythmic units, regardless of the prevailing meter (barlines): $\frac{3}{4}$ ♩♩ ♩♩ ♩♩♩ ♩ | ♩ ♩♩ ♩♩ ♩♩♩♩ ♪♩ ♪♩♩. ‖

This method helps the performer musically but is apt to make him lose the beat, and thus his place in the ensemble. It should therefore be employed only in music for a single performer, although there are certain exceptions (see Choices 1b and 2b below).

2. CHANGING METERS
Although the beaming remains as in 1 above, the meter now changes in accordance with the irregular rhythmic groupings, i.e., beaming and meter no longer contradict each other:

$\frac{2}{4}$ ♩♩ ♩♩ | $\frac{3}{8}$ ♩♩♩ | $\frac{2}{4}$ ♩♩ ♩♩ | $\frac{3}{8}$ ♩♩♩ | $\frac{2}{4}$ ♪♩ ♪♩ $\frac{3}{4}$ ♩. ‖

SUMMARY
Both of the above methods have advantages and drawbacks. Choices must be made from case to case. Particularly in ensemble music one must always keep in mind that the performer who has the cross rhythms must be able to relate his part to the ensemble and to the beats of the conductor (if any).

B. Polymetric Textures

This concerns different meters and rhythmic patterns performed simultaneously. The pattern above is to be combined with the following rhythmic pattern:

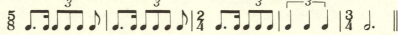

Several methods of combining these two patterns are available, and although none of them is entirely satisfactory, some are more practical than others:

1. THE ORIGINAL METERS ARE RETAINED

The two patterns are notated one above the other, each retaining its own metric divisions:

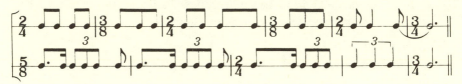

This method was used quite frequently in the early days of twentieth-century polyrhythmic experimentation, but in spite of its musical clarity it was abandoned as being too impractical in actual performance.

2. ONE OF THE ORIGINAL METERS SERVES BOTH LINES

The problem is to determine which of the two metric divisions functions best as common denominator (i.e., as a reference meter) for both patterns.

CHOICE 1

The original $\frac{3}{4}$ meter of the first rhythmic pattern (A*1:* Constant Meter) becomes the common denominator for both.

a. Both patterns are beamed according to the regular beat-units of the   meter; articulation marks are added to clarify the two conflicting patterns:

* The slurs have been placed above the notes to distinguish them from the ties, which appear in their regular position at the note-heads.

b. The same superimposed $\frac{3}{4}$ meter, but now each pattern is beamed in accordance with its own rhythms, whether they coincide with any $\frac{3}{4}$ beat-units or not (most of the time they do not):

Neither of these two notations is entirely satisfactory, because the $\frac{3}{4}$ meter of the first pattern is so alien to the second pattern that it is difficult to perform it properly. This is particularly noticeable in the triplet in measure 2, which has become unnecessarily difficult in this metric context.

CHOICE 2

The original metric notation of the second rhythmic pattern (B*1*) becomes the common denominator for both.

a. Both patterns are beamed according to the $\frac{5}{8}\text{-}\frac{2}{4}\text{-}\frac{3}{4}$ beat-units; articulation marks are added to clarify the two conflicting patterns:

b. Both patterns are beamed according to their respective rhythms (i.e., not according to the beat-units unless they happen to coincide with the rhythms):

Neither of the above solutions is ideal; each is a compromise at best, demonstrating the dilemma of our time in the field of rhythmic notation, as elaborated in the following analysis:

The $\frac{5}{8}$ meter as common denominator causes less distortion of the first rhythmic pattern than the $\frac{3}{4}$ meter did to the second pattern. One could conclude, therefore, that in choosing a meter suitable to two different rhythmic/metric patterns, the meter of the more complex pattern may be better suited than that of the simpler one (in this case the first pattern).

Expressed differently, one might say that a simple pattern is likely to remain recognizable even in a more complex metric context, while a complex pattern is easily lost in a metric context not its own. Even so, one must not consider this observation a hard and fast rule; music is too diverse to permit generalities.

Since in most polyrhythmic textures it is virtually impossible to find a common denominator equally suited to all the different rhythmic progressions and patterns involved, it is advisable occasionally to add rhythm cues wherever a pattern becomes unrecognizable even when equipped with accents and other articulation marks.

c. Choice 2a with an added rhythm cue:

SUMMARY

Two polymetric parts are best notated in the metric division of one of them—often that of the more complex one. If needed, a metric cue line showing the proper metric organization of the relatively obscured other part may be added wherever it can help to clarify the rhythm.

As for the treatment of polymetric and polyrhythmic textures in general, one rule is of principal importance: In polymetric or other rhythmically irregular ensemble music, and especially in music requiring a conductor, all parts should have the same time signature(s), if at all possible. Furthermore, all beaming should be done in accordance with these common time signatures. Articulation, stresses, etc., which used to become apparent through the notes' positions within the measure and through the beaming, must now be taken care of by accents and other articulation marks.

3. COMPROMISE METERS (REFERENCE METER)

If neither metric scheme of two different rhythmic/metric lines can accommodate both lines satisfactorily, a third, compromise meter must be worked out to coordinate the incompatibles with a minimum of distortion. Wherever possible, this compromise meter should match at least one of the lines' own metric divisions, i.e., intrinsic divisions should be given preference over compromise divisions wherever possible.

The following is an example from Leon Kirchner's *Concerto for Violin, Cello, Ten Winds, and Percussion*, first movement, mm. 114–17.

Line 1 (flute) as it might have been notated by itself, according to its intrinsic articulation

Line 2 (violin) as it might have been notated by itself, according to its intrinsic articulation

Lines 1 and 2 combined under a common "compromise" meter, as notated in the score of the Concerto

* This syncopated entrance has been changed to a strong first beat in the "might-have-been" versions above because in a metric context of constantly changing time signatures, syncopations cannot really be perceived as such by the listener.

C. Different Rates of Speed

The foregoing examples all show how different rhythmic patterns and metric divisions can be combined under a common metric denominator, because all of these patterns have some metric unit in common—usually a rather short one, such as an eighth or sixteenth. The chief difference lies in the stresses.

The following examples are marked by a notationally more irreconcilable difference: the individual parts do not only have different metric divisions, but they proceed at different rates of speed, so that there are often no common metric units by means of which one can arrive at a common metric denominator.

Although several methods of dealing with this problem are available, none is entirely satisfactory if absolute durational precision is wanted.

The most precise method is that demonstrated in the excerpt from Elliott Carter's *Second String Quartet* (opening of the second movement, quoted on page 91). The violin II part, which has a different tempo from the other three parts, was broken down into very small note-values, and groups of these small units were then made to fit approximately into the metric framework of the other parts. Absolute accuracy could not always be achieved. Besides, the part's simple rhythm (only eighth notes) looked so complicated that an explanatory footnote as well as a rhythmic cue line with a different time signature and metronome indication had to be added to prevent any misinterpretations.

In order to operate with finer divisions of note-values than those provided by our rather crude traditional geometric progressions (1, 2, 4, 8, 16, etc., meaning whole, half, quarter, eighth, and sixteenth notes for bipartite values, and the equally unwieldy tripartite progression of 1, 3, 6, (9), 12, etc.) it is necessary to become equally familiar with two additional progressions, to be used singly or in combination. They are:

1. the nonnotational "trick" of gradually changing metronome speeds;

2. arithmetical rather than geometric progressions of note-values (1, 2, 3, 4, 5, etc.) as shown on the facing page.

With the durational "raw material" shown on page 121 as a basis, a very large number of polymetrical problems can be solved, and if the notation becomes too complicated, a rhythm cue here and there will help the performer. Admittedly, it is not easy. Traditional notation, obviously, is not ideal for polymetric textures. But it is the only system in general use, and we have to make do with certain compromises if no other possibilities are available.

For a particularly good example of a wealth of polymetrics, controlled accelerandos and ritardandos, and metric modulation, see the score of Elliott Carter's *String Quartet No. 3* (1971), published by Associated Music Publishers, Inc., New York.

SUMMARY

In polymetric and other rhythmically or durationally disparate textures, all parts should have the same time signature(s), i.e., a common reference meter.

Since it is unlikely that the different elements comprising such textures are articulated in accordance with the prevailing reference meter(s), dynamics, phrasing slurs, and other marks of articulation must be notated carefully. The beams, however, should not be used for articulative purposes; they must follow the reference meter (beaming by beat-units), thus acting as an aid to synchronization.

If a reference meter and the note-values of a given part obscure the indigenous musical rhythm and/or phrasing to such a degree that correct performance is endangered, metric/rhythmic cue lines should be added to the part in question for clarification.

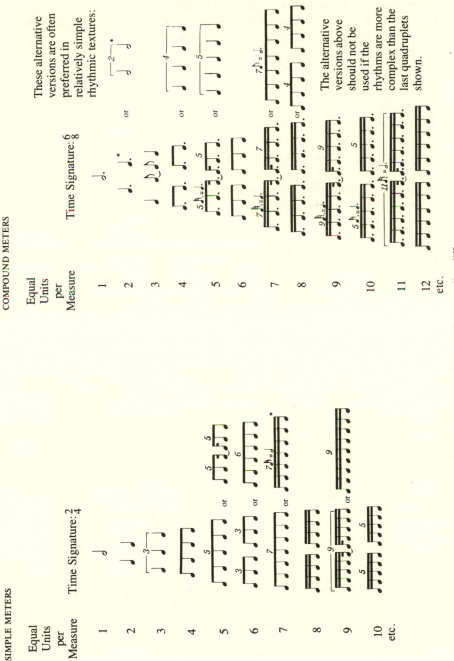

SIMPLE METERS

COMPOUND METERS

These alternative versions are often preferred in relatively simple rhythmic textures:

The alternative versions above should not be used if the rhythms are more complex than the last quadruplets shown.

* For the difference between single-beam and double-beam notation of septuplets, as well as different duplet notations, see Irregular Note Divisions, page 111 ff.

Similarly, if the necessarily complicated notation of a controlled accelerando or ritardando does not readily convey to the performer that a smooth increase or decrease of durations is intended (what Hugo Cole calls a "tempo glissando"*), a broken slur ending in an arrowhead and covering the entire passage in question should be used:

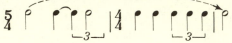

D. Spatial (or Proportional) Notation

If the music's rhythmic complexities do not require the kind of precision performance that necessitates the highly involved and subtle symbolic notation discussed above, spatial (proportional) notation will serve adequately and, moreover, is a great deal easier to work with. Furthermore, if the music is intended to be performed somewhat freely, this type of notation actually is preferable to symbolic notation.

Examples from the literature have been discussed above (page 96 ff).

Detailed instructions for the use of spatial notation will be found in a separate chapter below, beginning on page 136.

---

* Hugo Cole: *Sounds and Signs* (see Bibliography).

IV. *Duration and Rhythm: Individual Items*

Appoggiatura
see page 22 fn.

*Beamed Accelerando and
Ritardando*   *124*

Clusters
see pages 57, 102, and 259

Dotted Notes   *125*
A. *Dot Positions in Double-Stemmed
Two-Part Notation*   *125*
B. *Dot Positions in Dotted Unisons*   *125*
C. *Dot Positions in Unisons of a
Dotted and an Undotted Note*   *125*

Durational Equivalents   *127*
A. *Different Durational Units
(Beat-Units)*   *127*
B. *Identical Durational Units
(Beat-Units)*   *127*
C. *Metronome Marks*   *128*
D. *L'istesso tempo*   *128*

*Fermatas, Commas, and
Double Strokes*   *128*
A. *Fermatas*   *128*
B. *Commas and Double Strokes*   *128*

Glissando
see pages 19 and 63

Hemiola   *129*

Irregular Note Divisions   *129*
A. *Septuplets*   *130*
B. *Duplets*   *131*
C. *Specifications*   *132*

Rests   *133*
A. *Positions in the Measure*   *133*
B. *Full-Measure Rests*   *135*
C. *Full- and Multiple-Measure Rests
in Parts*   *136*
D. *Vertical Alignment of Rests*   *136*

*Spatial or Proportional
Notation*   *136*
A. *Definition*   *136*
B. *Spatial Notation versus Traditional
(Symbolic) Notation*   *137*
C. *Duration Beams*   *138*
D. *Note-Head Extenders*   *139*
E. *Details*   *140*
F. *Performance Materials*   *142*

Tempo Indications   *145*

Ties   *146*

Time Signatures (Meter)   *146*
A. *Meter Changes (Placement)*   *146*
B. *Reference Meter*   *147*

Tremolos   *147*
A. *Introductory Note*   *147*
B. *Details: Measured Tremolos*   *148*
C. *Details: Unmeasured Tremolos*   *150*
D. *Additional Items*   *151*

Beamed Accelerando and Ritardando

Accelerandos and ritardandos occurring in individual parts of an otherwise regular, metered context should be noted as follows:

If the accelerandos or ritardandos extend beyond a single measure, the beams should be lengthened accordingly:

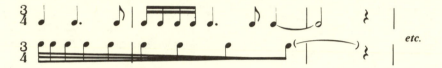

Note that beaming by beat-units has here been replaced by longer beams, since the accelerando and ritardando flexibilities take precedence over any exact beats. Besides, the gradual increase or decrease in the number of beams makes exact indications of beat-units impossible.

If beamed accelerandos or ritardandos are to be performed within a specific duration—for example that of a quarter or half note—the respective note-value should be placed at the beam side of the group, the same way as, for example, a triplet numeral, though always enclosed in horizontal brackets:

Beamed accelerandos and ritardandos of tremolos:

Accelerando and ritardando beaming is occasionally found in scores notated in spatial notation. This is not recommended, since durational spacing of note-heads in spatial notation makes such beaming redundant.

One sometimes finds such beaming in spatially notated music for a single player. This, too, is usually unnecessary, because in solo music there is no problem of synchronization, the problem for which such beaming was invented.

Dotted Notes

A. Dot Positions in Double-Stemmed Two-Part Notation

1. If an upstemmed note is on a line, the dot should be placed in the space above the line: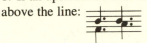

2. If a downstemmed note is on a line, the dot should be placed into the space below the line:

The reason for these rules will be apparent if the following example is considered:

Correct placement of dot   *Incorrect*

In the first notation, the low dot clearly shows that the lower note is dotted.

In the second notation, where the dot appears above the line, it is not clear whether the dot refers to the upper or the lower note, unless the system of lowering the dot for a dotted downstem note is adhered to, in which case the dot must belong to the upper note. For additional examples concerning this problem, see page 165.

B. Dot Positions in Dotted Unisons

If the note-values of the two parts are the same, the rule for single-stemmed notes should be followed, namely to use only one dot for both: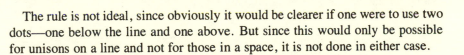

The rule is not ideal, since obviously it would be clearer if one were to use two dots—one below the line and one above. But since this would only be possible for unisons on a line and not for those in a space, it is not done in either case.

C. Dot Positions in Unisons of a Dotted and an Undotted Note

In traditional music it was customary to use only a single dotted note-head, even though one of the two parts of the unison is not dotted. The performers are expected to figure out whether the dot refers to the upstemmed or the downstemmed part by scanning the notes that follow the unison. Since rhythm in traditional music of the seventeenth to early twentieth centuries largely conforms to standard patterns, this is not as difficult as it may seem:

Dotted unisons in a space

Dotted unisons on a line

In music of greater rhythmic complexity, however, it is more practical to use two note-heads instead of one, with the undotted note-head preceding the dotted one. This is especially helpful for unisons in a space, since such unisons do not permit up or down positions of the dot. Following, you will find the examples above renotated with two note-heads:

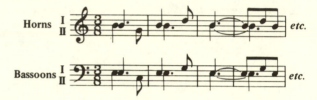

A more involved passage, typical of much recent music, demonstrates the absolute necessity for two note-heads instead of one. In the first version, the unisons are notated in the traditional manner with a single note-head. The passage is almost impossible to read:

The same passage notated with two note-heads for each unison consisting of a dotted (or double-dotted) and an undotted note:

For general rules for unisons, including undotted ones, see Pitch, Unisons, page 78. For dotted rests, see page 134.

---

* Note that double dots are treated the same way as single dots.

Durational Equivalents

A. Different Durational Units (Beat-Units)

1. IN THE COURSE OF A LINE

Center the equal sign over the barline, place the preceding note-value before the equal sign, place the new note-value after the equal sign, add small arrows right and left:*

Either   *Or, to make doubly sure*

2. FROM ONE LINE TO THE NEXT

End of line   *Beginning of next line*

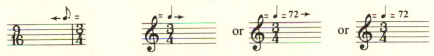

Note that the equal sign in line-to-line equivalents is not centered over the barline. At the end of the line it usually appears above the new time signature; at the beginning of the next line it generally appears just before the new time signature.

B. Identical Durational Units (Beat-Units)

If the note-values of the equation are identical , no arrows are needed:

A still better procedure is to use only one note, with arrows to both sides:

---

* The arrows are advisable to avoid confusion with the traditional practice of placing the new note-value first and the preceding note-value after the equal sign, followed by the Italian word *precedente* (preceding) or without any verbal indication:

Either   *Or without* **precedente**

(I.e., the quarter note equals the preceding dotted eighth.)

Note that the indication is placed at the beginning of the new measure, not above the barline. This method is not recommended.

C. Metronome Marks

It is often advisable to add metronome marks to the new note-value:

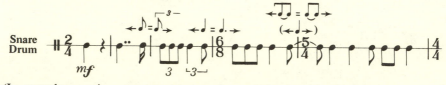

A selection of durational equivalents

(In complex music, repeat metronome in parentheses on each new page.)

D. L'istesso Tempo

The term *l'istesso tempo* (the same tempo) should be avoided because it is too ambiguous in the context of twentieth-century music.

Fermatas, Commas, and Double Strokes

A. Fermatas

These prolong sounds or silences. They may be placed above notes, rests, commas, and other signs indicating pauses, and in empty spaces of scores in spatial or free notation.

The progression from short to long fermatas runs as follows:

traditional (relatively short):	⌢		
longer:			
specified duration (by seconds):	2″		
approximate durations:	2″+	2″−	2″±

B. Commas and Double Strokes

These indicate silences only:

short: ,

longer: **||**

As mentioned above, both of these signs may be modified for longer duration by placing a fermata above them: 𝄐 ⅋ etc.

Hemiola

A hemiola may be defined as a temporary slowing of a triple pulse to twice its value:

Hemiolas were used a great deal from the fifteenth century into the eighteenth, and again sporadically by Schumann and frequently by Brahms. Although they are rarely used in twentieth-century music, they do figure in our current efforts to revive music of the Renaissance and Baroque.

Editors of new editions of old music are divided with respect to the notation of hemiolas. In the early days of publishing new editions of old music, the notation of hemiolas was modernized according to Brahms's music:

This notation, however, implies syncopations—a different concept from the original idea of merely "stretching" the regular three beats.

Since the notation at the top (which includes the change of meter) often causes difficulty in rehearsals of amateur choruses, and since the modernization distorts the composers' intentions, a compromise is suggested:

Irregular Note Divisions

Our durational notation operates with bipartite and tripartite units, i.e., with undotted and dotted notes, respectively. The bipartite units divide into two parts (one half note into two quarter notes; one quarter note into two eighth notes, etc.), while the tripartite units divide into three parts (one dotted half note into three quarter notes; one dotted quarter note into three eighth notes, etc.):

Bipartite   ***Tripartite***

If a bipartite or tripartite unit is divided irregularly, such as a half note into three parts instead of the regular two, or a dotted half note into two or four parts instead of the regular three, we have *irregular note divisions,* or triplets, duplets, and quadruplets, respectively:

The charts in the following two sections (A. Septuplets, and B. Duplets) show the notation of all bipartite regular and irregular divisions, as well as that of their tripartite equivalents. The only controversial irregular divisions are septuplets and duplets, as explained below:

A. Septuplets

The predominant practice is to retain the note-values of a regular note-division for the faster, irregular pattern, until the next, shorter regular division, and thus the next shorter note-value, has been reached:

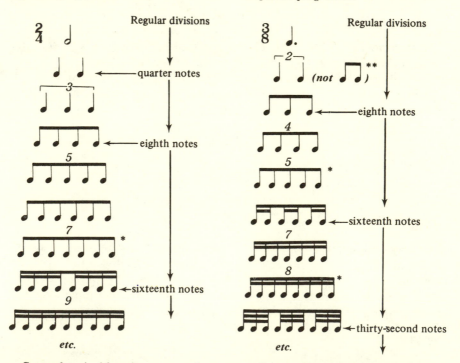

Septuplets in bipartite progressions, as well as quintuplets and octuplets in tripartite ones (all marked * above), are occasionally notated with the next shorter note-values (see the next example). Proponents of this notation argue that, for example, a septuplet in a bipartite progression is closer to the regular sixteenth notes than to the regular eighth notes, for which reason it should be notated as a group of sixteenths, rather than eighths:

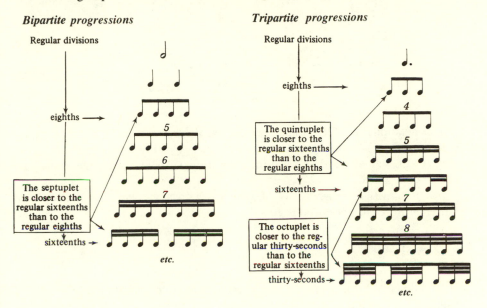

This compromise is not in general use today, and it is not recommended.

B. Duplets

(See ** on page 130.)

If, in tripartite progressions, eighth notes are used for duplets whose total duration equals one dotted quarter, it would mean that eighth notes occur before as well as after the regular eighths (duplets—regular eighths—quadruplets-—quintuplets), i.e., eighth notes would represent durations both longer and shorter than regular eighths, plus regular eighth durations as well, an obvious source of confusion. It is recommended, therefore, that only quarter notes be used for such duplets:

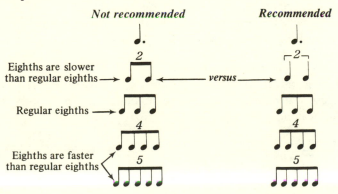

Another alternative, favored by French and French-influenced composers, is to use two dotted notes for a duplet:

This notation is as efficient and "correct" as that recommended above, except that performers generally perceive the "irregularity" of duplets more readily if they see the telltale numeral 2 and the truly irregular note-values, rather than a pair of dotted notes.

For arithmetical progressions of note divisions, see Practical Examples: Different Rates of Speed, on page 119.

C. Specifications

1. SINGLE NUMERALS

Traditionally, small numerals (italic type) are used to indicate irregular note-values (*2* for duplets; *3* for triplets, etc.).

2. EQUATIONS—NUMERALS ONLY

As rhythmic complexity has grown, it has become necessary to identify not only irregular note-values, but also the number of regular values that would normally comprise the group. For example, the equation *7:5* in the following example means 7 irregular eighth notes or rests in the normal time span of 5 regular eighths:

Both numerals must always refer to the same note-values. The first numeral refers to the irregular values; the second to the regular ones.

It is suggested that the customary colon be replaced by an equal sign: 7 irregular values equal 5 regular ones, i.e., *7 = 5*.

3. EQUATIONS—NUMERALS AND NOTES

If the rhythmic texture of the music becomes so complex that it is not easy at a glance to grasp which note-values the equation refers to, small notes should be used for clarification:

or even more explicit:

Small notes (instead of numerals) may also be used to show the total duration of an irregular group:

The last-mentioned method is particularly useful where septuplets are notated in sixteenth notes instead of the more frequent eighths (or equivalent situations). If instead of a mere numeral 7 the group is identified as $7\flat = \delta$ (or $7\flat = \delta$, depending on the composer's preference) all ambiguity is eliminated.

4. NOTES ONLY

In approximate notation, where the specific individual durations (notes and rests) of a particular group are indeterminate, a small, bracketed note should be used to show the total duration of the group:

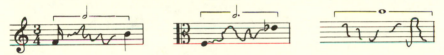

See also Beamed Accelerando and Ritardando, page 124.

Rests

A. Positions in the Measure

1. SYNCOPATED RESTS

Rests should not be placed in syncopated positions, the only and recent exceptions being dotted eighth, sixteenth, and thirty-second rests, etc., in binary contexts:

Traditional

More recent

N.B.: Syncopated rests should not be used in larger note-values, i.e., from dotted quarter rests up.

2. BINARY METERS

In binary meters, rests should not cross the middle of the measure:

Correct

Incorrect

3. TERNARY METERS

In ternary meters, no two-beat rests are used; each of the three beats must have its own rest:

Correct

Incorrect

4. DOTTED RESTS

a. SIMPLE METERS

In simple meters, dotted rests lasting 1½ beats should not be used at the beginning of a measure:

Correct

Incorrect

Dotted rests lasting 1½ beats may be used on the second beat of $\frac{3}{4}$ and on the third beat of $\frac{4}{4}$:

Such rests must, however, not be used on the second beat of $\frac{4}{4}$ because they would then cross the middle of the measure:

Correct   *Incorrect*

b. COMPOUND METERS

In compound meters, the same principle must be followed:

Correct   *Incorrect*

c. COMPOSITE METERS

In composite meters, the rests must conform to the respective subdivisions of the measures:

Correct

Incorrect

B. Full-Measure Rests

Whole rests are used as full-measure rests for all meters* less than $\frac{4}{2}$ (see page 136).

All whole-measure rests must appear in the center of the measure, regardless of all other notes and rests above and below in the same measure. (This rule does not apply to the whole *note,* which is centered only if no shorter note-values appear simultaneously):

If two parts are written on the same staff, whole rests for the upper part should hang from the top staff-line; those for the lower part should hang from the bottom staff-line:

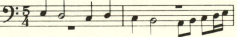

---

* A number of composers have tried during recent years to replace the "universal" whole-measure rests with rests that represent the measures' actual values, but these efforts have thus far failed to gain widespread acceptance (see page 46 f).

As shown in the examples above, whole rests are used for a full-measure rest regardless of the measure's actual duration ($\frac{5}{4}$ in the previous example; $\frac{3}{4}$ in the one before that). If, however, the total value of a measure reaches eight quarters ($\frac{4}{2}$ measures), a double whole-rest should be used:

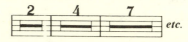

C. Full and Multiple-Measure Rests in Parts

Single measure

Two or more measures

D. Vertical Alignment of Rests

All rests must be aligned vertically (i.e., rhythmically) with the notes or rests above and below. Only whole-measure rests are centered:

Spatial or Proportional Notation

A. Definition

Spatial or proportional notation is a system in which durations are "translated" into horizontal distances instead of duration symbols (as in traditional notation), so that if, for example, the duration of a half note is made equal to one inch of horizontal space, a quarter note equals half an inch, and so forth:

Symbolic notation (spread out as if it were spatial notation)

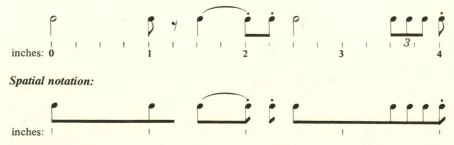

Spatial notation:

In short, all durations must be notated in spatial relationship to each other. Consequently, all duration symbols (white and black note-heads, beams, flags, prolongation dots, rests, etc.) become irrelevant. Note-heads now are needed only as pitch indicators (black note-heads are preferred), and only one kind of horizontal line (either a single beam, or an extension line at the level of the note-head) is needed to show the durations of sustained notes. Blank spaces mean silences (rests).

The spatial example above shows black note-heads and (single) duration beams. (For extenders at the note-head level see page 139.)

B. Spatial Notation versus Traditional (Symbolic) Notation

1. MUSICAL ASPECTS

The musical advantage of spatial over traditional notation is that the number of durations which can be notated is not confined to the available symbols, but is unlimited. Thus, spatial notation is ideally suited to smooth accelerando and ritardando passages, as well as all other aperiodic progressions difficult or impossible to express in symbolic notation.

The following example shows a written-out ritardando (Flute I) and accelerando (Flute II), to be performed simultaneously:

Performances from spatial notation are never as rhythmically precise as those played from traditional, symbolic notation, because counting regular beats is far more accurate than judging distances:

To summarize, spatial notation is the ideal graphic vehicle whenever rhythmic flexibility or durational vagueness is desired, while symbolic notation must be used whenever rhythmic/durational accuracy is needed.

2. PRACTICAL ASPECTS

The following two examples show the same music notated symbolically and spatially:

a. Symbolic notation

b. Spatial notation

In example *a.*, the extra horizontal space required for the two sharps does not affect the durations of the sixteenth notes, since they are not governed by spacing but by the "symbolic" sixteenth beams. Neither does the subsequent half note require more than a token space to show that it is longer than the sixteenths.

In example *b.*, the distances between notes of equal duration must be equal throughout. Since extra space is needed for the two sharps on one of the sixteenth beats, all other sixteenths must also be spaced that far apart, and the (former) half note now requires eight such sixteenth spaces.

Obviously, the symbolic system of durational notation is much more economical. Moreover, its horizontal flexibility is particularly practical for page layouts because it can be expanded or contracted without impairing rhythmic clarity, which means that good page turns in performance materials (a very important consideration) can generally be achieved quite easily.

Spatial notation, by contrast, depends for its durations on absolute rigidity of horizontal spacing. This inflexibility is not only uneconomical, but also creates serious problems of practical page turns, especially since spatial notation is almost always performed directly from the score. (For details concerning performance materials see page 142 ff.)

C. Duration Beams

The durations of long (sustained) notes are indicated with duration beams: the longer the beam, the longer the note: ♩__ ♩__

Uninterrupted progressions of notes are connected to the same duration beam: 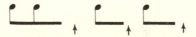 .

Interruptions of duration beams (gaps between beams) mean silences (rests):

If the last note of a beamed progression of two or more notes is too short to warrant a duration beam, or if a short note occurs by itself, unconnected to a beam, a vestigial, slanted duration beam (beamlet) is attached to the right side of the stem, similar to a flag:

Beamlets (and their stems) may be omitted altogether, so that only note-heads appear, a procedure favored for extended passages of disjunct, short notes, as is shown at the end of the example below.

Articulation marks, such as slurs, staccato dots, tenuto lines, etc., are the same as in traditional notation.

The following example demonstrates in context the various items discussed above:

D. Note-Head Extenders

The rules governing duration beams are equally applicable to note-head extenders (except for a few additions listed below). The following is an exact transcription of the duration-beam example immediately above:

This method of notation is best suited for vocal music or music for single-tone instruments. It becomes troublesome when used for close-textured intervals and chords because the extenders are likely to run into each other.

Moreover, the lack of stems makes clear graphic distinctions between two or more parts on the same staff virtually impossible unless vertical connectors are added to show the progress of the individual parts in cases of voice crossings or other ambiguous situations:

As the example shows, however, the connectors are not always possible: while one can connect the first, sustained F-sharp to the lower G, the same can not be accomplished from the G to the high grace note A because the G, being short, has no extender to which the connector can be attached.

Thus, although the extenders do possess a welcome graphic immediacy, they should be used only for simple, single-line parts, such as occur in the example of the *Rondes* by Aribert Reimann, page 97.

The following example, written with duration beams, depicts the voice leading of the music above much more clearly:

E. Details

1. CUT-OFFS

Since the durations in spatially notated music are approximate, it is necessary to indicate precise cut-offs where wanted. A short vertical stroke at the end of the duration beam or note-head extender will serve:

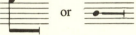

2. NOTES HELD FROM ONE LINE TO THE NEXT LINE OR PAGE

The duration beam or note-head extender should end with an arrowhead at the end of the line:

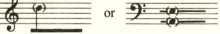

and begin on the next line or page a little before the held note, whose note-head should be placed in parentheses:

Some composers use ties, but these are redundant in combination with duration beams or note-head extenders.

3. GRACE NOTES

Grace notes are used in the traditional manner. In slurred passages they should be included under the slur (see page 21 f):

The difference between grace notes and the unstemmed note-heads mentioned above is that grace notes belong to a main note, while the unstemmed note-heads are generally independent short notes.

Grace notes could be written as small unstemmed note-heads, but such notation has proven to be unclear:

Not recommended

Another solution is to use an extra beam with slash for grace notes:

This notation is more legible because all note-heads are equally large. Its drawback is that full-size grace notes generally take up more horizontal space than they should in spatial notation.

4. TREMOLO

Wide-trill notation (see pages 76 and 147 ff) is recommended, but with full-size note-heads and tremolo bars:

5. ACCELERANDO AND RITARDANDO BEAMS

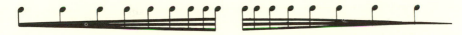

Theoretically, accelerando or ritardando beaming should not be necessary in spatial notation, since the horizontal spacing of the note-heads takes care of such matters. However, the spreading and diminishing beams are so expressive of what is wanted that one should not be too dogmatic about banning them altogether from spatially notated music.

For their use in the context of symbolic notation, see page 124.

6. CHANGES FROM SPATIAL TO TRADITIONAL NOTATION AND VICE VERSA

From spatial to traditional notation (0 = spatial)

From traditional to spatial notation

The "zero" time signature should be used only in music that alternates between spatial and traditional notation.

7. BLACK AND WHITE NOTE-HEADS

A fair number of composers have been unwilling to forego white note-heads altogether, since the psychological effect of white (relatively long) versus black (shorter) and cue-size (very fast) is undeniable and can be very useful:

The obvious drawback of this system lies in the ambiguity of the terms "relatively long" and "relatively short." It has been included, however, because of its advantages mentioned above. The final choice should rest with each composer.

8. MIXED NOTATION

It is possible to create a framework of measured notation, filled with durationally free or at least flexible sounds or silences. The example below covers several possibilities. With these as a basis, others can easily be accommodated.

The passage is organized in regular beats indicated by arrows pointing upward.* Above each event is a brief characterization.

The arrows may also be placed above the music, pointing downward, depending on the general setup.

F. Performance Materials

1. SCORES

Spatial notation is best performed from the score, so that all participants may see how their durations fit spatially into the total rhythmic/durational texture.

N.B.: Playing scores must be transposed, i.e., not "in C."

---

*See also Scores and Parts, Conductor's Signs, page 158 f.

a. PLANNING THE SCORE: SHORTEST NOTE(S)

The first step in preparing a definitive score is to examine the entire composition or movement for the shortest note(s), in order to arrive at the proper minimum unit of horizontal spacing. (Note that accidentals take up horizontal space, too, and must therefore be included in the durational measurements.) All longer durations are multiples of the shortest note(s).

b. TEMPO AND TIMING

The next step is to decide on the desired tempo or timing devices (horizontal brackets, vertical arrows, barlines, etc.). (See page 158 f for conductor's signs.) N.B.: Vertical lines must not take up any space of their own.

c. TEMPO CHANGES

If the music alternates between fast and slow sections it may become advisable to change the spatial proportions along with the tempos. In such cases the changing proportions must be indicated clearly and prominently:

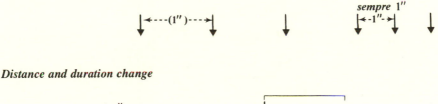

Distance between arrows remains the same; duration of beats changes
(prevailing duration of beats 1 second)

Distance between arrows changes; duration of beats remains the same

Distance and duration change

d. PAGE TURNS

Since music notated spatially does not possess any horizontal flexibility (see page 137 f), it may be necessary occasionally to forego consistent widths of right-hand pages in order to create workable page turns for the performers. However, there is generally very little leeway for such changes. (Vocal parts need not be considered, since a singer's hands are free to turn pages.)

In the following example, the normal page turn would be at arrow 17, but this is awkward for Flute II; therefore it would be better to end the music just before arrow 17, at the Flute I cut-off:

Best spot for
a page turn

e. SYNCHRONIZATION

Simultaneous entrances or cut-offs should be marked with dotted vertical double arrows (centered on the note-heads or cut-off strokes, resp.):

Dotted arrows are also useful to bring other events, especially entrances and cut-offs, to the conductor's attention.

Furthermore, dotted arrows may lead from instrument to instrument (in which case they may be slanted or vertical, depending on the situation), to coordinate entrances or cut-offs that depend on certain events in other instruments.

Sometimes the white arrows for subdivisions of main beats (▽) may be preferred to the double arrows shown above (see lowest example on page 145; see also page 159 f).

For still other cuing devices and procedures in scores, see page 160 ff.

f. PARTIAL SCORES

If the score is too large and unwieldy for use by all performers, partial scores must be made. Each such score will include a selection of parts, depending on the character and instrumentation of the full score. A constant cue line with the most audible music of the remaining parts, notated on one or two staff-lines, must also be included so that the performers can see their respective roles in the total durational context. (See also page 172.)

2. PARTS

If possible, individual parts should be avoided in spatial notation, since they invariably require elaborate cuing. Parts should be used only when the music is characterized by a predominance of regular beats or, conversely, when it calls for great independence of execution with only occasional conductor's signs indicating changes from one playing mode or event to another.

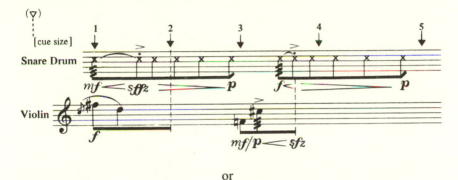

or

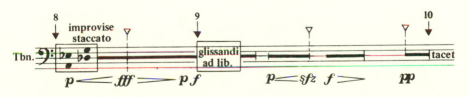

The discussion above pertains to relatively controlled scores. With increasing indeterminacy of notation, fewer and fewer of the listed precautions become necessary, just as standard notational devices become increasingly inappropriate as music becomes more aleatory.

Tempo Indications

When tempo indications were introduced into music, the languages used were almost exclusively Italian and, to a lesser extent, French. Generations later, composers began to substitute their native languages to express some of the finer shadings, and often all indications.

In the present century, when music is performed and studied more internationally than ever before, composers should use terminology that is as widely understood as possible. Often a return to the basic traditional Italian terms is useful where there is a choice (for example, *Allegro/Fast/Schnell/Vif,* etc.), especially since most verbal tempo indications can be accompanied by clarifying metronome marks or with beat-indications in seconds, wherever appropriate.

Of course, verbal instructions of this kind may be omitted altogether, as long as metronome or beat-indications are used, but it is definitely more evocative to refer to an *Adagio* passage or a *Vivace* section than to a quarter-equals-48 movement.

Concerning verbal modifications of basic directions, the best thing to do is to exercise restraint.

For proper placement of tempo indications, see page 32.

See also Spatial or Proportional Notation, page 143, *b* and *c*.

Ties

As a rule, ties should lead to the nearest main beats of a measure rather than pass over them, even if this makes an additional tie necessary. The following examples will illustrate this complex-sounding rule:

<table>
<tr><td align="center">***Correct***</td><td align="center">***Do not use***</td></tr>
</table>

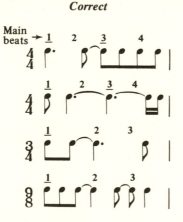
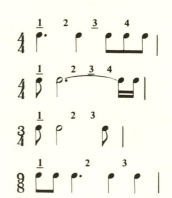

See also Slurs and Ties, page 36, B, ff.

Time Signatures (Meter)

A. Meter Changes (Placement)

1. AT A BARLINE

If a meter change takes place at a barline, the new time signature is placed after the barline: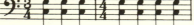

2. FROM LINE TO LINE

If a meter changes from one line to the next, a warning time signature is placed at the end of the line after the barline (which should be placed a little to the left of the end of the staff-lines), to signal that the next line begins with a new meter:

   *Next line*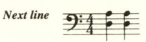

3. FROM METERED TO UNMETERED (FREE OR SPATIAL)

If a metered section of music changes to an unmetered one, a cancellation sign ⚏ should be used (see page 141 f).

Compare Clef Changes, pages 46 and 57.

See also Scores and Parts, Time Signatures, page 177 ff.

B. Reference Meter

A reference meter is one that acts as a metric common denominator in a polymetric texture (see pages 90 f and 116 ff).

Tremolos

A. Introductory Note

The term *tremolo* (trembling) and the different kinds of tremolo notation in present use are a source of frequent confusion. (For specific definitions see page 74 ff.)

There are two durational tremolo categories, and two pitch categories. The durational ones are:

> measured tremolos and unmeasured tremolos

The pitch categories are:

> repeat tremolos and trill tremolos

A further complication lies in the fact that measured tremolos are not true tremolos, but actually represent a form of shorthand for repeated or alternating notes—a notational convenience which is in the process of going out of fashion in "serious" music.

The unmeasured ("as fast as possible") tremolos—repeat tremolos as well as trill tremolos—continue, however, to be an important component of our notational resources, even though the notation of the trill tremolo is somewhat perplexing, as will be seen below.

It is suggested that the various tremolos be dealt with as follows:

1. MEASURED TREMOLOS

Although their usefulness is limited in today's art music, they are of true value in entertainment and show music, as well as in opera-vocal scores and similar keyboard reductions. Thus, measured tremolos should be used, but only where they are truly appropriate.

2. UNMEASURED TREMOLOS

Here, the repeat tremolo presents no problem. As for the trill tremolo, the traditional notation continues to be the ''safest,'' although wide-trill notation is gaining ground (see pages 76 and 151 for wide-trill notation).

B. Details: Measured Tremolos

1. REPEAT TREMOLO

For a regular repetition of a note, interval, or chord, short, slanted tremolo bars are drawn through the stem, or centered above or below a whole note depending on the stem direction if the note had a stem.

The note shows the duration of the tremolo, while the tremolo bars show the note-values of the repeated notes.

The tremolo bars should be a little thinner than beams, and as long as or a little longer than the width of a note-head.

A single tremolo bar = eighth note repeats

Other examples

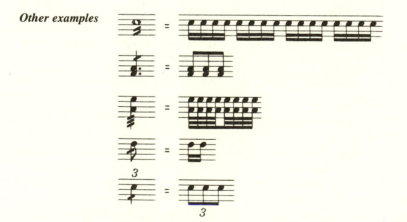

On beamed notes the tremolo bars usually slant slightly more than the beams:

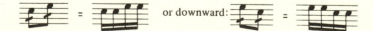

(Note that the tremolo bars always slant upward, regardless of the beam-slant.)

BROKEN TIES

If a tremolo continues without break from note to note within a measure or across a barline, broken ties should be used:

(When joined by broken ties, accidentals must be repeated from measure to measure.)

2. TRILL TREMOLO

The notation of a trill tremolo is an anomaly in that its total duration is given twice. For example, if a tremolo is to last one half note, two half notes are written, with tremolo bars between them:

Total duration   *Notation*

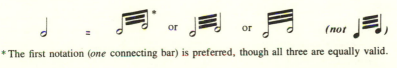

* The first notation (*one* connecting bar) is preferred, though all three are equally valid.

Only half notes, because of their white note-heads, permit being connected by one or all tremolo bars without thereby changing their value. If quarter notes were connected in this way, they would appear to be shorter note-values. For example, would become . The same is true of beamed notes: only their own beam(s) can connect them; if the tremolo beams were to do so, the note-values would change, for example, from to .

The following is a systematic list of tremolo bars and corresponding note-values:

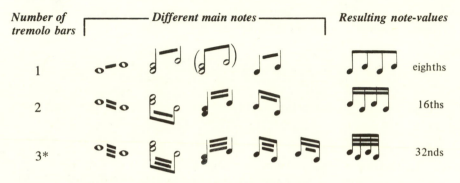

Number of tremolo bars	Different main notes	Resulting note-values
1		eighths
2		16ths
3*		32nds

*Actually, thirty-second-note tremolos are so fast that they are rarely if ever considered "measured," except in very slow music (see Unmeasured Tremolos, below).

C. Details: Unmeasured Tremolos

1. REPEAT TREMOLOS

The rules governing measured repeat tremolos also apply here, except that the number of tremolo bars should always convey a relatively fast tremolo, from two in fast music to a maximum of four in very slow tempos.

In addition, the abbreviation *trem.* may be placed above the first tremolo in an extended passage.

2. TRILL TREMOLO

The same rules apply as above.

Chord tremolos   *Single-note tremolos*

3. WIDE TRILL

As mentioned on page 76, single-note trill tremolos may also be notated as wide trills. Thus the total duration of the tremolo is represented only once instead of twice.

Single-note trill tremolos notated as wide trills:

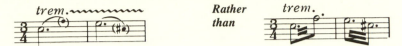

D. Additional Items

1. RHYTHMIC ALIGNMENT

If trill tremolos occur simultaneously with nontremolo notes, they must be placed into proper rhythmic alignment:

2. STEM DIRECTIONS

In general, the stem direction should be the same for both notes of a tremolo, even if one of the stems thus points the "wrong" way:  . However, upstem and downstem combinations are acceptable if the interval is very wide, such as an octave:

3. TWO-STAFF NOTATION

If trill tremolos occur in two-staff notation and go from one staff to the other, the tremolo bars should be placed between the staves:

For tremolo notation in spatial notation, see page 141.

v. *Indeterminate Events*

Alternative Events (Choices)	152	Indeterminate Repeats	154
General Observation	153	Different Kinds of Repeats: a Selec-	
Choices (Other than Above)	153	tion	154

Alternative Events (Choices)

Alternative passages (phrases, rhythmic patterns, pitches for improvisation, etc.), to be chosen by the performer(s) on the spur of the moment, should be notated above and/or below the "regular" music and enclosed in fairly heavy frames or boxes:

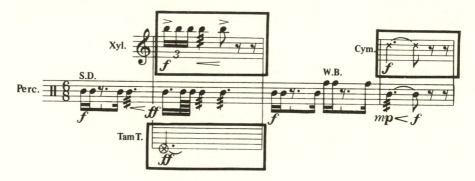

Alternative notation:

N.B.: The location of the alternatives—above, below, or on the regular staff—does not constitute preference. Each alternative is equally valid.

General Observation

The heavy box is not only used for choices, as above, but has other functions as well. For example, in piano music, such boxes may be used to distinguish music to be played inside the piano from regular notation (see page 263).

Boxes are also used for choices of different playing modes or dynamics (see below), or for different pitches, etc., with which to improvise (see page 156), and so forth.

If different kinds of boxed events occur in the same composition, it is recommended that boxes be used for one type of event only, and that other means be devised for the other event(s). For example, if a composition includes choices such as those above, and also contains boxed pitches for improvisation, the latter may be boxed, while the former can be distinguished with vertical brackets connected by broken horizontal lines:

Above the staff   *Below the staff*

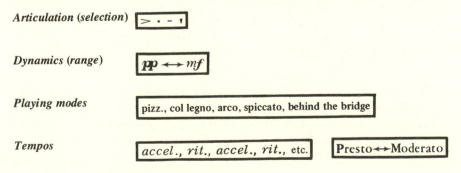

Choices (Other than Above)

In general, a heavy box drawn around elements indicates that the performer is to choose from the material in the box. The elements may consist of a selection of pitches, rhythms, signs of articulation, dynamics, or tempos. In addition, entire phrases or similar events may be boxed, thus becoming alternate versions to choose from.

Articulation (selection)

Dynamics (range) $\boxed{\textbf{\textit{pp}} \longleftrightarrow \textit{mf}}$

Playing modes $\boxed{\text{pizz., col legno, arco, spiccato, behind the bridge}}$

Tempos $\boxed{\textit{accel., rit., accel., rit.,} \text{ etc.}}$ $\boxed{\text{Presto} \longleftrightarrow \text{Moderato}}$

See also Indeterminate Repeats, below.

Indeterminate Repeats

Indeterminate repeats are used to create a mixture of controlled and chance elements. Usually, each part repeats different material (see below for a selection of types of material). An indeterminate repeat passage might look as follows:

The curved flanges at the repeat signs serve to distinguish them from ordinary repeats.

The total duration of a repeat passage is usually given in seconds, but it may also be ended at the conductor's discretion or, in metered music, at a particular measure. Thus not all indeterminate repeats have the same kind of indications of their total duration. If, however, the duration is given in seconds, this information should be located at or near the beginning of the passage (not at the end, where it is frequently found).

If indeterminate repeats run beyond a line or page, arrowheads should be drawn at the ends of the duration line and the duration bracket (if any):

Different Kinds of Repeats: a Selection

If the elements are ordered, such as given successions of pitches and/or short rhythms, repeat signs are used. If the material is unordered, i.e., if the performer must make his own choices from within a given pitch range and/or from a selection of note-values or rhythms, dynamic degrees, etc., these basic ingredients are placed in a heavy box followed by the usual duration line, and if applicable, topped by a duration bracket, as will be seen in the following specific examples.

N.B.: If complete phrases or patterns are given, the last repeat may occasionally go slightly beyond the cut-off point. If completion is desired regardless of the cut-off, the duration line should be prolonged slightly as a broken line with an arrowhead: ──────[- - →]

1. ORDERED ELEMENTS

Regular phrases

The four phrases differ in rhythm, duration, dynamics, articulation, and text. Each of them is to be repeated for 25 seconds. The tempos as well as the time intervals between the repeats are ad lib.

Pitches and text syllables are given; rhythm, articulation, tempo, etc., ad lib. The rhythmic patterns may be repeated or changed.

da day dee do

Rhythmic pattern is given; pitches, etc., ad lib.

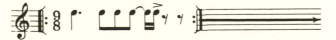

Rhythmic pattern is given; pitches are to be chosen from a given range

2. UNORDERED ELEMENTS

Improvise on given pitches (in any order)

Play open strings slowly, alternating playing modes (pizz., arco, col legno, etc.) in random order. Strings must follow each other according to given connecting lines, but the same string(s) may be repeated. Change dynamics ad lib.:

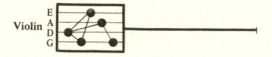

Improvise on three given rhythms (in any order)

If pitched instruments are used, vary pitches ad lib.

N.B.: Boxed selections or ranges of other elements, such as dynamic degrees, signs of articulation, playing modes, etc., may be added to any of the above examples.

3. MULTIPLE CHOICES

Multiple choices from the material to be repeated are indicated by horizontal sub-divisions within the box:

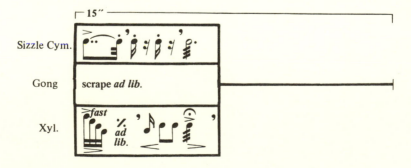

If there are three players, each performs one box. If two or one, choose.

Instead of boxes followed by duration lines, the boxes may be continued with broken lines for the entire duration:

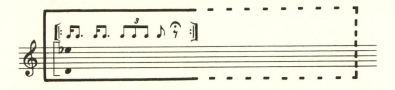

Either type of box may be used, but once decided upon, the same type must be used throughout a given composition.

While the elongated boxes may be more self-explanatory, they are less versatile in cases of approximate endings and of indications to complete the respective patterns after cut-off.

VI. *Scores and Parts*

Conductor's Signs   158
A. *Time Signatures with Specified Subdivisions*   158
B. *Metronome Marks*   159
C. *Beats or Other Subdivisions in Seconds (Spatial Notation Only)*   159
D. *Free Subdivisions*   159
E. *Free (Unconducted) Passages*   160

Cues   160
A. *Entrance Cues in Parts (Traditional)*   160
B. *Playing-Cues for Missing Instruments or for Reinforcement*   161
C. *Rhythm Cues*   161
D. *Signals from Player to Player or to and from the Conductor*   161
Tape Cues, see page 317

Group Stems   162

Parts: Miscellaneous Details   162
A. *Mutes*   162
B. *Page Turns*   163
Repeated Patterns, Measures, etc., see pages 33 and 154
Rests, see page 135
C. *Tempo Indications*   164
See also page 145

Parts: Divisi (Two or More Parts on a Single Staff)   164
A. *Instrumental Parts*   164
B. *Choral Parts*   165
C. *Accidentals and Cancellations*   166
D. *Slurs and Ties*   167

Rehearsal Letters/Rehearsal Numbers/Measure Numbers   168
A. *Rehearsal Letters*   168
B. *Rehearsal Numbers*   168
C. *Measure Numbers*   168

Score Setups   170
A. *Traditional Orchestra Scores*   170
B. *Scores for Chamber Ensembles*   172
C. *Special Score Setups*   172
D. *Extraneous Designs*   172
E. *Band Scores*   173
See also page 176

Solo/Tutti Indications   175
A. *In Orchestra Scores*   175
B. *In Band Scores*   176

Time Signatures: Placement   177
A. *In Scores*   177
B. *In Performance Scores*   182
C. *In Parts*   183
D. *General Note*   183

Conductor's Signs

A. Time Signatures with Specified Subdivisions

If specific beat-patterns are desired, parenthetical numerals and plus signs are generally preferred to beating signs:

$$\left|\begin{smallmatrix}8\\8\end{smallmatrix}\right. \text{(3+2+3)} \quad \left|\begin{smallmatrix}5\\4\end{smallmatrix}\right. \text{(2+3)} \quad \left|\text{(3+2)} \quad \right|\text{(4+1)}$$

not: $\left|\begin{smallmatrix}8\\8\end{smallmatrix}\right.$ △ ⊔ △ $\left|\begin{smallmatrix}5\\4\end{smallmatrix}\right.$ ⊔ △ *etc.*

See also Time Signatures: Placement, page 146 f.

If dotted barlines are used to show subdivisions of measures, they must all correspond to the specified conductor's beat patterns. Cross rhythms (if any) must be indicated by other means.

B. Metronome Marks

1. IN SYMBOLIC NOTATION

The usual indications should be used, but large enough for easy reading.

2. IN SPATIAL NOTATION

Black arrows should be used for main beats; white arrows for subdivisions:

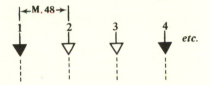

Metronome indications should be centered between beats, with arrows to each side, as in the preceding example.

C. Beats or Other Subdivisions in Seconds (Spatial Notation Only)

Durations are marked from arrow to arrow:

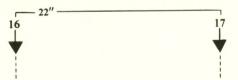

Note that all arrows are numbered consecutively, the numerals functioning as rehearsal numbers.

D. Free Subdivisions

White arrows with heavier frames than the subdivision arrows should be used. A numeral inside the white arrow indicates the number of unspecified beats or gestures (subdivisions) desired. These arrows may have to be drawn quite large so that the numerals inside are clearly visible:

E. Free (Unconducted) Passages

If the conductor is to stop beating altogether, the following sign should be used to show the end of a conducted passage:

Any other conducting instructions should be given verbally.

Cues

A. Entrance Cues in Parts (Traditional)

When choosing an entrance cue, one must always bear in mind that it is more important for the performer to be able to hear the cue clearly than that the cue be musically significant. For example, a trombonist in a large orchestra is more likely to hear the snare drum than the English horn, especially in a loud passage.

All cues must be in the same tuning (actual sound or transposed) as the part in which they occur. For example:

Passage to be cued

In the Flute

In the Bassoon

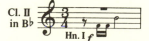

In the B-flat Clarinet

In Horn II in F

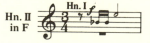

B. Playing-Cues for Missing Instruments or for Reinforcement

It may sometimes be expedient to have an instrument which is not playing fill in for a missing instrument or reinforce a part. Such playing-cues are notated like traditional entrance cues (see above): cue-size notes predominantly stemmed in the wrong direction, and full-size rests, with an instruction saying either "Play in the absence of———," or "Play at conductor's discretion."

If the two instruments in question happen to have different tunings, the playing-cue must of course be transposed. Thus if a B-flat clarinet is to play an oboe passage, that passage must be transposed into B-flat:

In the score, such playing-cues need not be written out. It suffices to direct the conductor's attention to the fact that the part of the substitute instrument contains the respective cue:

C. Rhythm Cues

See examples on page 91 (excerpt from Carter's *Second String Quartet*); page 112 (excerpt from Babbitt's *Composition for Twelve Instruments*); and page 118.

D. Signals from Player to Player or to and from the Conductor

1. IN PERFORMANCE SCORES, PARTICULARLY THOSE IN SPATIAL NOTATION

A medium-sized arrow pointing to a performer's staff indicates that a signal is to be received from the conductor or another performer:

A medium-sized arrow pointing away from a performer's staff indicates that a signal is to be given to another performer or to the conductor:

The arrows must be heavier than those denoting microtonal inflections (↑), but not so heavy that they could be mistaken for conductor's beating signs.

The arrows referring to the conductor should always be above the staff; the others should be above or below the staff, depending on the position of the instrument or voice on the score page.

Unlabeled arrows are useful in music such as *Texture* by Elliott Schwartz (see excerpt on p. 101), but in small combinations (instrumental duos, songs for voice and piano, etc.) they are superfluous.

2. IN PARTS, SPATIALLY OR OTHERWISE UNTRADITIONALLY NOTATED

Use the same kind of cues and signals as described above, but with one exception: All arrows should appear either only above or only below the staff, since the up and down positions on the score page do not apply to separate parts.

Group Stems

If, in a score, some or all parts form a homorhythmic progression, they may be stemmed together, especially in spatial notation, as shown in the example on the next page. In traditional notation, group stems are equally possible but rarely employed.

Conductors are far from unanimous in their reaction to this notation, their frequent objection being that there are too few duration bars to make the character of held chords sufficiently apparent. (The author agrees.)

Parts: Miscellaneous Details

A. Mutes

Brass: when mutes are to be applied it is helpful, as a warning, to add the instruction ''take mute'' or simply ''mute'' following the end of the last unmuted section. The same applies to the end of a muted section: ''mute off.'' (Such instructions do not appear in scores.) At the beginnings of the muted or unmuted sections the instruction must be repeated: ''mute'' and ''open.''

Bowed Strings: Use the same procedure as for brass, except that Italian equivalents are customary: *sord.* (*sordino*) and *via sord.* (''mute off''). At the beginning of the unmuted section the instruction is *senza sord.*

B. Page Turns

As mentioned elsewhere in this book, good, practical page turns are of the utmost importance. (In divisi parts it is sufficient if one of the players at the same desk has enough rests to turn the pages.)

C. Tempo Indications

Metronome indications need not be included in orchestra parts (i.e., in conducted music) as long as the verbal tempo indications appear. If there are no verbal indications, the metronome marks must of course be included.

Parts: Divisi (Two or More Parts on a Single Staff)

A. Instrumental Parts

1. TWO DIFFERENT PARTS

If two different parts, to be played simultaneously, are written on a single staff, they must be for identical instruments, such as Flutes I and II, not Flute and Oboe, and never, of course, for instruments having different transpositions.

If both instruments have the same rhythm, single-stem notation is acceptable, but double stemming is generally preferred.

2. VOICE CROSSINGS

Occasional crossings in two-voice parts written on a single staff are permissible. In intervals of a third and wider, the note-head of Part II (see below) must be lined up slightly to the left of that of Part I so that each stem touches one note-head only:

In intervals of a second, the note-heads must be a little farther apart than normally so that the stems will not run into each other:

If accidentals are involved, they are placed in front of the stems, except in intervals of a second where the position is normal:

If dots are involved, they must be placed after the stems:

In seconds in which only one part is dotted, it is not always clear to which part the dot refers unless certain notational rules are suspended, as follows:

Correct

Incorrect

1. Dot on D *up,* even though it is the lower part.

2. Upper note before the lower note to indicate clearly that the dot belongs to the lower note; in the second incorrect solution, the notes are too far apart.

3. No compromise needed.

4. Although the note-heads are separated by the dot, the preferred solution clearly shows that the dot belongs to the D.

If both notes are dotted, there is no danger of ambiguity.

For other dot positions, see Dotted Notes, page 125 ff.

3. THREE DIFFERENT PARTS

If three different parts are to be written on a single staff, they must be very simple rhythmically because only two stems are available to accommodate them, i.e., at least two of the parts must go on one stem. Thus, either the upper or the lower two parts must have the same rhythm:*

Permissible   Flutes I, II, III

The limit of permissible complexity

B. Choral Parts

All divisi places should be written with double stems. The same goes for regular double parts (Sopranos I and II, Soprano and Alto, etc.), unless they are in unison. If a part divides into more than two, an extra staff should be added unless the texture is very simple and the divisi passage very short.

---

* More sophisticated stemming is of course possible, but it is not practical for use in instrumental parts and choral music.

Tenors and basses require separate parts unless the tenors are notated in bass clef. This, however, is never done in open score—only in two-staff notation, such as in church hymnals.

Alternations between open score (with tenors in G-clef) and close score (tenors in bass clef) are not desirable, although the vocal scores of some larger church works do sometimes have choral movements in open score and chorales on two staves.

C. Accidentals and Cancellations

1. ONE PLAYER

In double-stemmed notation for a single player (keyboard, etc.), accidentals and cancellations apply to all identical notes (same octave, same clef) in the same measure on the same staff.

2. MORE THAN ONE PLAYER

In divisi parts, i.e., parts combining music for more than one performer on a single staff, each line must have its own accidentals and cancellations, even though this may at times look rather redundant:

For piano (right hand)

For Oboes I and II

To assure correct reading, it is necessary, in divisi parts, to use accidentals and cancellations where none would have been required if the parts had been written on separate staves (see notes marked with an asterisk in the following example).

Single-staff notation

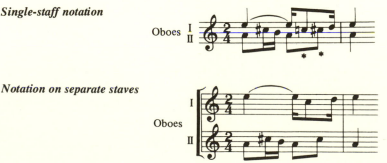

Notation on separate staves

D. Slurs and Ties

1. SINGLE-STEMMED DIVISI

Single-stemmed divisi passages, whether for a single player or for two or more performers, require only one slur, but all tied notes must have their own ties:

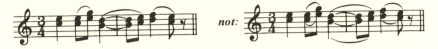

2. DOUBLE-STEMMED DIVISI

In double-stemmed divisi passages, slurs must be placed above as well as below:

In double-stemmed unisons, two ties are used:

When, in a divisi passage, only one part has a tie, or in a three-part divisi, only one or two parts have ties, the tied and untied notes should have separate stems:

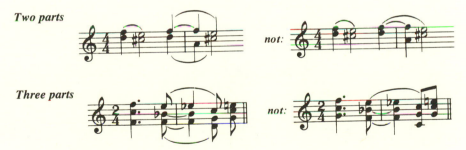

Two parts

Three parts

It is best to begin and end the double stemming in accordance with a short pattern or phrase. The following versions of the examples above look awkward because they both change back to single stemming before the end of the slurs (marked with an asterisk):

Do not use   *Do not use*

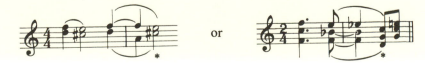

or

Rehearsal Letters/Rehearsal Numbers/Measure Numbers

A. Rehearsal Letters

Rehearsal letters should be used only in extended compositions where they serve to flag passages likely to require attention in rehearsals and lacking other identifying features such as new tempo indications. If the composition has more than one movement, the letters should continue through all the movements. If more letters are needed than are contained in the alphabet, double letters are used (. . . X, Y, Z, AA, BB, etc.).

B. Rehearsal Numbers

Rehearsal numbers are less practical than letters because they are easily confused with measure numbers, for which reason they should be avoided.

C. Measure Numbers

Measure numbers are the most practical rehearsal aids. Counting begins with the first complete measure (upbeat measures are not counted). The customary method is to mark every fifth measure by placing a numeral above the barline at the beginning of the measure to be designated:

Boxed measure numbers are placed above the barline or slightly to the right:

Once in a while one finds the five-measure (or ten-measure) segments marked 1, 2, 3, etc. This usually avoids three-digit figures in extended works but nevertheless should not be employed because of the inevitable confusion with measure numbers.

There is little agreement about numbering the measures of first and second endings in repeats. The most practical (although rather illogical) method is to ignore the fact that first and second endings are involved and simply count all measures, regardless of repeat signs, etc.:

If repeats are written out in the score and not in some or all parts (or vice versa), the last-mentioned method will invariably cause serious confusion in rehearsal. Score and parts, therefore, must either follow identical repeat procedures, or must use rehearsal letters or numbers instead of measure numbers, and mark written-out repeats by using the same letter or number over again, followed by a small "a."

1. PLACEMENT OF MEASURE NUMBERS

Orchestra scores: above the score and above the strings;

Band scores: above the score and above the brasses;

Vocal scores: above the voices (if more than one) and above the piano;

Choral scores with accompaniment or keyboard reduction: above the voices and above the accompaniment or reduction.

If a measure number coincides with a tempo indication or other instruction appearing above the staff, it is placed above such instructions.

If it is found desirable to frame the measure numbers to make them more prominent, a square or rectangular frame is more practical than a circle, because it can be widened as the numbers grow in width: ⑤ ⑮ ⑯

2. MEASURE NUMBERS IN PARTS

These must of course match those in the score. This means that multirests (²̲ , ⁴̲ , etc.) must not be longer than five measures if the measures are numbered in segments of five, and ten measures if numbered in segments of ten:

3. MEASURE NUMBERS AT THE BEGINNING OF EACH LINE OR SYSTEM

This is another method often encountered. In scores, such numbers should appear just right or left above the first top clef of each brace (though not on the opening measure of the movement), and in the parts, the numbers may either appear above the clefs or in front of each line, i.e., in the left margin. (Note that this system permits longer multirests.) Needless to say, the actual numbers will be different from part to part.

POSITIONS OF MEASURE NUMBERS

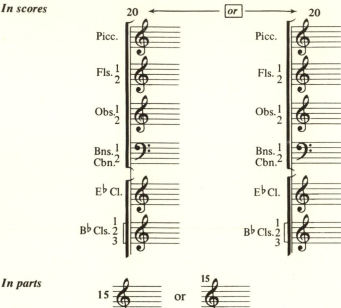

In scores

In parts

Score Setups

A. Traditional Orchestra Scores

The traditional organization of a score page reflects the classical orchestra's division into choirs: woodwinds, brasses, and strings. Anything that does not belong in these three basic groups is placed between the brasses and the strings.

A word of advice: the first page of the score should show all instruments needed for the entire composition. If the orchestra is so large that the page is not high enough to accommodate a complete listing, the complete instrumentation must appear on the page preceding the music.

All subsequent pages may contain only the instruments actually playing. Nonetheless, the barlines must continue to be governed by instrument families, i.e., according to the system established on the first page of the score.

In more recent music, the orchestra is often treated as an ensemble of individual instruments of equal importance instead of choirs of instrument families. This change in attitude has brought about a variety of novel arrangements on the score page. Most of these, however, have not proven to be more practical than the traditional setup, and by now tradition has largely won out.

The example shows a typical score for a large, conventional orchestra (Anton Webern, *Passacaglia, Op. 1*).

The piece has a key signature of one flat in the C instruments, which means that the transposing instruments have different key signatures: B-flat instruments—one sharp; F instruments—no sharp or flat. (Although the English horn is an F instrument, it is not customary to mark it "in F.") Nontonal scores have no key signatures to tell whether the score is in C or transposed. For this reason it is doubly important to indicate "Transposed Score" or "Score in C."

A few details: in the original score, the timpani appear directly below the tuba, followed by the rest of the percussion.

Until quite recently, few percussion details, if any, were indicated in the score. The names of the respective instruments only appeared at their points of entry. The present score represents a slight improvement: the percussion instruments required are listed on a separate page as triangle, cymbals, tam-tam, and bass drum. The number of timpani is not specified, nor does the mere word *cymbals* reveal that a suspended cymbal and a crash cymbal are required. (For details concerning percussion scores, see page 215 ff.)

This score setup does not contain solo staves (as in concertos) or vocal and/or choral staves. All of these would go above the violins. If tempo indications appear above the violins, the solo or vocal staves are placed above such indications.

Note that the barlines connect the major families of instruments: woodwinds, brass, strings. Instruments appearing between the brass and string sections are generally barred individually, but certain circumstances may make connecting barlines for some of these instruments preferable.

B. Scores for Chamber Ensembles

Chamber scores are organized along the same principles that govern the grouping of instruments in orchestra scores, except that practically all small chamber ensembles containing a piano or other keyboard instrument are notated with the keyboard instrument at the bottom.

C. Special Score Setups

If two or more orchestral or choral groups are to perform in different locations of the hall, they should be notated separately in the score, one above the other(s). Good examples are Elliott Carter's *A Symphony of Three Orchestras,* and many of the works of Henry Brant.

If two or more conductors are used for different groups, and if the total score thus becomes too large to be manageable, each conductor should have a partial score showing his own ensemble in full, with the other ensemble(s) indicated by one or more cue lines. A good example, written in spatial notation, is Witold Lutosławski's *Trois poèmes d'Henri Michaux,* for twenty-part chorus and orchestra. (See also page 145.)

D. Extraneous Designs

It has once again become fashionable occasionally to arrange the staff-lines in such a way that they form either abstract designs (circles, spirals, rectangles, crosses, and more elusive shapes) or pictographs (hearts, bells, crucifixes, etc.). While such designs can be quite ingenious and even beautiful, they usually are troublesome for the performers.

Only in a few circumstances are unconventional designs of practical advantage; for example, circular arrangements of events that are to be performed clockwise or counterclockwise, beginning with any event chosen at random. The events may be pitches, durations, rhythms, or completely written out fragments, etc. In all such arrangements, the music should be written horizontally to avoid having to rotate the page:

Preferable

Impractical

E. Band Scores

Unlike orchestral scores, band scores are not yet completely standardized. As shown on page 171, orchestra scores are divided into three basic families— woodwinds, brasses, and strings, with percussion and "odd" instruments or voices between the brass and the strings.

Band scores also begin with woodwinds—flutes, oboes, and English horn— but since the clarinets in bands are so numerous, they form a group of their own. The bassoons are placed either below the clarinets, but barred separately, or below the English horn, barred with the upper woodwinds. Over the years, the latter solution has become the preferred one. (See example of band score on page 174.)

Next are the saxophones, which bridge the gap between woodwinds and brasses, being a bit of both.

The brass instruments follow, but their order differs from that in orchestra scores: The positions of the horns and trumpets are reversed. The trumpets, moreover, are often interchangeable with cornets, in which case they are marked "Bb Cornet (or Bb Trumpet)" or "Bb Cornet/Trumpet." If cornets and trumpets have separate parts, the cornets are placed above the trumpets.

The baritone is occasionally placed between the horns and trombones, but since it often doubles the tuba in the upper octave, its preferred position is above the tuba and below the trombones. The proper notation of the baritone is also in question: whether as a B-flat instrument, notated in G-clef, transposing a major ninth down, or as a C instrument, in bass clef, at concert pitch. The C notation has become preferred in scores, but the parts usually include both notations, at the player's option.

As the example shows, the top of the brass group in band scores is equivalent to the top of the strings in orchestra scores. Solo instruments appear above the brasses, as do tempo indications and rehearsal numbers or letters. However, band scores have no standard place for "odd" instruments, except for keyboard and/or harp parts, which are generally placed at the bottom of the score, below the percussion.

The example shows a fairly typical score with a key signature of three flats in the C instruments, and appropriately different signatures in the various transposing instruments.

In nontonal music there are no key signatures, regardless of whether the score is transposed or in C.

Solo/Tutti Indications

The term *solo* has three different meanings:

1. a "true" solo, i.e., the solo part(s) of a concerto or concert aria, etc.;

2. a passage in which one or a few instruments are exposed because the balance of the ensemble has rests;

3. a passage which must be given prominence.

In solos of the first kind, the indication *Solo* must appear in score and parts; in the second and third meanings, *Solo* need only appear in the part(s).

In addition, there are situations which call for only one player of a section or one desk or stand, for reasons of balance, etc.

To avoid ambiguity, the following nomenclature should be used:

A. In Orchestra Scores

Solo: a single player has prominent material. For the strings the following refinements are available:

One Solo: a single player. (*Solo* without *One* could mean that an entire section plays prominently.)

Two Soli: two players have prominent material.

One player; two players; one desk; etc., are indications of balance, rather than of solo material.

In general, no indications are given to show the end of a full-section or single-instrument solo.* However, if the solo was played by fewer instruments than the full section, the word *Tutti* must appear when the full section resumes playing.

When the section is divided between one or more solo strings and the other players, the latter group is marked *gli altri* or *the others.*

When a string section is divided equally, it is marked *div.*, and when it resumes playing in unison, it is marked *unis.* (not *a 2*). However, if the strings play double stops, then play two notes divisi, and then play double stops again, they should be marked *non div.*, rather than *unis.*

When two similar instruments, such as two flutes, are notated on a single staff, they must be marked as follows:

a 2 if they are to play in unison;

div. (*divisi*) if they are to play different parts.

For three instruments the markings are *a 3* and *div. a 3*, respectively.

*But see Levels of Prominence, page 17 f.

N.B.: Although the Italian words have been italicized above, all these terms customarily appear in roman type in the music, italics being reserved for expression marks and dynamics. Thus:

Solo, Tutti, a 2, div., non div., unis., gli altri, etc.; but *espressivo (espr.)*, *marcato (marc.)*, *crescendo poco a poco,* etc.

It is strongly suggested that these two different typefaces be maintained, because musicians have become accustomed to them and quick reactions are essential for good musical performances.

B. In Band Scores

Unlike the instruments in orchestra scores, which are usually identified with roman numerals (Flute II, Horn IV, etc.), band instruments generally take arabic numerals for identification (2nd Flute or Flute 2; Horns $\frac{3}{4}$, etc.). As a result, a clear distinction must be made in band music between numerals that identify instruments (1, 2, etc.) and spelled-out numerals which indicate the number of players (one, two, etc.).

Thus, instructions such as the following should be used:

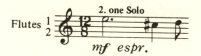

One second flutist plays solo

All available third horns play solo

No need for a numeral since the baritones have only one part, but the word all *after* Solo *indicates that all baritone players have a prominent phrase*

Other typical indications:

one player

two players

the others (The Italian *gli altri* is not used in band scores.)

1. two Soli div.

one stand

Exception: In spite of what has been said above about spelling out the number of players, the instruction *a 2* must have a numeral *2*.

Time Signatures: Placement

(For irregular subdivisions of measures, see Conductor's Signs, page 158 ff.)

A. In Scores

1. TRADITIONAL PRACTICE

The traditional practice is to put the time signatures into all staves of the score. They are thus quite small, and in printed scores, which are usually reduced versions of the original "master copy," the individual signatures are invariably too small for conductors to read during performances. Fortunately, however, the meter in traditional music rarely, if ever, changes, so that the size of the time signatures is not crucial.

In more recent music, however, this is no longer so: the meter usually changes a great deal, so that the conductor must be able to spot and read the signatures more easily. Consequently, larger signatures have been introduced.

These new, larger signatures may be written in one of two ways: 1) between or through the staves; or 2) above the score and, if it is a large score, again further down, usually above the strings.

The signatures that go between or through the staves, although quite popular, have the disadvantage of interrupting the horizontal flow of the music; those going above the score have only the nonmusical disadvantage of requiring extra vertical space. If space permits, the latter placement is preferred.

Large signatures going through or between the staves are placed after the barlines:

a. Time signatures through the staves

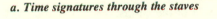

(In example *a,* the large time signatures are at best an unnecessary encumbrance: since the music is for string quartet, a conductor's concern with legibility is not at issue. Yet one encounters such notation quite frequently.)

b. Time signatures between the staves

Large signatures going above the score and, if possible, above one or two sections below, should be placed just to the right of the barlines or centered above them. Examples will be found below and on pages 179 and 180.

NUMERALS ONLY:

2. OTHER PRACTICES

If vertical space is limited, the two numerals of the time signature may be replaced by one numeral and a note, placed next to each other. The numeral represents the number of beats; the note indicates the beat-unit.

(Continued on page 181.)

From Hans Werner Henze, Versuch über Schweine (Essay on Pigs) for Voice and Orchestra (**1969**)

Another example of this style of notation:

From Elliott Carter, A Symphony of Three Orchestras *(1976)*

AMP-7715

© 1978 by Associated Music Publishers, Inc. Used by permission.

See also the examples on pages 94 f, 101, and 284 f.

THE SAME METERS NOTATED WITH NUMERALS AND NOTES NEXT TO
EACH OTHER: (Note the changes in the compound meters!)

A score page notated in this style:*

From Milton Babbitt, Composition for Twelve Instruments *(1948/54)*

AMP 96418-52

© 1964 by Associated Music Publishers, Inc. Used by permission.

*See also page 217.

c. AT THE PAGE TURN

In scores of rhythmic complexity and frequently changing time signatures, it is strongly suggested that the prevailing time signature be repeated in brackets at the beginning of all left-hand pages:

End of right-hand page

Beginning of subsequent left-hand page

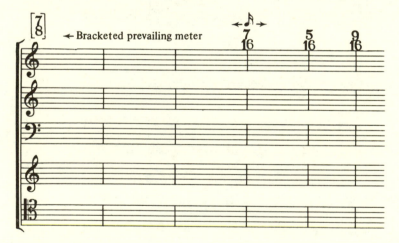

← Bracketed prevailing meter

B. In Performance Scores

If the music is performed directly from the score, the traditional time signatures within the staves must be retained so that each performer (reading horizontally) has all signatures in his own part:

C. In Parts

If separate parts are extracted, they should have the traditional time signatures within the staves only.

D. General Note

Avoid half-beat time signatures: for example, instead of $3\frac{1}{2} \over 4$ use $7 \over 8$ wherever possible; or break a measure in half ($\frac{4}{8}+\frac{3}{8}$, or $\frac{4+3}{8}$, etc.), either with a double signature (as shown above) or as two separate measures.

Part Two: Specific Notation

For easy reference, the instruments (or instrument groups) in this section appear in score order, and the subheadings in each chapter in alphabetical order.

VII. *Wind Instruments: General Topics*

Air Sound or Breathy Sound 186
A. *Pitched Sounds* 186
B. *Unpitched Sounds* 186
C. *Tongued Air Sounds* 187
D. *Breathing In and Out* 187
E. *Combined Effects* 187

Bending the Pitch 187

Flutter Tongue 188

Humming While Playing 188

Tonguing 188
A. *Single Tonguing* 189
B. *Staccato Tonguing* 189
C. *Legato Tonguing* 189
D. *Double Tonguing* 189
E. *Triple Tonguing* 189

Transpositions
see *page 71*

Unpitched Sounds 190

Air Sound or Breathy Sound

The generic symbol for creating a breathy sound by blowing air through an instrument is:

A. Pitched Sounds

Sounds that are to be more pitch than air are notated as follows:

Specified pitches

Approximate pitches

Articulation syllables may be added.

B. Unpitched Sounds

Sounds that are to have more air than pitch are notated as follows:

With articulation syllables

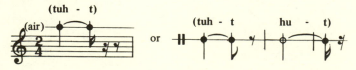

With words (whispering) *

or

C. Tongued Air Sounds (tuhh and whht)

The word *air* and the syllables need only appear at first occurrence. The player exhales, unless *inhale* is specifically stated, either verbally or with IN←.

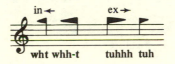

N.B.: The stem indicates the exact metric position of the "t" sound; the duration of the wedges is approximate.

D. Breathing In and Out

For quick alternations of inhaling and exhaling, IN← and EX→ should be used (see Voice, page 295).

E. Combined Effects

The effects described above—especially the tongued air sounds—may be combined with others, such as the key slap:

Bending the Pitch

A "contour" line is drawn at the level of the note-head:

* A stem going through a round note-head always indicates that air is blown through an instrument, as differentiated from vocal whisper notation, where the stem does not go through the note-head (see Voice, Whispering, page 304 f).

Flutter Tongue

For individual notes, tremolo bars should be used:

(The addition of *fl.* for *flutter tongue* is optional.)

For approximate pitch notation, such as the following, the abbreviation *fl.* followed by a wavy line must be used because there are no stems on which to place tremolo bars:

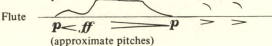

For other tonguing techniques see Tonguing, below.

See also Brass Instruments, Growl, page 199.

Humming While Playing

To indicate hummed pitches, small notes should be used, along with the verbal direction *hum*. (The instrumental notes remain full-sized.)

If specific octave positions for the hummed pitches are desired, and if such pitches are very far from the instrumental ones, an extra cue-sized staff should be added. Preferably, however, the octave position for hummed tones should be left to the performer, since vocal ranges vary greatly.

The humming notes must appear in the same transposition (if any) in which the instrument is notated.

Tonguing

No special signs need be employed, since the traditional notation is entirely sufficient.

A. Single Tonguing

Music written without slurs or other articulation such as staccato dots or accents, calls for single tonguing.

B. Staccato Tonguing

Same as above, with staccato dots.

C. Legato Tonguing

Two or more different, tongued tones played with one breath may be notated with slurs and staccato dots or with slurs and tenuto lines, the former being a little lighter in character:

D. Double Tonguing

A series of quickly repeated (or successive) tones, played with one breath, and with a tongue movement similar to pronouncing *ta-ka*.

Double tonguing should be notated either with slurred staccato dots (for a rather light form of double tonguing), or with slurred tenuto lines (for a slightly heavier version). The written-out notation of dotted repeated notes may be followed by an abbreviation: single notes with two slurred dots each, as shown below. Successive notes and notes with tenuto lines can not be abbreviated.

With abbreviations

E. Triple Tonguing

The same as double tonguing, but for three notes (tongue movement similar to pronouncing *ta-ka-ta**):

For flutter tongue, see page 188.

---

* If different kinds of tonguing (hard to soft) are wanted, they should be indicated: *ta-ka—ta-ga—da-ga*, for example, and for triple tonguing: *ta-ka-ta—ta-ga-da—da-ga-da*, or *ta-da-ga*.

As for the vowel, *a* is more universal than the *u* found in much American music, because unlike the *u*, a short *a* sounds quite similar in most languages.

Unpitched Sounds

Unpitched sounds should, as a rule, be notated on an extra line outside the regular staff (preferably above).

Most unpitched sounds should be notated with x-shaped note-heads and identified verbally, since the large number of possible unpitched sounds makes identification by individual symbols impossible.

The verbal identifications should be spelled out at first occurrence and abbreviated at subsequent entries.

If several different unpitched sounds are to be produced simultaneously or in quick alternation, different stem directions should be used and/or extra lines added. The extra lines should always be farther apart than the normal staff-lines.

If unpitched sounds are used for protracted periods, the regular staff should be discontinued and replaced by a single line (as a continuation of the middle line of the regular staff) or by as many lines as needed.

See also Air Sound or Breathy Sound, page 186 f; Key Slaps, page 192; Smacking Sound or "Kiss," page 195 and 203; Fingernails, page 198; Valve Click, page 204.

VIII. *Woodwinds*

Air Pressure   191

Alternate Fingerings
  see *Trills (Other than Conventional)*, page 196

Embouchures (Lip Positions)   192
A. *Single and Double Reeds*   192
B. *Flutes*   192

Fingering
  see *Multiphonics*

Harmonics   192

Key Slaps   192

Multiphonics   193
A. *Fingering*   193
B. *Precise Pitches*   194

C. *Mixtures of Precise and Approximate Pitches*   194
D. *Approximate Pitches*   194
E. *Cluster Notation*   195

Muted   195

Octave Sign   195

Smacking Sound or "Kiss"   195

Sub Tone (Clarinets)   195

Trills (Other than Conventional)   196
A. *Double Trill*   196
B. *Timbral Trill*   196
C. *Trills with Harmonics*   196

Air Pressure

Verbal instructions generally are considered preferable to signs or abbreviations. However, if air-pressure variations occur frequently, the following combination of abbreviations and signs should be used:

Pr = pressure. The abbreviation should be cancelled with *ord.* or *norm.* or simply *n* for *natural*.

+ Pr = much pressure (*molto*), i.e., more than normal

− Pr = little pressure (*poco*), i.e., less than normal

< Pr = increasing pressure

Pr > = diminishing pressure

Embouchures (Lip Positions)

A. Single and Double Reeds

⬛ = normal lip position

⬜ = lips at the tip of the reed(s), or toward the tip

⬛ = lips at the base of the reed(s), or toward the base

B. Flutes

No trend toward specific symbols has emerged, nor are signs for lip positions on the flute used with sufficient frequency to warrant suggestions for standardization. If such signs are wanted, it is recommended that they be based on those for mouth positions in the voice section of this book, i.e., that rectangles and squares be used and that circles be avoided because they are likely to be mistaken for harmonics or fingerings, etc.

Harmonics

In traditional notation, crosses (+) as well as circles (o) above the notes are used to signify harmonics. In present-day notation, however, it is strongly suggested to use only circles, since they have increasingly become the generic sign for harmonics, while crosses are now frequently used to signify other effects:

(The note indicates the sounding pitch.)
See also Trills (other than conventional), page 196.

Key Slaps

The generic symbol for key slaps is an x or an x-shaped note.

Pitched key slaps   key slaps

(The sounding pitches are indicated*.)

---

* The pitches indicated by the x-shaped notes in the staff sometimes require fingerings different from those which would produce these pitches as regular tones. (In transposing instruments, these "sounding pitches" are notated in transposition, the same as the regular pitches.)

Unpitched key slaps

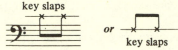

Regular tones beginning with a key slap or a key slap grace note

Key slaps with embouchure hole closed (flute only)

Add on first occurrence: *c.* (= closed or *chiuso*)

Key-slap trills

For half and whole notes the x is encircled.

Multiphonics

A. Fingering

Since the playing of multiphonics involves certain variations of timbre, it is often necessary to indicate fingerings to insure the desired sound. These should be indicated with representations of the holes and/or keys, and with letters, rather than with numerals or words.

The graphics for diagrammatic representation are:

○ = open

● = closed*

In addition, there are the two following symbols:

◕ = half-open

∅ = rim only

---

* Composers and arrangers who are faced with having to mark a great number of fingering indications are advised to draw an open hole in black ink and have a rubber stamp made. They can then stamp the hole wherever needed, filling it in as required.

Right- and left-hand holes are separated by a short line, either horizontal or slightly slanted (see below).

Extra keys may be indicated with symbols (for example, in flute fingering) or pitch letters with accidentals, if any (such as in oboe fingering). Identification of extra keys by numbers is not recommended because there is too little uniformity in the meaning of such numbers.

B. Precise Pitches

1. FLUTE

Double stops *Triple stop*

2. OBOE

Double stops *Triple stop*

C. Mixtures of Precise and Approximate Pitches

Only the precise pitches are notated; the wavy lines cover areas of indeterminate sound.

Flute

D. Approximate Pitches

The lengths of the wavy lines and their positions on the staff show the approximate areas of sound. In order to signify half notes and whole notes, encirclings should be used, the way x-shaped note-heads are encircled for the same purpose.

E. Cluster Notation

The notation of indeterminate or approximate clusters is in the process of becoming the preferred notation for approximate multiphonics as well. This would make the last example appear as follows:

Muted

Since the quick alternations between muted and open, typical for brass instruments, are not at all typical for woodwinds, there is no real need for a symbol. A verbal instruction, possibly with an explanation concerning how to mute the instrument, would be most practical. If, however, signs are wanted, the following should be used:

$$+ = \text{muted}$$
$$\circ = \text{open}$$

Octave Sign

Very high notes in the flute should be written out (if vertical space is available) instead of being notated with an 8va sign. There is no rationale for this rule other than a strong tradition and the fact that flutists are used to reading notes with many leger lines.

Smacking Sound or "Kiss"

The notation for a smacking sound (double reeds only) is as follows:

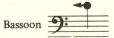

Sub Tone (Clarinets)

Notate sub tone on the clarinet as follows:

Trills (Other than Conventional)

A. Double Trill

Alternate fingerings enable the player to produce very fast double trills, but their number is limited and varies from one instrument to another. Before writing such a trill, it is important to ascertain whether it can actually be realized.

(The addition of fingering is optional.)

B. Timbral Trill

Timbral trill (unison trill), or trilling with the same pitch, is notated as follows:

(The addition of fingering is optional.)

C. Trills with Harmonics

See also Pitch, Vibrato/Tremolo/Trill, page 74 and Brass, page 203.

IX. *Brasses*

"Cracked" Tone	197	C. *Grid Notation*	201
		D. *Hand Stopping (Horn)*	201
Fingering	198	E. *Rhythmic Muting*	202
Fingernails	198	*Portamento (Trombone)*	
		see *Glissandos, pages 19 and 63*	
Growl	199		
		Rip	202
Half Valve	199	A. *Broken-Line Notation*	202
A. *Glissando Effect*	199	B. *Slur*	202
B. *Individual Tones*	199		
		Smacking Sound or "Kiss"	203
Horn Transpositions	199		
		Timbral Trill	203
Mouthpiece Pop (Hand Pop)	200		
		Tongue Positions (for	
Mutes	200	*Changes in Timbre)*	204
A. *Mute Designations*	200		
B. *Mute Manipulations*	201	*Valve Click*	204

"Cracked" Tone

Add a bold, upper-case **K** to the dynamic marking:

If too little space is available to place the **K** after the dynamic marking, it may appear above the note or below the dynamic. (The **K** should not be too far from the note-head.)

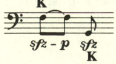

Notes may be cracked above or below the given note. If the composer wishes to specify the direction, the symbols are: **K↑**   **K↓**

Fingering

Diagrammatic representations of the valves are preferred to numbers, letters, or words. The valves should be indicated by the following symbols:

o = open valve

◑ = half valve (but see the entry Half Valve for glissando effects)

● = closed valve

o → ● and ● → o = gradual changes from open to closed valve and vice versa

ø = valve trill

Valves and corresponding fingers   *Specific examples*

Fingernails

The unpitched sound most frequently encountered in the brass section consists of tapping the bell of the instrument with fingernails. This should be notated:

fingernails on bell

Growl

Growl refers to a low-pitched flutter tongue (usually pedal tone). It may be notated on a specified pitch with the word *growl* added:

If the growl is to sound more like a noise than a discernible pitch, an x-shaped note-head is more appropriate:

Half Valve

A. Glissando Effect

Diamond-shaped note-heads and the verbal instruction ½v. (half valve) should be used. The ½v. need not be repeated, except as an occasional reminder. The abbreviation *ord.* should appear after the completion of the half-valve effect.

B. Individual Tones

If individual tones are to have half-valve timbre, they are notated as above: diamond-shaped note-heads and the verbal instruction ½v. For approximate pitches in full staff notation a verbal indication is recommended:

Horn Transpositions

While G-clef notation is always written a fifth above actual sound, bass-clef notation used to be written a fourth below actual sound, and often still is. It is becoming common practice, however, to write a fifth above in both clefs. To avoid confusion regarding the intended transposition in bass-clef passages, a small numeral should be added to the bass clef, as follows:

To sound
a fifth lower
(now preferred)

To sound
a fourth higher

Actual sound
in both notations

If verbal instructions are preferred, a clear wording would be "Horn sounds a fifth lower, regardless of clef."

Mouthpiece Pop (Hand Pop)

The following notation for mouthpiece pop should never be used without verbal identification at first occurrence.

Pitched sounds

Unpitched sounds

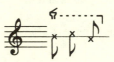

Mutes

A. Mute Designations

The names of the mutes, rather than pictographs, should be used. They should always appear above the music.

Trumpet and trombone mutes:

"straight" or "straight mute"; after first occurrence, use "st."
"cup mute," followed by "cup"
"harmon mute," followed by "harmon"
"solotone" (no abbreviation)
"plunger" (no abbreviation)

Horn and tuba: "mute" (do not confuse with hand-muting of the horn)

N.B.: "Wa-wa" is not a mute but an effect produced with a harmon mute or a plunger.

For removing the mute, the term *open* should be used, unless a succession of relatively rapid changes, or half muting, is desired (see below).

B. Mute Manipulations

1. SYMBOL KEY FOR ALL MUTES
(but see Hand Stopping, Horn, below):

+ = muted (closed)
⊕ = half closed
O = open
+ ➤ O and O ➤ + = gradual changes from one mute position to another
O|+ and +|O = sudden changes

2. SPECIAL SYMBOLS FOR THE HARMON MUTE

✦ = mute in; hand over stem-cup (i.e., closed)
✦ or ✦ = mute in; stem-cup half closed
+ = mute in; stem-cup open
O = mute out (open)

3. "WA-WA" EFFECTS

✦┬+ = "wa." Instead of the symbols, the word "wa" may be used.

✦ ➤ + ➤ ✦ = "owwwaoooww"

N.B.: When the special symbols for the harmon mute are used, they must be explained in the performance instructions or at first occurrence.

C. Grid Notation

If more subtle mute manipulations are desired, a grid should be placed above the staff and the mute positions indicated between the lines representing "open" and "closed":

D. Hand Stopping (Horn)

+ = stopped
● = half stopped
O = open

N.B.: Horns require the verbal indication "mute" unless hand-stopping is wanted.

E. Rhythmic Muting

Muting symbols may be combined with small notes for precisely specified rhythmic muting. The symbols and the notes should be placed above the staff, but no extra staff-line is necessary for the rhythm-cue notes:

Rip

The rip is essentially an arpeggiated glissando. It is notated either with a broken line (to symbolize the rip's irregular succession of pitches) or with a slurlike curved line.

A. Broken-Line Notation

The broken-line notation, which should include a slur and the word *rip,* is used for rips between two regular notes:

Solid-line notation is also used but is not recommended because of its similarity to glissando notation:

B. Slurlike Notation

The slurlike notation, which also includes the word *rip,* is used for quick, rhythmically somewhat indeterminate whipping or sighing lip glissandos:

The gracelike rip with specified pitches

The same with unspecified opening pitch

The rip from a main note with specified pitches

The same with unspecified final pitch

*The forced rip to the highest possible pitch,
usually called "shriek"*

Smacking Sound or "Kiss"

A smacking sound is notated as follows:

Timbral Trill

Timbral trill (unison trill), or trilling with the same pitch, may be notated as
follows:

More detailed notation, with fingering added   *Fingering ad lib.*

(If fingering is ad lib., the instruction *alternate fingering* should be added at
first occurrence, and the abbreviation *alt. fing.* thereafter.)

N.B.: The timbral trill is not actually a trill, but a repeat tremolo, inasmuch as
the pitch does not change (see Pitch, Vibrato/Trill/Tremolo, page 74). However,
since "trimbral trill" is the designation by which it is most widely known, any
attempt to change it would only add to the complexity of present-day notation.

Tongue Positions (for Changes in Timbre)

Different vowels are used to indicate different tongue positions. It is suggested that the International Phonetic Alphabet be used. If not, the language must be specified to assure the intended pronunciation.

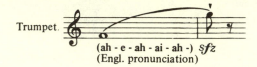

Trumpet.

(ah - e - ah - ai - ah -) *sfz*
(Engl. pronunciation)

Valve Click

As in the following example, there should always be a verbal identification for valve click at first occurrence. If the effect recurs after a lengthy interval, the abbreviation *v.c.* should be used.

valve click

X. *Percussion*

Instrument Abbreviations and
Pictograms   205

Stick, Mallet, and Beater
Pictograms   210

Ranges of Percussion
Instruments with Definite   213
Pitch

Score Order for Instrument
Families and Mixed
Ensembles   215
  A. *Single Instruments and Instrument
     Families*   215
  B. *Mixed Groups of Instruments*   216
  C. *Traditional or Typical Setups*   219

General Practices   219
  A. *Instrument Specifications*   219
  B. *Note Shapes*   219

C. *Beater Indications*   220
D. *Short-Decay Instruments:
   Rhythmic (Durational) Notation*   220
E. *Long-Decay Instruments: Rhythmic
   (Durational) Notation*   220
F. *Gong versus Tam-Tam Notation*   220
G. *Marimba*   221

Effects and Techniques   221
  A. *Brush Swishes*   221
  B. **Circular Rubbing or Scraping**   221
  C. *Dead Stick*   221
  D. *Grace Notes*   221
  E. *Gradual Changes of Location and
     Other Gradual Changes*   222
  F. *Locations on Cymbals, Gongs, etc.*   223
  G. *Locations on Drums*   224
  H. *Ride-Cymbal Technique*   224
  I. *Rim Shot*   224
  J. *Rolls*   225
  K. *Striking with Two Beaters*   225

Instrument Abbreviations and Pictograms

The instruments are listed on the following pages in the order in which they should appear in the score.

All instruments used in a given work should be listed on a prefatory page in the score. In the parts, all instruments of the percussion section should be listed in score order at the top of the first page of music, together with their abbreviations or pictograms. If there are several percussion sections, the part(s) of each section should list that section's instruments.

In the music, the name of each instrument should be given in full at first occurrence, with the respective abbreviation or pictogram added in parentheses if the instrument plays again later on. Thereafter, the abbreviation or pictogram is sufficient. For example:

First occurrence: *Suspended Cymbal* (⊥), or *Suspended Cymbal* (*S. Cym.*)

Subsequent occurrences: ⊥ or *S.Cym.*

In deciding whether to use pictograms or abbreviations (or fully written-out instrument names) one should bear in mind that although verbal indications are still more commonly used than pictograms, the latter are more universally practical because they do not depend on any specific language.

In each category or family, the instruments are listed from high to low (approximately).

Glass	Wind Chimes (Glass)	W. Chimes	
Metals	Triangle*	Trgl.	
	Crotale(s)** or Antique Cymbal(s)**	Crot. Ant. Cym.	
	Finger Cymbals***	Fing. Cyms.	
	Sistrum	Sist.	
	Sleigh Bells	Sl. Bells	
	Cymbal Tongs	Cym. Tngs.	
	Sizzle Cymbal*	Sizz. Cym.	
	Suspended Cymbal*	S. Cym.	
	Crash Cymbals*	Cym.	
	High-Hat Cymbals*	Hi-Hat	
	Cowbell(s)	Cowb. or C.B.	
	Herd Bell(s) or Almglocke(n)	Herd B. Almgl.	

* See also General Conventions, Note-heads, page 30 f.
** Suspended; struck with metal beater.
*** Rim against rim or clashed (with two fingers).

	Bell Plate(s)	Bell Pl.
	Bell(s)	Bell(s)
	Handbell(s)	Handb.
	Flexatone	Flex.
	Chinese Cymbal	Chin. Cym.
	Vietnamese ''Hat''	Viet. Hat
	Brake Drum(s)	Brake Dr.
	Tam Tam (without dome)	TamT.
	Gong (domed) (also called Nipple Gong)	Gong
	Gong (without dome)	Gong
Woods	Claves	Claves
	Board Clapper (Whip or Slapstick)	Bd. Clp. Slapst.
	Sandpaper Blocks	Sandp. Bl.
	Ratchet	Ratch.
	Guíro	Guíro

Maraca(s)	Mar.	
Cabaza	Cab.	
Wood Block(s) or Chinese Block(s)	W.B.	
Temple Block or Korean Temple Block	T. B. or Temp. Bl.	
Slit Drum	Slit Dr.	
Log Drum	Log Dr.	

Pitched	Orchestra Bells or Glockenspiel Keyboard Glockenspiel	Orch. B. Glsp. Glsp. (Kbd.)	*
	Celesta	Cel.	
	Xylophone	Xyl.	
	Vibraphone	Vib. or Vibes	
	Marimba	Mar.	
	Chimes or Tubular Chimes	Chimes Chimes	

* The symbol is the same for the different types of Glockenspiel. The prefatory list must indicate which type is wanted.

Membranes	Tambourine	Tamb.	
	Bongos	Bongos	
	Timbales	Timb.	
	Conga Drum	Conga	
	Snare Drum (with snares on)	S. D. (w. snare) or (w.s.)	or
	Snare Drum (with snares off)	S. D. (sn. off)	or
	Military Drum	Mil. Dr. or Mil. D.	
	Tenor Drum	Ten. Dr. or T. D.	
	Tomtom	Tomt.	
		(with wooden top:)	
	Bass Drum (upright)	B. D.	
	Bass Drum (on side)	B. D.	
Effects	Police Whistle	Pol. Whistle	
	Slide Whistle	Sl. Whistle	or
	Bird Whistle	(no abbreviations for effects from here on)	

Duck Call

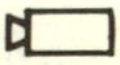

Wind Whistle or Mouth Siren

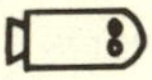

Siren

Klaxon Horn

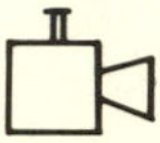

Auto Horn (Bulb Horn)

Gun or Gun Shot

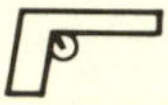

Lion's Roar

Wind Machine

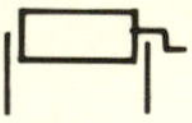

Thunder Sheet

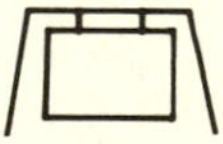

Anvil

Timpani   Timpano (Timpani)   Timp.*    or

Stick, Mallet, and Beater Pictograms

Snare Drum Stick | or | Snare Drum Stick with Plastic Tip |

When the beaters are drawn upside-down, it means that the player is to strike with the handle.

* The abbreviation *Timp.* is generally preferred, while the pictogram with the indication of the size of the drum is often used in prefatory diagrams showing the instrumental setup.

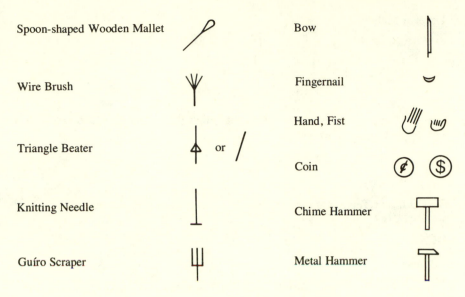

Spoon-shaped Wooden Mallet	Bow
Wire Brush	Fingernail
	Hand, Fist
Triangle Beater	
	Coin
Knitting Needle	Chime Hammer
Guíro Scraper	Metal Hammer

Pictograms Showing Degrees of Hardness and Other Characteristics of the Heads of Mallets and Beaters

Rubber and Plastic Heads for Xylophone and Orchestra Bells, etc.

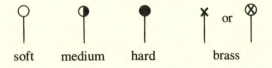

soft   medium   hard   brass

String- or Yarn-Wound Heads for Vibraphone, Marimba, and Suspended Cymbal, etc.*

soft   medium   hard

*Although ''woolly'' heads are frequently used, it has been found that such heads are often mistaken for poorly drawn round heads, while a ''hairy'' head will always be distinctive.

Timpani Mallets

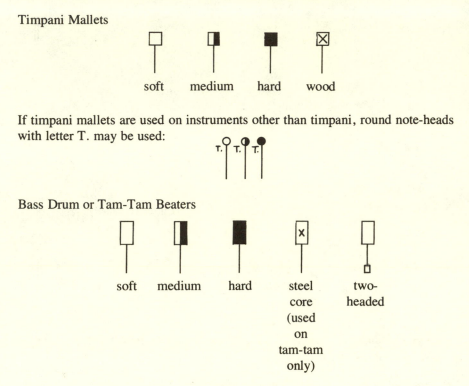

soft   medium   hard   wood

If timpani mallets are used on instruments other than timpani, round note-heads with letter T. may be used:

Bass Drum or Tam-Tam Beaters

soft   medium   hard   steel   two-
                       core   headed
                       (used
                       on
                       tam-tam
                       only)

Pictograms Showing Combinations of Beaters

N.B.: The pictograms are boxed to show that the beaters are to be used by a single player. The boxes must not be too heavy, so as not to be confused with choice boxes (see Indeterminate Events, page 152 f).

One beater in each hand:

Two beaters of the same kind in each hand:

Two different beaters in each hand:

Strike with handles (the beaters are drawn upside-down):

Indications to Add or Omit a Beater, Mallet, etc.

Add: Omit:

Ranges of Percussion Instruments with Definite Pitch

Almglocken: same range as Cowbells
Antique Cymbals: same range as Crotales

Bell Plates      sound: as notated

Bells      sound: as notated

Celesta      sound: as notated

Chimes (Tubular)    sound: as notated

Cowbells   sound: as notated

Crotales   sound: 2 octaves higher

Finger Cymbals: same range as Crotales

*The pitches of the lower register are quite indistinct.

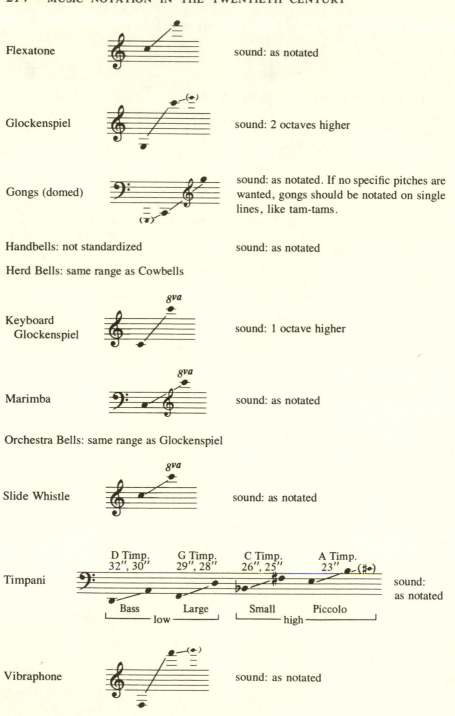

Flexatone   sound: as notated

Glockenspiel   sound: 2 octaves higher

Gongs (domed)   sound: as notated. If no specific pitches are wanted, gongs should be notated on single lines, like tam-tams.

Handbells: not standardized   sound: as notated

Herd Bells: same range as Cowbells

Keyboard Glockenspiel   sound: 1 octave higher

Marimba   sound: as notated

Orchestra Bells: same range as Glockenspiel

Slide Whistle   sound: as notated

Timpani

D Timp. 32", 30"   G Timp. 29", 28"   C Timp. 26", 25"   A Timp. 23"   sound: as notated

Bass   Large   Small   Piccolo
low   high

Vibraphone   sound: as notated

Xylophone   sound: 1 octave higher

Score Order for Instrument Families and Mixed Ensembles

A. Single Instruments and Instrument Families

One instrument: use a single staff-line, note-heads on the line, stems up or down (upstems are preferred because they bring dynamics and articulation closer to the note-heads):

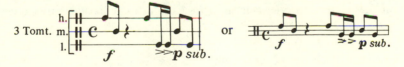

BY FAMILIES

Two instruments: use a single line, note-heads above and below the line:

or use two lines, bracketed in front:

Three instruments: use three lines (preferred), bracketed in front:

or use two lines, bracketed in front:

or (rarely) one line:

Four or more instruments: for more than three instruments of the same family a regular five-line staff, rather than a four-line grid, should be used. Performers can grasp positions on regular staves more easily than on four-line staves, and especially on four-line grids:

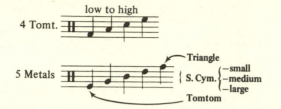

All stems should point in the same direction in single-line notation as well as in grids of widely spaced lines, but on regular staves they should follow the general rules of stem directions, up and down, space permitting. Membranophones (drums, etc.), when notated on a regular five-line staff, should be placed in the spaces, while nonmembranophones should be notated on the lines.

B. Mixed Groups of Instruments

Percussion groups of mixed instruments should be scored in the following order from top to bottom:

glass, metals, and (most) hanging objects

woods (nonpitched)

pitched instruments in keyboard arrangement

membranophones (nonpitched)

effects (auxiliary instruments)

timpani (may alternatively be placed at the top of the percussion since their musical material is often related to the bass instruments above the percussion)

In general, each type of instrument should be notated on a separate staff-line or staff, while instruments belonging to the same family should be notated on grids. The lengths of vertical brackets at the beginning of the lines, as well as that of the barlines, must be decided from case to case; percussion scores are too diverse to permit rigid rules. There is, however, one principle which should never be ignored: No matter which kind of notation and score order has been chosen, it must be adhered to throughout a given composition or movement.*

*The *Handbook of Percussion Instruments* by Karl Peinkofer and Fritz Tannigel (Clifton, N.J.: European American Music Distributors, 1976) contains an exceptionally comprehensive sampling of percussion notation and score setups.

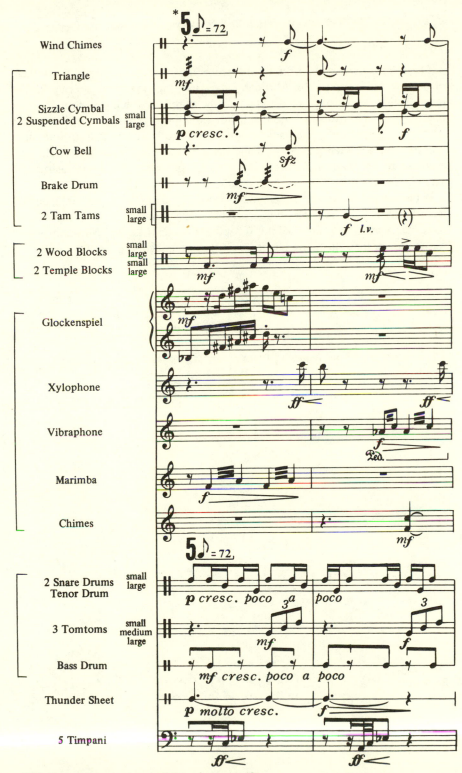

*This kind of time signature is discussed on page 181.

SAMPLE PERCUSSION SCORES

The sample percussion score on the preceding page demonstrates the principles suggested on page 216. Musically speaking, this arrangement is by far the most explicit, but in large scores (such as the sample), which require more than one player, it fails to show the conductor how the instruments are distributed among the performers. Such scores, therefore, are better broken up into subgroups—one for each player—and the parts extracted accordingly. Each subgroup score, however, must still follow the same general principles of instrument succession.

If unrelated instruments are played as a unit by a single player, adjustments must be made. For example, while cowbells and snare drum normally appear rather far apart in the score below, if a phrase occurs like the two-line passage further down, they should be notated as if they belonged to the same family:

Complete score

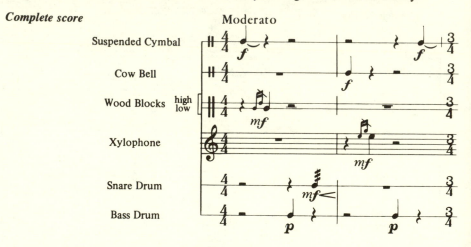

Continued with cowbell and snare drum passage

or

C. Traditional or Typical Setups

The following three setups are among those considered standard. Given the diversity of twentieth-century music, however, the situations in which standard setups are called for are quite rare.

Traditional mixed groups consisting of snare drum, bass drum, and cymbal are usually notated on a five-line staff:

General Practices

A. Instrument Specifications

Instrument specifications may be placed in the left-hand margins or above the pertinent staff-line(s), depending on the complexity of the notation and the available space.

Specific identifications, such as sizes or pitches, may be added to the pictograms, preferably inside if possible:

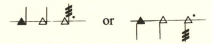

B. Note Shapes

Because percussion groups differ from score to score, more pictograms or verbal indications are required than in other instrument categories. A limited but helpful reduction of this clutter of indications can be achieved by using different note shapes for certain instruments. Two of these have become more or less standard:

Triangle: triangular note-heads   or

Cymbals: x-shaped note-heads for black notes; open diamond-shaped note-heads for half and whole notes:*

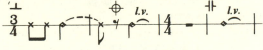

*But see pages 30–31.

C. Beater Indications

Beater indications should be placed above the pertinent staff-line(s). They should be rather small and boxed.

If rest measures appear before a new beater is to be used, the beater indication may be placed ahead of the entrance of the actual music, i.e., above the rest measure(s). In such cases it is necessary to precede the indication with the word *take* (e.g., take ⬚), and always to repeat the indication at the beginning of the pertinent passage of music.

D. Short-Decay Instruments: Rhythmic (Durational) Notation

It is neither practical nor, in fact, possible to notate exact durations of short-decay instruments. For these reasons, relatively simple rest- and note-values should be used, especially in complex, syncopated rhythms:

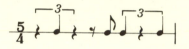

rather than:

If very short durations (quick damping) are wanted, staccato dots are preferable to additional rests.

E. Long-Decay Instruments: Rhythmic (Durational) Notation

Exact note-values (exact durations):

(For damping, ⋁, ▼, or ❜ may be used instead of ⊕.)

Indeterminate durations:

(*l.v.* is optional.)

F. Gong versus Tam Tam Notation

Gongs should be notated as pitched instruments (five-line staff) unless no specific pitch is wanted, in which case normal notes on a single line are equally acceptable, depending on the overall score setup.

Tam tams should be notated as nonpitched instruments (one-line staff or, if a five-line staff is used, with x-shaped note-heads).

G. Marimba

For the kind and number of beaters needed, see the pictograms under Instrument Abbreviations and Pictograms, page 211.

For the many playing techniques special to the marimba, such as ripple rolls, mandolin rolls, single-bar rolls (with one hand and with two), interval rolls, bowing, and so forth, it is best to use verbal instructions and their abbreviations. The field of sophisticated marimba playing is still fairly new, and very little marimba notation has as yet emerged that is used widely enough to warrant endorsements for eventual standardization.

Effects and Techniques

A. Brush Swishes

B. Circular Rubbing or Scraping

This pertains to any instrument with a sounding surface that permits circular rubbing or scraping:

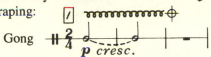

C. Dead Stick

Press down stick so it will not rebound: Mil. Dr.

But see also Striking with Two Beaters, page 225.

D. Grace Notes

Single (flam)

Double (drag or ruff)

Multiple

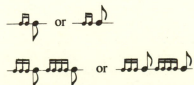

Use either ♪ or ♪ consistently throughout a composition. If both are used in the same piece they imply a durational difference which is virtually never intended.

The short, slanted stroke is optional and often omitted.

Grace notes should not be notated with ties to the main note unless such ties are actually intended to produce a single stroke immediately before the beat, and none on the beat itself:

See also General Conventions, Stems: Grace Notes, page 21 f.

E. Gradual Changes of Location and Other Gradual Changes

If the beating surface of a percussion instrument produces different sounds when struck in different locations (such as the center versus the edge of a drum head or a gong), a location line moving between two fairly widely separated staff-lines should be drawn above the regular staff or staff-line. The movement of the location line will then show which location is to be struck.

Gradual changes of location on xylophone bars

Gradual changes of location on a drum head

In isolated instances, changes may be indicated without extra staff-lines:

N.B.: If such locations are clearly separate, such as the rim or shell of a drum versus the drum head, no gradual changes are possible and individual staff-lines must be drawn for each location (see below).

The location line is also used for gradual changes of timbre produced by methods other than moving across the beating surface, such as the gradual opening and closing of the two hi-hat cymbals:

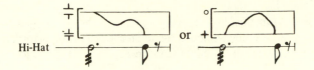

Hi-Hat   or

Gradual changes of the pitch of a drum head may also be notated with a location line, but when produced by controlled hand or elbow pressure on the drum head, the use of note-heads between the two lines is preferred:

F. Locations on Cymbals, Gongs, etc.

Dome (or cup or bell) of suspended cymbal or domed gong

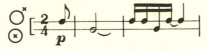

Center of flat gong, tam-tam

Play near the edge

Play on the edge

Combinations and alternations of locations

Gong

Gradual changes from one location to another

Gong

Actually, there is no genuine need for the pictograms shown above; verbal indications would do just as well. It should be noted, however, that the edge and near-edge locations are placed above the center location, in accordance with the approximate pitches which should always descend from high to low.

See also page 222 f.

G. Locations on Drums

Head: play near the center ⓧ   or verbal instruction *center*

Head: play near the edge   ⓧ   or verbal instruction *near edge*

Play on the rim (use extra staff-line above):

Rim shot: see below.

Play on the shell (use extra staff-line below):

Combinations or alternations of locations (rim, normal, shell):

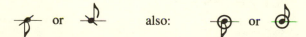

H. Ride-Cymbal Technique

Alternation of dead and ringing strokes on suspended cymbals

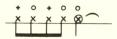

N.B.: Add verbal instructions on first occurrence:
+ = damp*
o = let ring

I. Rim Shot

⨍— or ⨎—   also: ⊕— or ⊕—

*In general, the sign for damping or muffling should be ⊕. However, since the damping in ride-cymbal technique does not stop the sound but only mutes it, the + is actually more appropriate (cf. muted brasses, for example).

Both notations are employed. The second has the advantage in that it cannot be mistaken for a crossed-out note.

It is advisable to add the words *rim shot* at first occurrence.

J. Rolls

Slanted tremolo bars should be used:

Note that broken ties are used if a continuous roll is wanted. When there is no tie (see the last two notes above) the note after the roll is separated slightly from what precedes it. If rolls for tuned instruments (timpani, xylophone, etc.) go across a barline and the note to be rolled has an accidental, that accidental must be repeated at the beginning of each new measure:

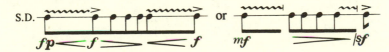

N.B.: Use only slanted bars for rolls; horizontal bars should be reserved for use as abbreviations for fast metered strokes:

Some composers prefer the trill line (wavy line) to tremolo bars, especially in spatial notation where the wavy line shows the duration of the roll more graphically. If the wavy line is used for rolls, the initial *tr* should be omitted:

Single-pitch roll

Only in real (two-note) trills should the *tr* be used. See also page 75 ff.

K. Striking with Two Beaters (Sticks, Mallets, etc.)

(both sticks)

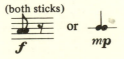

XI. *Harp*

Preliminary Remarks 228

Aeolian Rustling (S)
  see *Rustling Glissando, page 238*

Aeolian Tremolo (S)
  see page 250

Arpeggio/Non Arpeggio 228

Bending the Pitch 229

Bisbigliando (Whispering) 229

Brushing the Strings, Hand Slides
  see *Whistling Sounds, page 255*

Clusters 231
  A. *Plucked Clusters* 231
  B. *Hand-Slap Clusters* 231

Damping/Muffling (Étouffer) 231
  A. *General Damp Sign* 231
  B. *Damp All Strings* 232
  C. *Damp Only the Low Strings* 232
  D. *Damp with Both Hands* 232
  E. *Damp at Specific Points* 232
  F. *Damp Specific Strings* 233
  G. *Damp Specific Pitch Areas* 233
  H. *Damp All Strings below the Written Note* 233
  I. *Damp All Strings from the Small Note on Down* 234
  J. *Damp in a Patting Motion* 234
  K. *Isolated Sounds (S)* 234
  L. *Repeated Pattern Indication* 234
  M. *Staccato Damping* 234

Fingernail Buzz 235

Fingernail Plucking 235

Glissandos 236
  A. *Cluster Glissandos* 236
  B. *Two-Tone Glissandos* 236
  C. *Glissandos for Three or More Tones (Fingers)* 236
  D. *Fingernail(s)* 236
  E. *Combinations* 237
  F. *Gushing Chords (S)* 237
  G. *Non Glissando* 237
  H. *Rustling Glissando* 238
  I. *String Noise* 238

Half Pedal 239

Harmonics 239

Isolated Sounds (S) 234

Laisser vibrer (l.v.): Let Vibrate 240

Metallic Sound (S)
  see *String Noise, page 238*

Muffling
  see *Damping, page 231*

Muting 240
  A. *Mute Near the Sounding Board* 240
  B. *Mute and Pluck Near the Sounding Board* 241
  C. *Mute and Pluck In or Near the Middle of the String* 241
  D. *Harmonics* 241
  E. *Muting with the Fingernail* 241
  F. *Muting with Foreign Objects* 241
  G. *Muting with the Tuning Key* 242
  H. *Snare-Drum Effect (S)* 242

Non Glissando 237

Pedal Buzz
    see Half Pedal, page 239

Pedal Noise   242

Pedal Slide   243

Pedal Trill   243

Pedals   244
A. Pitch Letters   244
B. Pedal Diagrams   244
C. One Foot, Two Pedals   245
D. "Wrong" Foot   245

Placement of Playing
Indications   246

Plectrum   246

Près de la Table (Play near the
Sounding Board)
    see pages 248 and 253

Près des Chevilles (Play at the
Upper Ends of the Strings)
    see pages 250 and 253

Range   246

Scordatura (Abnormal
Tuning)   246
A. Actual Sound ("Concert Pitch")   246
B. Transposed   247

Scraping a String
    see Measured Scraping, page 253

Slap Pizzicato   247

Snare-Drum Effect (S)   242

Sounding Board   248

Striking the Body or the
Sounding Board   248

Striking the Strings   249

Strumming   250

Tam Tam Sound (S)
    see Striking the Strings, page 249

Thunder Effect (S)
    see String Noise, page 238

Top (Upper Ends of Strings)   250

Tremolos   250
A. Aeolian Tremolo (S)   250
B. Thumb Tremolo   251

Trills   251

Trilling (Vibrating) between
Two Strings   251

Tuning, Abnormal
    see Scordatura, page 246

Tuning-Key Slides   251

Vertical Locations on the
Strings   252
A. Changing Vertical Locations   252
B. Playing near the Bottom   253
C. Playing near the Top   253

Vibrato   253

Whistling Sounds (S):
Fingernail Scrapes   253
A. Measured (Slow) Scraping   253
B. Very Fast Scraping   254

Whistling Sounds (S): Hand
Slides   255
A. Measured (Slow) Vertical Slides   255
B. Damping   255
C. Very Fast Slides   255

Preliminary Remarks

Much of the notation recommended in this chapter hails from Carlos Salzedo's virtually clairvoyant *L'Étude moderne de la harpe* of 1918, including his colorful terminology for many of the effects. Wherever this terminology has been retained, it has been identified with a parenthetical S.

The large number of effects, their notational devices and practices included in this chapter, and the abundance of practical information for the actual production of these effects—an expansiveness not found in most of the other chapters—is attributable not only to the considerable versatility of the harp, but also to the widespread ignorance of its resources among otherwise well-informed musicians.

Arpeggio/Non Arpeggio

For general instructions, see page 3 f.

All unmarked chords and intervals are played arpeggio or non arpeggio ("flat") at the discretion of the harpist. Traditional practice, especially in romantic music, favors a slight rolling of the chords. In twentieth-century music, unrolled playing has become more common. To avoid ambiguities it is strongly suggested that clear instructions be given concerning the desired style of playing, as follows:

Indicate at the beginning of a composition or movement either *sempre arpeggio* or *sempre non arpeggio,* unless no predominant style of playing is desired.

In a piece marked *sempre arpeggio,* no additional arpeggio signs need be marked, except:

1. When the direction or speed of the roll is specified (see page 4);

2. When occasional non arpeggio intervals or chords appear. These must be marked with non arpeggio brackets ([ ), and as a precaution, an arpeggio sign must be placed before the first chord or interval (in both hands) when the prevailing arpeggio style is to be resumed. (The cautionary arpeggio signs serve the same purpose as the words *ordinario* or *normale* in music for other instruments.)

Conversely, in a piece marked *sempre non arpeggio,* no additional non arpeggio signs are needed, except when occasional arpeggio intervals or chords appear. These must be marked with appropriate arpeggio signs, and a non arpeggio bracket must be placed before the first chord or interval (in both hands) when the prevailing non arpeggio style of playing is to be resumed.

Note that harp music frequently combines non arpeggio in one hand and arpeggio in the other. These playing modes must be marked meticulously:

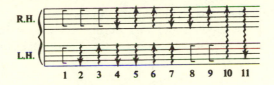

In 1, 4, 5, 6, and 7 both hands play together;
in 2, 3, and 10 the left hand precedes the right hand;
in 8, 9, and 11 the right hand precedes the left hand.

Bending the Pitch

The player is to insert the wooden part of the tuning key between two strings, then pluck one of them and twist the key so as to raise the pitch slightly. Always indicate whether the tuning key is to be inserted near the sounding board (p.d.l.t. = *près de la table*) or in the center of the strings.

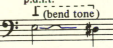

Bisbigliando (Whispering)

This is a form of tremolo for two hands.
The notes for the right and left hands are notated either in the same staff, with up- and downstems, and with tremolo bars above or below:

or on the upper and lower staves, with stems, if any, pointing toward each other, and tremolo bars as shown:

Whole notes   *Half notes*   *Quarter notes*

As demonstrated above, the arpeggio signs should have arrowheads to indicate the directions. The most common directions are down for the right hand and up for the left.

If arpeggios for both hands go in the same direction, one hand after the other, it is best to notate the chords above each other, with one continuous arpeggio sign, and with tremolo bars above or between the chords, depending on available space:

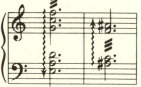

If specific starting and/or ending notes are desired, grace notes should be placed before and/or after the main notes, and a slur should be added:

If three-note or four-note chords are to be played in an order other than rolled up or down, the order must be written out:

bisbigliando

If the notes are to be played in random order, the pitches should be notated with note-heads only, in parentheses, with tremolo bars placed between the staves:

N.B.: It is advisable always to add the word *bisbigliando* or its abbreviation *bisb*.

Clusters

(For a general discussion of clusters, see page 57 ff.)

A. Plucked Clusters

These should always be written out, i.e., treated as ordinary chords (which essentially they are). They should not exceed four notes per hand:

B. Hand-Slap Clusters

These are most effective in the lowest register of the harp. Here pedal settings become immaterial because the pitches can no longer be heard clearly.

In the upper registers, hand-slap clusters will become audible only if the strings are struck with a very short rubbing impact. Pitches are more likely to be heard in the upper registers than in the bass.

It is advisable to add the words *hand-slap cluster* on first occurrence.

Cluster glissandos, see page 236.

Strummed clusters, see Muting: Snare-Drum Effect, page 242, and Strumming, page 250.

Damping/Muffling (*Étouffer*)

A. General Damp Sign

The sign ⊕ is usually placed close to the note(s) or rest(s) involved: right hand—above; left hand—below:

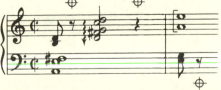

B. Damp All Strings
The sign ⊕ is placed between the staves:

C. Damp Only the Low Strings
The sign ⊕ may be placed between the staves, or below the lower staff:

D. Damp with Both Hands
The sign used: ⊕⊕

E. Damp at Specific Points
It is not always possible to damp at every rest. Therefore, arrowed signs ⊕ ⊕ should be used where damping is essential:

F. Damp Specific Strings

One string   *Two strings*   *Three strings*

etc.

The sign is placed near the note(s) involved:

p.d.l.t.

ord.

L.H.   R.H.

G. Damp Specified Pitch Areas

The sign used:

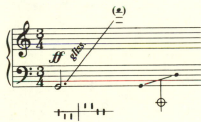

ff *gliss.*

H. Damp All Strings below the Written Note

I.e., keep only the top note ringing:

ff   *f* *gliss.*

I. Damp All Strings from the Small Note on Down
The sign used:

J. Damp in a Patting Motion
(Gradually muffle the strings upward or downward according to the short horizontal strokes after the damping sign.)

First damping sign: after the first glissando, damp low strings upward to the small note-head;

Second damping sign: after the second glissando, damp strings from any pitch downward.

K. Isolated Sounds (S)
Damp each sound simultaneously with playing the next, so that no sounds run together:

(Put *ordinario* [*ord.*] at end of arrowed passage.)

L. Repeated Pattern or Playing-Mode Indication

M. Staccato Damping
This is distinct from other forms of damping.

Second-Finger Staccato
Thumb Staccato
Two-Handed Staccato
} All staccato effects are notated with staccato dots. If special techniques are desired, verbal instructions must be added:

See also Muting, page 240 ff.

Fingernail Buzz

The player places the back of a fingernail against the middle of a vibrating string (best in the low register). The nail may be moved lightly against the string and away, in rhythm.

N.B.: The nail symbol here assumes the role of a note-head—black and white, and in the second measure, dotted.

Fingernail Plucking

Since fingernail plucking requires a bit of time to place the nails in the proper position, the most practical use of this technique is on single strings, although intervals and chords are also possible. Unmarked intervals and chords are played "flat." Even so, it is advisable to specify the playing mode. Arpeggio with fingernails is difficult and should be avoided.

The fingernail symbol may also be drawn: ⌒
For other fingernail effects, see Glissando: Fingernail(s), page 236 f; Muting: with Fingernail, page 241.

Glissandos

For a general discussion, see pages 19 ff and 63 f.

A. Cluster Glissandos

The harp does not lend itself to regular clusters, because its pitch resources are diatonic and sound essentially tonal, especially in glissandos, where the sequence of pitches always remains the same.

Thus the broad bands of sliding, chromatic clusters used for the notation of cluster glissandos in string sections or string ensembles in Polish and Polish-influenced music of the 1950s and later are not useful for the harp. Instead, the starting pitches of glissandos and the pedal settings should always be written out.

It should also be borne in mind that on the harp, one- and two-finger glissandos are more resonant and louder than those played with three or more fingers.

B. Two-Tone Glissandos

One hand

Two hands

Near the sounding board

Instead of 〰〰〰 , p.d.l.t. (*près de la table*) may be used.

C. Glissandos for Three or More Tones (Fingers)

These follow the same notational principles as those for two.

D. Fingernail(s)

For fingernail glissandos, only the back of the fingernail is used. Upward glissandos thus can only be played with the back of the thumbnail, while downward glissandos are played with the fingernails.

One finger   *Thumb*

(The instruction *Back of nail* is optional.)

Two and three fingers

E. Combinations

Back of thumbnail plus (regular) second and third fingers

Back of fingernails of second and third fingers, plus (regular) thumb

F. Gushing Chords (S)

These are very fast glissandos: Short   *Held**

If the final note is to be plucked, this must be indicated verbally.

G. Non Glissando

Occasionally it is desirable to begin or end a glissando with a fingered scale. Such portions should be written out and marked *non gliss.*

Non gliss. may also be added in other situations, to avoid ambiguity.

*The note-value indicates the duration of the resonance.

In spatial notation:

H. Rustling Glissando

This is a glissando played with the open hand (all five fingers, spread apart), which gradually moves upward or, less frequently, downward, resulting, as its name implies, in a rustling sound. It is notated with a random number of short, curved lines between the glissando lines, or with short arrows (for the effect shown in the second example below):

| *Upward; final pitches not specified* | *"Up-up-up" from the same pitches* | *Upward to specified pitches* | *Up and down; final pitches not specified* |

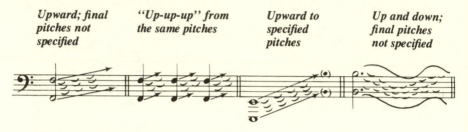

I. String Noise

1. METALLIC SOUND OR THUNDER EFFECT (S)

This is a rapid, forceful glissando on the wire strings, causing them to strike against each other:

With specific string indications   *With approximate string indications*

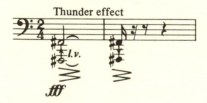

(same as strumming)

It is suggested to add the verbal instruction *Thunder effect* on first occurrence.

2. NONMETALLIC SOUND

Same as above, but the pitches must lie above the wire strings and the verbal instruction must be *String noise* instead of *Thunder effect:*

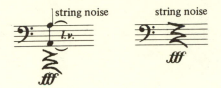

Half Pedal

Hold pedal halfway between two notches to allow the string to vibrate against the tuning gear. Then proceed in one of two ways:

1. Set pedal(s), then pluck

One string

D♮♭♭

Two strings

A♮♭♭
D♮♭♭

2. Pluck first, then slur into half-pedal effect

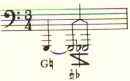

G♮
♭♭

This effect is possible only on low strings, because they have the long vibration time required.

For extended passages with the pedal(s) moving the tuning notches against and away from the string(s), see Pedal Trill, page 243.

Harmonics

Three harmonic pitches are used: the octave, twelfth, and seventeenth. (The last two are usually referred to as the fifth and the third, respectively, in spite of their actual distance from the fundamentals.)

The octave harmonic is notated with a full-size note-head for the string to be played (the fundamental), and the familiar small circle above.

The other two harmonics are notated as follows: The string to be played (fundamental) is notated full size with a diamond-shaped note-head; the sounding pitch is notated with a small regular note-head in parentheses. The small circle and the numerals 5 or 3, resp., may be added above for instant recognition.

Octave      *Sounding*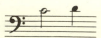

Twelfth (Fifth)   optional

Seventeenth (Third)   optional

N.B.: Because of the general lack of uniformity in the notation of harmonics, it is strongly suggested that the notational system used be indicated at the beginning of the composition.

Laisser vibrer (l.v.): Let Vibrate

In symbolic notation

(The *l.v.* is optional.)

In spatial notation, the duration beam should be extended to the length of desired audibility; then, a short slur is added if no actual cut-off (damping) is wanted.

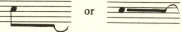

Muting

It is necessary to indicate exactly where the string is muted and where it is plucked, as follows:

A. Mute Near the Sounding Board
Pluck in the middle of the string ["Xylophonic Sound" (S)]:

or p.d.l.t.

B. Mute and Pluck Near the Sounding Board

C. Mute and Pluck In or Near the Middle of the String

This mode of muting can either produce harmonics or avoid them, depending on the position of the muting finger.

E. Muting with the Fingernail

Mute by placing the back of the fingernail lightly against the middle of the string:

F. Muting with Foreign Objects

Muting by weaving a strip of paper, material, yarn, tin foil, etc., into the strings or by placing objects between the strings requires somewhat lengthy operations. For this reason no signs or abbreviations are needed—verbal instructions are sufficient.

G. Muting with the Tuning Key

Pluck the notated strings; then hold the wood of the tuning key against the vibrating strings, thus producing a percussive effect and a considerable change of timbre. (The moment of contact must be notated rhythmically.)

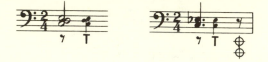

See also Muting, Snare Drum Effect (S), below.

H. Snare-Drum Effect (S)

1. MUTING WITH PALM OF HAND

Mute low strings near the top with the palm of the left hand; produce a short, forceful strum upward with a fingertip or the back of a fingernail of the right hand:

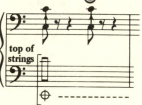

2. MUTING WITH TUNING KEY

Instead of the palm of the left hand, hold the wooden part of the tuning key against the strings (see above):

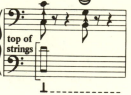

Pedal Noise

This refers to motion of the pedals only, i.e., without plucking the respective strings.

When notating such pedal motion remember that the highest position of the pedals flattens the pitch and the lowest sharpens it. This fact is often misconstrued, since musically it would be more logical to equate a sharp with up and a flat with down.

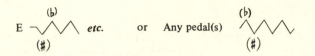

N.B.: This effect is controversial not only because the sound can be negligible (though it might be strengthened electronically), but also because some harpists contend that it is damaging to the mechanism.

Pedal Slide

The pedal position is changed without replucking the string. This is notated as follows:

The lines show that a
pedal slide is wanted.

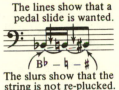

The slurs show that the
string is not re-plucked.

The pedal slide has to be made rather quickly, so that the aural effect is almost no slide at all. If the pedal is moved more slowly it creates a buzz, which is a separate effect (see Half Pedal, page 239).

Pedal Trill

This effect consists of fast, repeated pedal slides (see Pedal Slide above). Since the trill is rather slow, the sound is likely to die out before much trilling has taken place. It is of longest duration in the low register.

As in the pedal slide, the string is not replucked.

Short, thin lines must connect the notes. They must slant up or down, according to the direction of the pitch changes. A final note must be indicated if a specified final pitch is desired:

Trill with lower note

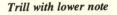

Trill with upper note

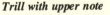

See also Half Pedal, page 239, and Vibrato, page 253.

Pedals

Pedal indications are properly the province of the individual harpist, particularly because harpists rarely agree on when to change which pedals. Moreover, many composers are not truly familiar with the most practical strategy of harp pedaling. In general, therefore, it is best not to indicate pedaling, but to leave ample blank space below the music or between the staves for the harpists to mark their own pedaling.

The following rules and practices thus should be considered with the caveats mentioned above in mind.

Pedal settings are indicated either with pitch letters and accidentals or with pedal diagrams.

A. Pitch Letters

These are given in the order of the pedals—the four right-foot pedals above, the three left-foot pedals below. All letters are followed by their respective accidentals or natural signs. For example:

Eb F♯ C♯ A♮
D♯ Cb B♮

B. Pedal Diagrams

Pedals are shown left and right of the dividing line.
The three basic positions are:

Flats

(Db Cb Bb Eb Fb Gb Ab)

Naturals

(D♮ C♮ B♮ E♮ F♮ G♮ A♮)

Sharps

(D♯ C♯ B♯ E♯ F♯ G♯ A♯)

Here is a pedal diagram showing the same pedal setting as in the pitch-letter example above:

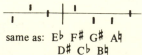

same as: Eb F♯ G♯ A♮
D♯ Cb B♮

Complete pedal settings should appear at the beginning of a composition (preferably below the bottom staff), at or preceding glissandos, and at likely rehearsal stops. Ideally, each line of music should begin with the pedal setting needed at that point.

Pedal changes should be indicated with pitch letters (placed below the bottom staff or—less desirable—between the staves), regardless of whether the complete settings are shown with letters or with diagrams.

Although pitch letters and diagrams are equally useful for complete settings, the preferred system consists of a combination of both methods: diagrams for complete pedal settings; pitch letters and accidentals for changes of one or more pedal positions between complete settings. For example:

First setting (beginning of a composition or movement)	Change F♯ to F♮	Change D♯ and A♮ to D♭ and A♭	Change G♯ to G♮, then to G♭	Second complete setting (first rehearsal stop)	etc.

(D♯ C♭ B♮ E♭ F♯ G♯ A♮)   F♮   D♭ A♭   G♮— ♭   (D♭ C♭ B♮ E♭ F♮ G♭ A♭)

Each diagram shows the complete setting at the point of its appearance in the music. (Needless to say, the parenthetical pitches that appear below the diagrams in the above example would not appear in actual practice.)

Occasionally, another compromise may prove practical: the use of diagrams only, with the changing pedals encircled:

A practical suggestion: In order not to lose track of the pedal settings when marking a composition, it is helpful to draw a line on a sheet of paper and place coins where the short strokes representing the pedals appear in the diagram, moving them up and down as the pedals change.

C. One Foot, Two Pedals

One foot changing two pedals simultaneously with one motion is notated with a single bracket in front of the pedal indications: D♭ C♭

The bracket must be quite heavy so that there is no doubt that the pedal change is to be carried out with one foot only.

D. "Wrong" Foot

A pedal change with the "wrong" foot, i.e., the foot that would not normally be used for the pedal in question, is notated with boxed pedal indication: G♭

This indication should be used only if many such instances occur in the respective composition, and even then there should be an explanatory note on first occurrence.

See also Half Pedal, page 239.

Placement of Playing Indications

If possible, all playing indications for the right hand should appear above the top staff of a system, and those for the left hand below the bottom staff, regardless of whether they are symbols or verbal indications.

Plectrum

Plucking the string with a plectrum is notated as follows:

Be careful to round the corners of the symbol for the plectrum, so that it will not be mistaken for an accent ▾ .

Range

The range of a full-size concert harp is:

Note that the pedals do not affect the top G and the bottom C and D.
The wire strings of the harp range from down to the lowest string.

Scordatura (Abnormal Tuning)

If one or more strings are tuned to pitches other than the normal ones, a tuning chart is placed at the beginning of the music, for example:

Such tunings are called scordatura.
Music that includes scordatura may be notated in two ways:

A. Actual Sound ("Concert Pitch")

All notes are notated according to their actual pitches, regardless of the abnormal tuning of some of the strings. The pedal settings are notated according to the mechanical actions the player must perform, again regardless of the resulting pitches, but in order to remind the player of the discrepancies between the pedal settings and the notes in the music, the discrepant pedals are repeated in parentheses above the notes.

The following examples operate with the scordatura given above:

B. Transposed

All scordatura notes are notated according to what the player must do to achieve the desired pitch. The actual pitches are added in small notes outside the staff, near the notes to be played. The pedal settings, too, are notated according to the mechanical actions, rather than the actual sounds.

Here is a second version (transposed) of the previous example:

The first method of notation (actual sound) is preferable because

1. The music can be read easily, without knowledge of the notational complications resulting from the scordatura tuning;

2. It is simpler to draw the additional discrepant pedal settings than the small staves, clefs, and notes.

N.B.: Scordatura should be used with great discretion. It had its just place before the invention of pedals. In our era's music it should be resorted to only if certain effects are impossible to produce by regular means.

Slap Pizzicato

Plucking the string *près de la table,* so that the finger slides forcefully to the sounding board, creates a sharp, knocking sound in addition to the pitch:

Note the similarity with the sign for the "Bartók pizzicato" in bowed string instruments, where the string is to be plucked vertically from the fingerboard, slapping the wood as it is released—an effect not too different from the sound of the slap pizzicato of the harp, i.e., a string/wood combination.

Sounding Board

The symbol for the sounding board is a bold **T** (from the French *table*). For playing near the sounding board (*près de la table*), p.d.l.t. is the most commonly used abbreviation, but a wavy horizontal line is almost equally common:

either

See also Striking the Body or the Sounding Board, below, and Vertical Locations, page 252 f.

Striking the Body or the Sounding Board

Use **B** for body and **T** for sounding board (*table*), and give verbal instructions, such as *strike, slap, tap, knock, drum,* etc. Indicate *knuckles, fingertips,* etc.

If mallets, etc., are to be employed, use pictograms (see Percussion, page 210 ff) but identify the pictograms in the front matter or on first occurrence. If no pictograms are available, use verbal descriptions.

Harpists will strike, scratch, rub, etc., the most resonant part of the body or sounding board—ususally around the center—unless directed otherwise.

Notate all effects (striking, tapping, etc.) with x-shaped* notes, either between the staves or above the top staff, for example:

* Actually, Salzedo's large, round note-heads outside the staff are more familiar to harpists,

but since the tappings and strikings of all other instrument bodies, etc., are notated with x-shaped notes, it is desirable to have the harp follow suit.

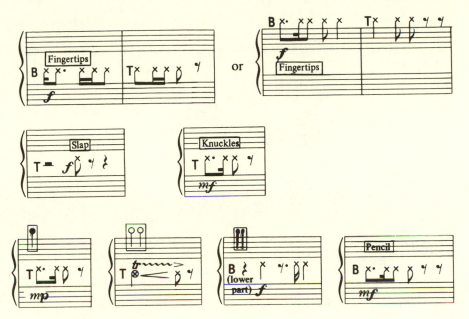

N.B.: The sounding board produces not only more volume but also more timbral variety than the body of the harp.

Striking the Strings

Strike a low string with a flick of a fingernail or other implement (pencil, ivory stick,* etc.).

Use verbal instructions on first occurrence.

Specific strings

Any (low) string(s)

* Salzedo calls this ''Tamtam Sound.''

**For further pictograms see Percussion, page 210 ff.

Strumming

Short, rapid strumming on consecutive strings (actually clusters) are noted as follows:

For small clusters

(up)   (down)

For larger clusters

(Same notation as for Gushing Chords, see page 237.)
    For muffled strums see Muting, Snare Drum Effect, page 242.

Top (Upper Ends of Strings)

To indicate playing at upper ends of strings (*près des chevilles*), it is best to use verbal indications instead of the abbreviation *PC*, which is not known beyond harpist circles. ("Play near the screws" is not recommended because it is unclear whether to play above or below the screws.) For a symbol, see page 253.

Tremolos

A. Aeolian Tremolo (S)

    Rub strings (between notated pitches) very rapidly, back and forth, with open hand, fingers pointing up:

N.B.: It is important that pedal indications for the strings be given between the notated notes.

B. Thumb Tremolo

    Brush strings rapidly back and forth with the side of the thumb:

Trills

With one hand (use single stem)   *With two hands (use double stems)*

A one-handed trill is necessarily slower than a two-handed one. Harp players will usually perform a two-handed trill wherever practical, often despite the notation. It is recommended, therefore, to leave this particular decision to the performers.

Trilling (Vibrating) between Two Strings

Verbal instructions should be used, with or without the wavy line.* (This effect is quite soft.)

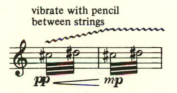

Note the curve showing the up-and-down motion of the playing implement.

Again, note vertical motion.

Tuning-Key Slides

The following effects can only be produced with old-fashioned tuning keys of uncovered wood and metal.

---

*Indicating the changing vertical locations of the implement is optional. If the wavy line is used, it should be drawn as close to the music and/or instructions as space permits.

⊥   tuning-key pictogram.* (For single-string slides, the metal part of the key is used; for two-string slides, the wooden part.)

indicates that the string is plucked and specifies the rhythm of the plucks, including the duration of subsequent sliding motion(s) (if any) of the key. The notes are stemmed down to free the area above the note-heads for the slide indications.

indicates the vertical motion of the tuning key along the string(s).

(•)   indicates approximate pitches (if desired). The pitch of the slide will always be at least one third higher than the string plucked.

indicates instantaneous, fast slides (here the note-values show the duration of the resonance).

indicates a two-string slide (the wooden handle of the tuning key is inserted between two adjacent strings).

An example showing these devices

Vertical Locations on the Strings

A. Changing Vertical Locations
Gradually move to a higher location on the string while playing:

*The symbol for the tuning key must not be reversed when placed below the left-hand staff, because this would change it into a **T**. It must always be ⊥.

Gradually move to a lower location on the string while playing:

N.B.: This effect is best suited for the lower strings.

See also Sounding Board, page 248.

B. Playing near the Bottom
Abbreviated p.d.l.t. (*près de la table*), this effect is indicated:

C. Playing near the Top
The indication for this effect is: ΛΛΛΛΛ/\/ but see page 250.

Vibrato

Insert the metal or wooden part of the tuning key between two strings and immediately after plucking vibrate it against the notated string:

See also Pedal Trill, page 243.

Whistling Sounds (S): Fingernail Scrapes

One or two wound strings are scraped up or down with one fingernail per string.

A. Measured (Slow) Scraping
The pitches of the notes indicate the strings to be scraped, not their normal pitches, since these cannot be discerned during the scraping action. (It is for this

reason that the note-heads are placed in parentheses.) The note-values indicate the durations of the scrapings; the slanted arrows or contour lines show the directions of the scraping. The fingernail symbol (‿) is placed below the staff, and the Pan-pipes pictogram (⫴) below the fingernail symbol.

If a succession of scrapings occurs, a dotted extension line should be used.

If implements other than fingernails are to scrape the strings, the nail symbol must of course be replaced with a different one or a verbal indication.

If two adjacent strings are to be scraped simultaneously, two notes must be written, with one vertical line for each:

N.B.: The longest strings are the most suitable ones for scraping.

B. Very Fast Scraping

This is notated with an arrowhead on the vertical lines that rise from the note-head(s), and without a slanting arrow. Furthermore, since the strings now are left to vibrate after the scraping, their normal pitches become audible. The note-heads are therefore drawn without parentheses, and the note-values now include the scraping and the reverberations. (To avoid misunderstandings, it is suggested that *l.v.* be placed where appropriate.)

N.B.: As with the measured scrapings, verbal explanations must be present at first occurrence.

Whistling Sounds (S): Hand Slides

Hand slides are best executed on low, wound strings.

A. Measured (Slow) Vertical Slides

These go along the wire strings, either up or down:

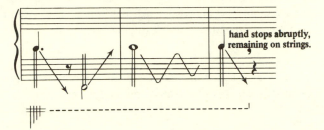

The note-heads must be well away from the staff so they will not be mistaken for pitches. The note-values indicate the duration of the sliding motion, not that of the reverberations. Up and/or down directions of the slides are shown with arrows or contour lines after the vertical double line. The Pan-pipes pictogram, although strictly speaking superfluous, should be placed at the bottom because harpists recognize it readily. If a succession of slides occurs, an extension line should be used:

B. Damping

The hand may stop the sound abruptly at the end of the slide by remaining on the strings. There is no generally recognized notation for this effect. A comma and a verbal instruction such as "hand stops abruptly, remaining on strings" must be added, since the effect is quite different from ordinary damping.

C. Very Fast Slides

*hand stops abruptly,
remaining on strings.

The notation of the fast hand slide differs from the slow slide (see above) in the following details: The note-value shows the duration of the reverberations, not that of the sliding motion which must be as fast as possible. An arrowhead is drawn through the vertical double line to indicate that a very fast slide is wanted, as well as its direction.

1. NON L.V.

The hand may stop the sound abruptly at the end of the slide by remaining on the strings, which should be indicated with the verbal instruction *non l.v.* (A staccato dot is not recommended, since it implies raising the hand.)

2. NON STACCATO

The hand leaves the strings at the end of the slide, letting the sound ring. This need not be notated, since it is understood, but an *l.v.* may be added.

XII. *Piano*

Braces and Barlines   257
A. *Ordinary Two-Staff Notation*   257
B. *Three- and Four-Staff Notation*   258
C. *Four-Hand Music*   258

Clusters   259
A. *Specified Pitches*   259
B. *Chromatic Clusters*   259
C. *Indeterminate Boundary Notes;*
   Approximate Pitches   260
D. *Spatial Notation*   260

Crossing of Hands   260

Harmonics   261

Inside the Piano   262
A. *Preliminary Remarks*   262
B. *Finger Damping*   263
C. *Glissandos*   264
   Harmonics, see page 261
D. *Muffle or "Stop" the String with a*
   Finger (Before Playing)   265

E. *Pizzicato*   265
F. *Scraping Up or Down One or Two*
   Wound Strings   266
G. *Striking the Strings*   267
H. *Strumming*   268
I. *Sweeping Back and Forth with*
   Fingers across the Strings   269

Pedals   269
A. *Abbreviations and Signs*   269
B. *Order*   270
C. *Depression and Release*   270
D. *Half Pedal*   270
E. *Gradual Pedal Depression,*
   Change, and Release   271
G. *Pedal Sound Only*   271

Silent Depression of Keys   272

Staccato Reverberations   272

Tied Notes from One Hand to
the Other   273

Braces and Barlines

A. Ordinary Two-Staff Notation

B. Three- and Four-Staff Notation
This is to be used for very complex textures only.

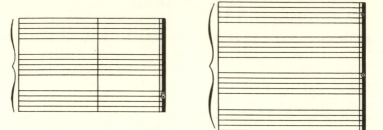

If the distribution of the music between left and right hand is regular, the barlines may be interrupted to reflect such regularity.

C. Four-Hand Music

Traditionally, four-hand piano music (piano duet) was notated on facing pages (preferably of oblong format), the left-hand pages marked *Secondo,* the right-hand pages marked *Primo:*

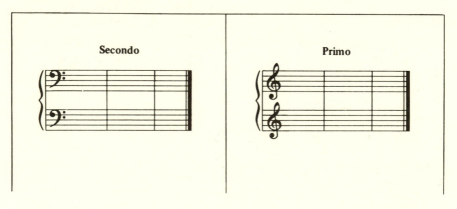

With the growth of musical complexity, notation in (upright) score format has become the preferred method:

Two-piano music is also usually notated in score form. When the two pianos are part of an ensemble, each pianist often plays from a separate part, thereby reducing the number of page turns by one half. The two pianos are marked I and II, rather than *Primo* and *Secondo*.

Clusters *

(For a general discussion of clusters, see page 57 ff.)

A. Specified Pitches

The note-heads of the outer pitches of a cluster are connected in the center with a heavy line.

The stem (if any) is attached to the top or bottom note, according to the rules of stem direction. Ties should connect only the top and bottom note-heads.

For white-key clusters, natural signs are placed above the right-hand clusters and/or below the left-hand ones.** For black-key clusters, sharps or flats are placed above and/or below the clusters:

B. Chromatic Clusters

Chromatic clusters do not require accidentals, since it is generally understood that clusters without accidentals are chromatic. If, however, a composition includes only one type of cluster (in keyboard music usually white-key clusters), a note should be placed at the beginning of the music or at the first cluster, stating which type of cluster is wanted, thus making further identification unnecessary.

It is desirable to indicate whether the clusters are to be played with the fist— tightly closed or relaxed—palm of hand, edge of hand, forearm, etc. Clusters may also be played with suitable objects.

All such special instructions must be given verbally.

---

* Notation invented by Henry Cowell.

** White-key and black-key clusters may also be identified by large natural signs or accidentals, respectively, placed in front of the clusters:

This notation obviates regular-size accidentals in front of the top and bottom notes. On the other hand, the large accidentals are not only rather unwieldy, but take up more horizontal space than ordinary accidentals, which can cause problems in spatial notation.

C. Indeterminate Boundary Notes; Approximate Pitches

Narrow vertical boxes replace the boundary note-heads.

The length of the boxes indicates the approximate width of the clusters.

For black-key or white-key clusters, accidentals or natural signs are placed above or below (or large ones in front—see preceding footnote).

Chromatic clusters do not require any accidentals.

or

If still greater indeterminacy of pitches is desired, single-staff-line notation may be used:

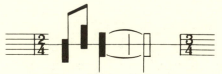

Indeterminate clusters such as these need not be provided with accidentals.

D. Spatial Notation

In spatial notation the duration of the clusters is shown by the length of the duration bars. Durational elongation of the cluster boxes themselves is not recommended. It needlessly interrupts the otherwise consistent notation. Besides, it is inappropriate for instruments such as pianos which have tones of short duration. For use of elongated cluster boxes, see Pitch, Clusters in Ensemble Music, page 58 ff.

Crossing of Hands

Music is too diverse to permit rigid rules for the notation of crossing hands. In general, however, the notes of both hands should remain in their respective staves during hand crossings. The word *sopra* (above) may be added for clarification, and in the less frequent cases where a hand is to cross below the other, the word *sotto* (below or under) should be used.

From the first movement of Beethoven's **Piano Sonata,** *Op. 57*

In certain situations the notational picture becomes clearer if the notes of the crossing hand are moved into the other hand's staff, showing the crossing graphically, as in the following example:

End of **Mazurka,** *Op. 63, No. 3 by Frédéric Chopin*

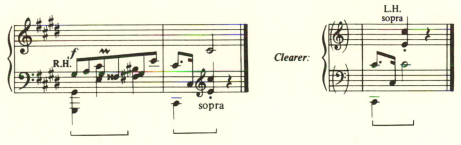

Harmonics

The keys notated with diamond-shaped note-heads are depressed silently by the right hand; the left hand then plays the regular staccato notes. This will create harmonics (resultants), which are shown with small parenthetical note-heads topped by the harmonics circle:

(The small note-heads showing the resultants are optional but advisable.)

Another method of creating harmonics is to touch the appropriate node of a given string inside the piano lightly before playing it. The string is notated full size, while the resultant is shown with a small, parenthetical note-head topped by the harmonics circle:

The verbal instruction need be added only on first occurrence. (The string node is not notated—the player must find it before the performance and should mark it with chalk.)

A third method is the same as the one just above except that the fundamental is played first and the string node touched subsequently:

Inside the Piano

A. Preliminary Remarks

1. IDENTIFICATION OF STRINGS

As long as piano manufacturers do not provide black and white dampers to duplicate the keyboard, pianists should either attach labels to the dampers of the specific strings to be used (using masking tape to insure easy removal) or mark all white-key dampers with white tape for general orientation. This would not only aid performances but also reduce the need for notational explanations.

2. STRINGS COVERED BY METAL BARS

The metal frames of different makes and vintages of pianos vary considerably with respect to which strings are covered by cross bars, and there are other structural variations which make it extremely unwise to call for specific pitches and effects as if all pianos were identical. This should be borne in mind when considering the following notational suggestions, whether additional warnings are included in their descriptions or not.

3. BOXED INSTRUCTIONS

Instructions for playing inside the piano can be reduced considerably by drawing heavy black boxes around the word *Inside* or around certain pertinent instructions, such as ┃ pizz. ┃, etc., depending on the context.

If an intermittent effect (such as a fingernail pizzicato or a sweep across the strings) is called for in an otherwise ordinary texture, the specific instructions and the staff with the pertinent notation may be placed in a box. This would obviate the boxed words Inside and the subsequent *normale* or *ord*.

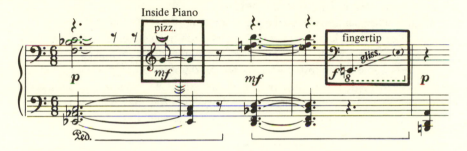

N.B.: In spite of what has just been said about labeling, the meaning of the boxes must always be indicated at least once, because boxes are also used for choices.

If all boxes in a given piece are used for playing inside the piano, or if all boxes enclose choices, only the first box needs a verbal explanation. However, if the meaning of the boxes changes from box to box, each must be labeled. (If the boxes are rather small, a fairly large *I* for "Inside" or *C* for "Choice," with an explanatory note on first occurrence, may be preferable to the spelled-out words.)

B. Finger Damping

Damp the string with a finger after playing:

If the note is played on the keyboard, but damped inside the piano, a verbal explanation is needed. In the example above, both events—the playing and the damping—take place inside the piano.

---

*The fingernail symbol may also be drawn: ◠ .

In the following example, the note is played on the keyboard and damped inside the piano:

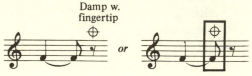

(See Harp, Damping/Muffling, pages 231 ff. for similar but more detailed situations.)

C. Glissandos

(For a general discussion of glissandos, see pages 19 ff and 63 f.)

1. GLISSANDOS WITH SPECIFIED PITCHES

A glissando, naturally, can be performed only on an unobstructed set of strings. Therefore, the pitch range of a glissando must be considered carefully because of the different kinds of metal frames used in different makes of pianos.

The note-value of the initial note shows the duration of the glissando, but not the total glissando's reverberations. These are expressed in the second note (note of destination). An open tie and/or the abbreviation *l.v.* may be added. A pedal indication can also show the desired duration of the sound:

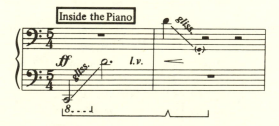

2. GLISSANDOS WITH INDETERMINATE PITCHES

Indeterminate glissandos are actually the "safest," considering the variations in metal frames.

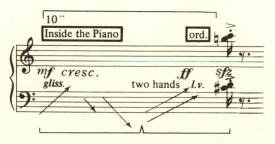

3. GLISSANDOS WITH FINGERNAIL (USUALLY BACK OF FINGERNAIL),
THIMBLE, OR OTHER IMPLEMENTS

The fingernail symbol (⌣) or appropriate pictograms should be used (for percussion beaters, see Percussion, page 210 ff), with a verbal explanation at first occurrence.

With a fingernail

D. Muffle or "Stop" the String with a Finger (Before Playing)

E. Pizzicato

1. FINGERTIP PIZZICATO

Abbreviation: *pizz.*

The dampers may be raised in three ways:

by playing the note on the keyboard and holding it;

by depressing the key silently (diamond-shaped notes);

by raising its damper (along with all others) with the pedal.

The following example shows the three methods in context (with boxed explanations):

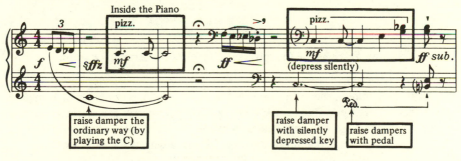

2. FINGERNAIL PIZZICATO

(Damper notation as above.)

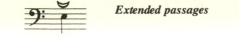

Extended passages

If a pizzicato passage extends to the next line, repeat *pizz.* in parentheses.

Plucking with plectra, thin knitting needles, and other suitable implements must be dealt with on an individual basis, but the beater pictograms in the percussion chapter would prove useful. These must be explained, however, because they are usually unfamiliar to pianists.

F. Scraping Up or Down One or Two Wound Strings

Fingernails or wooden or metal implements should be used. For fingernails, the ⌣ sign should be placed at the top of the vertical line(s); other implements require verbal indications.

1. MEASURED (SLOW) SCRAPING

a. WITHOUT PEDAL

The pitches of the notes indicate the strings to be scraped, not the resulting pitches, since these cannot be discerned during the scraping action. (It is for this reason that the note-heads are placed in parentheses.)

The note-values indicate the durations of the scrapings; the slanted arrows show the direction of the scraping.

Inside the Piano

Scrape with fingernail along string

senza ped.

If two adjacent strings of the same pitch are to be scraped simultaneously, two thin, vertical lines must be drawn. If two different pitches are wanted, two notes, each with its own line, are required:

N.B.: The lowest strings are the most suitable ones for scraping.

b. WITH PEDAL

In this technique, the strings are left to vibrate after scraping, which means that their normal pitches become audible. The note-heads are therefore drawn without parentheses. The note-values, however, still indicate only the duration of the scraping. The reverberations must be indicated with pedal extension lines or with *l.v.* (or both).

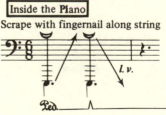

Inside the Piano

Scrape with fingernail along string

l. v.

2. VERY FAST SCRAPING

This is notated with an arrowhead on the vertical line that rises from the note-head, and without a slanting arrow.

Furthermore, since the strings here are left to vibrate after scraping, the note-heads are drawn without parentheses, and the note-values now include both scraping and reverberations. (To avoid misunderstandings, it is suggested that *l.v.* be placed wherever appropriate.)

N.B.: As with the measured scrapings, verbal explanations must be added at first occurrence.

G. Striking the Strings

1. WITH THE PALM OF THE HAND (RINGING SOUND)

The hand bounces off the strings after striking to allow the strings to reverberate (first chord in the example below).

2. WITH THE PALM OF THE HAND (DAMPED SOUND)

The hand remains on the strings after striking, thus damping the sound (second chord in the example below).

Verbal instructions must be added; pedal indications are essential.

3. WITH OTHER IMPLEMENTS

If the strings are to be struck with other implements, such as percussion beaters, verbal instructions or pictograms should be employed. The beater pictograms require verbal explanations on first occurrence.

4. STRIKING DIFFERENT REGIONS OF STRINGS

Although different makes of pianos have differently shaped metal frames, there generally are five reasonably similar areas within which the strings can be struck (or plucked, etc.).

If several specific regions are to be struck, it is advisable to notate such passages in tablature* and add a drawing that shows the regions with their identifying numerals:

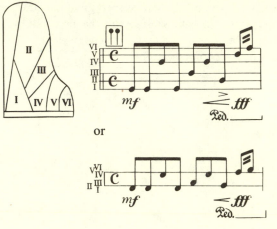

or

Since the piano, if played in this way, actually becomes a percussion instrument, the reader should turn to the Percussion section, page 205 ff, for pictograms of beaters and for other notational information.

H. Strumming

The notational symbol is borrowed from harp notation; it must be accompanied by a verbal indication at first occurrence:

1. CHROMATIC STRUMMING
Dampers are raised by keys :

2. NONCHROMATIC STRUMMING
Dampers are raised by keys. Although the finger strums across all the strings, only the undamped ones will reverberate:

---

*For further details concerning this kind of tablature notation, see Bowed String Instruments, page 307 f.

upper pitch ad lib.
= (any string above the B♭)

senza ped.

For slightly slower strumming, the arpeggio sign should be used, with an arrow above or below showing the direction:

I. Sweeping Back and Forth with Fingers across the Strings

A vertical line is drawn between two pitches to indicate the approximate range of the sweeps.

The note-values indicate the duration of the sweeping motion, not that of the reverberations. If reverberations are desired, they can be indicated with open ties from subsequent notes (see example), or by adding *l.v.* Pedal markings, which belong to this effect anyway, also show the desired duration of the reverberations.

A verbal instruction must be added, such as "sweep back and forth [across strings]," as well as indications for dynamics, pedaling, and the number of fingers to be employed.

Pedals

A. Abbreviations and Signs

℘ed. = damper pedal. (Do not use for any other pedals, including pedals on other instruments, such as organ or vibraphone, where the abbreviation Ped. in ordinary roman type is customary.)

Sost. Ped. = sostenuto pedal. (Although the shorter abbreviation *S.P.* is used quite often, it is undesirable because it might be mistaken for *Senza Pedale.*)

U.C. = *una corda.*

B. Order

The vertical order of pedal indications should be as given above.

C. Depression and Release

The traditional method of placing 𝄢𝄐. followed by ❀ below the music is often too vague for twentieth-century music. Besides, if more than one pedal are employed simultaneously, it is not always clear to which pedal the release star refers.

To remedy the situation, it is suggested that extension lines be used for all three pedals, with various graphic devices for indicating different ways of pedal depression and release, as follows:

1. DAMPER PEDAL

Note that only the first occurrence begins with 𝄢𝄐. . All subsequent indications within the same movement may omit the 𝄢𝄐. sign and begin with a mere downstroke.

Note also that the depression begins at the letter 𝄢 (and at the letters *S* and *U* for the other pedals), rather than at the beginning of the extension line.

2. OTHER PEDALS

Precede the extension line with *Sost. Ped.* or *U.C.*, respectively. Repeat the abbreviations as often as necessary to avoid ambiguity. (The abbreviations may be further shortened, after their first occurrence, to *S.* for sostenuto pedal and *U.* for *una corda*.)

3. PEDALING EXTENDING FROM ONE LINE TO THE NEXT

The damper pedal generally needs no identification; the other two pedals do:

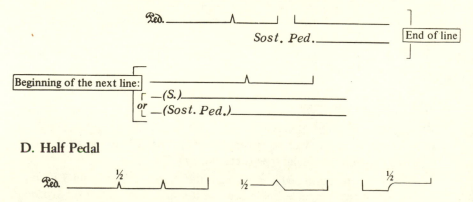

D. Half Pedal

Since the difference between full and half pedal indications is not easy to see, the ½ should be repeated at each occurrence of the half pedal, and if it continues from one line to the next, a ½ in parentheses should be placed at the beginning of the new line: (½)

E. Gradual Pedal Depression, Change, and Release

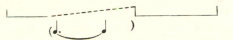

If a gradual depression begins after a 𝄃𝄃. sign, care must be taken to begin the dotted line high enough: 𝄃𝄃.----- _____|

If it is found desirable to notate the precise end of a gradual pedal release, a small corner bracket may be used: |_____.--⌐

If the duration of a gradual pedal movement is to be measured exactly, one or more notes in parentheses should be used:

For catching staccato reverberations with the pedal, see Staccato Reverberations, page 272.

F. Pedal Sound Only
Use diamond-shaped note-heads on a single line.

Single attacks

Tremolo

Verbal instructions should always accompany a pedal-sound effect.

Electronic amplification of the sound is suggested since the strings reverberate only very softly.

Silent Depression of Keys

This is notated with diamond-shaped, full-size notes:

See also Harmonics, page 261 f, and Inside the Piano: Strumming, page 268 f.

Staccato Reverberations

Catching the vibrations after a staccato attack may be effected in two ways:

By silently redepressing the key(s)

senza pedale

(The *senza pedale* is optional but advisable.)

By depressing the damper pedal immediately after leaving the key(s)

catch sound
with pedal

Tied Notes from One Hand to the Other

Ambiguity as to whether such notes are to be played again or merely taken over by the other hand can be avoided by notating them with diamond-shaped notes at the point of transfer:

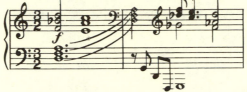

If further ties are needed after the transfer, normal notes are resumed:

XIII. *Organ*

Braces and Barlines	274	*Manuals*	277
Clusters	274	*Pedals*	278
Keys (Held and Released)	274	*Registration*	278
A. *Held Keys*	274	*Stops*	279
B. *Release of Keys*	275	A. *Individual Stops*	279
C. *Mechanically Secured Keys and*		B. *Stops by Pitch*	279
Their Release	276	C. *Stops by Timbre*	279

Braces and Barlines

The barlines must be interrupted between the manual and pedal staves.

Clusters

For short, rhythmic clusters, see Piano: Clusters, page 259 f. There is as yet no preferred style of notation for sustained clusters. It is suggested, however, to use the "Cowell system," including its indeterminate extensions (as shown in the chapter on Piano: Clusters), since it has proven to be the most efficient.

Keys (Held and Released)

A. Held Keys

GRADUALLY FILLED-IN CHORDS OR CLUSTERS

Each note or group of notes to be held is connected with a vertical line from the center of the note(s) to a heavy, horizontal "continuation bar."

B. Release of Keys

The notes (keys) may be released separately or all at once. The release is shown with x-shaped note-heads:

1. SIMULTANEOUS RELEASE

All keys are to be released at once; the continuation bar ends with ♪ :

If the continuation bar above must be interrupted because it proceeds from one line to the next, the held keys are shown in square brackets at the beginning of the new line (in the present case it is a cluster). Also, the continuation bar ends with an arrowhead at the end of the first line:

End of first line

Beginning of next line

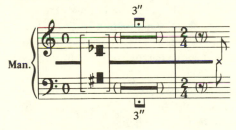

2. GRADUAL RELEASE

The keys are released one by one; x-shaped note-heads indicate which keys are to be released; at the last key to be released, the continuation bar ends with an x. (Note that only some of the keys played are also held, i.e., connected to the continuation bar.)

End of first line

Beginning of next line

In the example above, individual note-heads appear in the bracket at the beginning of the new line, unlike the example on page 275, which showed a cluster.

C. Mechanically Secured Keys and Their Release

The keys are held down by placing weights on them or by inserting wedges or pencils between them and the headboard. In general, this has to be done with assistance.

The notes to be held are notated with diamond-shaped whole notes. These are connected with heavy vertical lines (which should not actually touch the notes) from the center of the notes to a heavy, horizontal continuation bar, which continues as long as any of the held notes is still secured. The words "secure ◆-keys [with weights or wedges]" should be placed above the top staff or wherever convenient.

Dotted vertical lines may be drawn from the held notes to the regular ones to aid synchronization, but unless the texture is rhythmically complex these lines may not be necessary. (They do appear in the example below.)

To release the keys, x-shaped note-heads are placed at the point of release. These, too, are connected with vertical lines to the continuation bar. At the last key to be released, the continuation bar ends.

Since the mechanically held notes (keys) are usually played on a manual other than the regular one(s), each manual should be notated on a separate system.

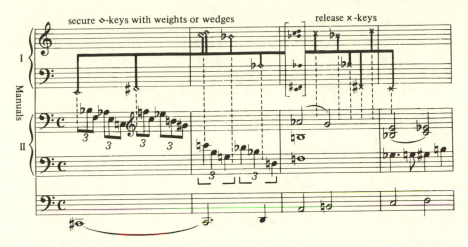

Manuals

The number of manuals varies from organ to organ—from a single keyboard to seven (very rare). Most organs have two to four manuals, in addition to the pedal keyboard.

The manuals are identified either by roman numerals or by their names. Since the numerals alone may be ambiguous, however, the names—in full or abbreviated—should always accompany them at the initial indication of required manuals. This indication should appear at the upper left of the first page of music. Thereafter, i.e., in the music proper, numerals suffice to indicate the respective manuals. (For further details, see Registration, below.)

The following list shows the manuals and pedal of a typical five-manual organ—first written out in full, then in the customary abbreviated form:

Manual I: Great Organ	I (Gt.)
Manual II: Swell Organ	II (Sw.)
Manual III: Choir Organ	III (Ch.)
Manual IV: Positive Organ (sometimes Solo Organ)	IV (Pos.) or (Solo)
Manual V: Echo Organ	V (Echo)
Pedal Organ	Ped.

Each manual indication, as well as the pedal, should be followed by a list of the stops to be used (again, see Registration, below).

Most organs have couplers which make it possible to add the stops of one manual to another or to the pedal. Such couplings are marked Sw. to Gt., Gt. to Ped., and so forth. In the music, these couplings would be indicated II to I, I to Ped., and so forth.

Pedals

The traditional signs for heel and toe should be used:

Heel: ∪   Toe: ∧

Markings for the right foot go above the staff; for the left foot, below.

Changing from heel to toe or vice versa on the same key: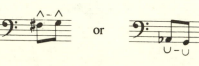

Sliding from key to key:

Registration

Since hardly any two organs are alike (except electronic instruments), it is strongly suggested that composers who provide exact registrations also show the specifications of the organ for which they are intended. In this way, other organists can adapt the required registrations more easily to the resources of their own instruments.

The following represents the most commonly used groupings when more general registration indications are sufficient:

Flues	Soft
Strings	Full (or Tutti)
Reeds (Solo Reed)	

If possible, these indications should include pitch-levels (octaves) for regular stops as well as for mixtures, etc. For example:

Flues 8′ 4′ 2⅔′	Soft 16′ 4′
Strings 8′	Ped. 16′ 8′
Solo Reed 4′	Full (or Tutti)

When notating an organ piece, the required manuals (see Manuals, page 277) and their stops should appear in the upper left of the first page of music, for example:

I (Gt.): Reed 8′
II (Sw.): Flues 8′ 4′
III (Ch.): Flues 8′ 2⅔′ 1⅓′ to I
Ped.: Flues 16′ 8′

If the stops remain the same throughout the movement, they are not mentioned again in the music itself; if they change, this must be indicated. For example, the

Swell of the example above might begin as II 8′, followed by +4′; or it might begin II 8′ 4′, followed by −4′, and so forth.

If manuals are to be coupled, a plus sign should be used in the music. *Coup. off* ends the coupled section.

The following example shows several changes, telescoped into a very short phrase to demonstrate the method:

I (Gt.): Reed 8′
II (Sw.): Flues 8′ 4′
III (Ch.): Flues 8′ 2′ 1′
Ped.: Flues 16′ 8′

Stops

The following recommendations apply to the operation of stops by assistants while the organist holds down keys.

A. Individual Stops

Tablature notation is recommended. In the organ part, the tablature must appear above the top staff so that it can be seen in context. For the assistants, however, only a stop part with proper entrance cues is needed.

or

Manual or pedal information must be indicated. Switching from one stop to another should be shown in the same manner as, for example, switches from flute to piccolo in a flute part (see switch to Sesquialtera in the example above).

B. Stops by Pitch

Verbal instructions must be given, such as:

Gradually add 2' stops.

Add 4' stops as quickly as possible.

Add stops from 4' up (may be abbreviated after first occurrence to 4' ↗).

Add stops from 4' down to 16' (may be abbreviated to 4' ↘).

Subtract all 8' stops gradually.

If such manipulations are to take place in specified rhythms, a tablature similar to the one above should be worked out. Arrows may also be used, such as:

Add any stops at the arrows   ↑↑↑   ↑   ↑   ↑

C. Stops by Timbre

Verbal instructions must be given, such as:

Add (subtract) all Reeds as quickly as possible.

Add Mixtures, one every 2 seconds.

XIV. *Keyboard Reductions*

Choral Scores   **281**   *Orchestra Scores*   **289**

Choral Scores

The sole purpose of keyboard reductions of choral music is to enable a rehearsal accompanist who is not able to play from open score to do a serviceable job. Consequently, such reductions should be kept as simple and "pianistic" as possible, even if the voice leading is obscured here and there. Since the open score always appears above the reduction, it can be consulted for clarification whenever needed, and if individual parts are to be rehearsed, they can be played directly from the score.

Although it is impossible to cover all eventualities, especially in complex music, the following thirteen rules might serve as very general guidelines.

1. Notes of equal duration should be on the same stem (for each hand) wherever possible, but changes from double to single stemming should not be made within a beat (see * in first measure of the Hindemith *Credo*, page 282 and the upper example on page 287).

2. Tacit parts need not be accounted for with rests unless this results in "dangling" note-values (see left-hand staff of same example).

3. Notes of different durations must never be on the same stem:

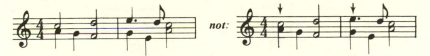

4. Tied notes should be stemmed separately from untied notes, even when their durations (not counting the ties) are the same:

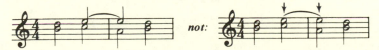

5. Voice crossings with equal note-values and in the same hand should be disregarded in the reduction (first measure, bottom of page 282).

6. Voice crossings with different note-values make double-stemming unavoidable, in which case the stems may as well show the crossings. How-

Paul Hindemith, Credo from the Mass, measures 9–11

ever, if notational simplification is possible, it is preferred (second measure of example):

* Although the last version is the most distorted, it is exactly as helpful for the chorus as the other

7. If notes of the inner voices go too high or too low for the respective hand to reach, the notes should be moved to the other staff and played by the other hand. This is preferable to using brackets or arrows to show which notes are to be played with which hand. Thin, slanted lines should indicate the change from staff to staff:

Hindemith, Benedictus from the **Mass,** *measures 28–32*

© 1963 by Schott's Söhne, Mainz. Used by permission.

The following, more complicated example is from the author's edition of *Dolcissima mia vita* by Carlo Gesualdo (c.1560–1613), measures 4–16. In this excerpt some of the slanting lines that show the voice leading are omitted in order to prevent too much clutter. In other instances, ties serve the same purpose as lines (see measure 16).

At times, the distribution of the notes between the two hands is so complex that indications of voice leading have to be reduced to a minimum or abandoned altogether (see, for example, measures 15 and 16).

(This reduction also shows many other features which are discussed in the rules that follow.)

---

two, and it is by far the easiest to play. For further examples of voice crossings, see the second example under rule 9 and the one for rule 12.

Carlo Gesualdo, **Dolcissima mia vita**, *measures 4-16*

*See page 181.

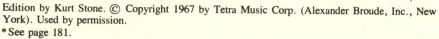

8. If the right and left hands reach a unison, one of the notes should be placed in parentheses, depending on the following criteria:

if the two notes are of different duration, the shorter note should be in parentheses;

if the two notes are of equal duration, the one less convenient to play should be parenthesized (see measure 15 of the preceding Gesualdo example);

if it is a matter of two voices singing a unison passage (i.e., not merely an occasional note) only one of the voices needs to be notated.

(The example for the next rule also includes situations described above.)

9. When a voice reaches a pitch already held by another, the long note of the first voice should be split into shorter values so that each subsequent voice entrance is made audible by a new attack. At the same time, the voice that enters the unison is also notated, to clarify the voice-leading. The shorter of the two unison notes should be placed in parentheses.

Example: the tenor reaches the E held by the alto

Example: the tenor, and then the bass, enter on the C held by the alto; later on, the alto reaches the B-flat held by the bass. (This example also includes some voice crossing.)

See also the Gesualdo example, measure 4: alto D joined by soprano II; measure 11: soprano II G joined by soprano I; etc.

10. If two voices reach a unison, one being tied over from the preceding note, the other not, the tie should be either omitted or placed in parenthe-

ses, since the pianist should produce an attack for the untied note. (See measure 16 of the Gesualdo example above. The situation is particularly awkward here because the tie also serves as a voice-leading guide in lieu of a slanted line.)

11. In general, if a note ends before the barline, the rest(s) may be omitted if another voice can seemingly continue where the first ended. Otherwise rests must be used (last measure):

See also Rule 2, page 281.

but:

12. Accidentals must be used in accordance with the needs of the reduction only. Thus, if, for example, the alto has a sharp, followed by another sharp for the same pitch in the soprano (in the same measure), there is no need to repeat the sharp in the reduction.

Similarly (continuing the above hypothesis of the sharps in the alto and soprano), if the measure that follows contains the same note without a sharp but in a different voice, a natural is required in the reduction.

In the following example, at the * in measure 1, the alto's sharp before D is not repeated in the reduction; and in measure 2 at **, the natural before D appears only in the reduction, not in the tenor part:

The Gesualdo example also provides numerous instances showing the proper treatment of accidentals. It should be noted, however, that in older music cancellations of accidentals are often self-evident, so that the rules recommended here need not always be followed as strictly as they should be in twentieth-century music.

13. Dynamics and articulation should appear in the reduction whenever possible, but reduced to a minimum (for example, if voices enter one by one, each having its own *mf,* the reduction requires only one *mf* at the beginning of these entrances). Syllabic slurs should not be included because they do not represent phrasing, but if the score contains genuine phrasing slurs, they should be included in the reduction.

Most of the examples above show some dynamics and articulation, but few show syllable slurs. None contains phrasing slurs, since these are rarely found in choral music.

A final note: While the choice of single versus double stemming is a mere matter of style or practicality in music up to four parts, it becomes a necessity as soon as five or more voices are involved. Obviously, the arranging of reductions becomes more difficult as the number of polyphonic parts increases. Only if the texture is predominantly homophonic is it possible to reduce multivoiced scores satisfactorily.

Furthermore, it is much easier to deal with traditional harmony than with more complex systems of pitch organization, because the harmonies permit the omission of certain chord tones if they are hard to reach, without distorting the music (for example, the fifth in a seventh chord). Also, multivoiced homophonic music contains many doublings that need not be included in the reduction.

All this is quite different in more recent music. For example, it would be utterly impossible to produce a truly representative and practical reduction of the excerpt from Luigi Nono's *La terra e la compagna* which appears on page 94 f. There, all six tenors sing on the same pitch, but their entrances occur at extremely subtly differentiated time intervals and with many timbral minutiae.

Quite another problem would be the reduction of a multivoiced twelve-tone choral piece, with each voice singing a different version of the row both as to rhythm and succession of pitches. There are no tones that permit omission, nor are there generally any doublings.

In short, choral music, especially if it has more than four parts, generally permits reductions for a single piano only if its tonal organization and texture are somewhat traditional (and not too polyphonic). Two-piano reductions, on the other hand, may be quite practical even if only one pianist is available: he or she might play the two parts in alternation each time the chorus repeats the piece or section. Certainly this is better than no reduction at all.

The example on page 290 shows an extreme case of multivoiced choral writing: the opening of the *Symphonia sacra "Nunc dimittis"* by Giovanni Gabrieli (ca.1555–1612)—three choirs; a total of fourteen parts. Of course, the music is old and thus does permit doublings and omissions. A similar score in an atonal idiom would not be reduceable for a single piano.

(The small notes in the reduction may be omitted.)

The final example, for four-part chorus divisi, is relatively homophonic, but it contains no doublings—each tone counts:

Ernst Krenek, opening of **Holy Ghost**

Orchestra Scores

The problems involved in reducing an orchestra score are basically the same as those concerning choral scores, except that they are more complicated. It is therefore of great importance to realize the purpose of an orchestral reduction before one even begins to produce one.

Giovanni Gabrieli, Opening of the Symphonia sacra, Nunc dimittis

In the days before recordings it was customary to publish every symphony in a piano version to enable music lovers to play the work at home. If the piece was sufficiently popular, reductions for four hands, two pianos, and even violin and piano would also be issued.

Today, piano reductions are no longer a source of enjoyment for music lovers, but of practical necessity, chiefly in the two areas of ballet and opera. Ballet reductions may eventually be replaced by a recording, but reductions of opera scores remain an essential part of rehearsals.

It is almost impossible to provide guidelines because of the immense dissimilarity of musical styles and attitudes of our era. Not only are twelve-tone and serial works difficult to reduce, there is virtually ''irreducible'' music too, such as scores with large, prominent percussion groups and/or electronic devices, i.e., music consisting mostly of timbres and few, if any, definable pitches. Still other scores may involve indeterminate sections which cannot and, for that matter, should not be ''petrified'' into an inflexible keyboard reduction.

In all such cases it may occasionally be possible to work out some sort of a skeletal piano sketch, but this can only be decided from case to case.

If, on the other hand, a score does lend itself to the production of a keyboard reduction, two general observations might be worth considering:

1. If in doubt whether to include certain secondary material or not, it is usually best to omit it or place it on a smaller staff outside the keyboard part proper. As in the considerations for choral reductions, one should always be guided by the fact that the reduction must be played, often at sight, by a rehearsal pianist, not by a virtuoso.

2. Wherever convenient, instrument abbreviations should be included in the reduction. They greatly help both singers and dancers when the actual orchestral sounds are heard for the first time after long periods of rehearsals with piano.

For examples, compare full scores of operatic and choreographic music with their reductions. This is not always easy, since full scores are rarely published these days; but some music libraries have a few.

To conclude: We have an arsenal of notational devices, old and new, to cope with a large number of musical situations, but when it comes to keyboard reductions, it is often the music itself which makes reductions impractical (if not impossible).

xv. *Voice*

Aspiration   292

Beams versus Flags   293

Clusters in Choral Music
  see *Pitch, Clusters, page 57*

Falsetto   293

Flutter Tongue   293

Highest Note/Lowest Note   294

Inhale/Exhale   295
  A. *Voiced (Pitched) Inhaling and
     Exhaling*   295
  B. *Unvoiced Inhaling and
     Exhaling (Air Sound)*   295
  C. *Instrumental Notation*   295

Interpretive Markings
(Articulation, Dynamics,
Expression Marks)   295

Mouth Positions   295

Nasal Voice   296

Phonetics   296

Portamento   296

Slurs   296

Sprechgesang,
Sprechstimme, *Spoken*   297
  A. Sprechgesang *or* Sprechton   297
  B. *Sprechstimme*   298
  C. *Spoken or Speaking*   298

Text Placement under the
Music   299
  A. *Centered or Flush-Left Alignment*   299
  B. *Extenders*   299
  C. *Articulation of Final Consonants*   299
  D. *More than One Line of Text*   300

Text Presentation   300
  A. *Adherence to the Original
     Presentation of Poetry or Prose*   300
  B. *Repeats or Partial Repeats of Text*   300
  C. *Syllable Division*   301
  D. *Foreign Languages and
     Translations*   301

Tremolos   301
  A. *Guttural Tremolo or Repeat
     Tremolo*   302
  B. *Hand Tremolo*   302
  C. *Trill Tremolo*   302

Unvoiced Vocal Effects   303

Vibrato/Non Vibrato   304

Whispering   304

Aspiration

The aspiration of a sound should be indicated with the abbreviation *asp.* and cancelled with *ord.:*

Beams versus Flags

The traditional system of beaming and flagging vocal music according to text syllables has been replaced almost universally with instrumental beaming, i.e., beaming according to beat-units or other metric divisions, with slurs indicating whenever more notes than one are to be sung on one syllable:

Traditional system

Instrumental beaming

Instrumental beaming with extended beams and stemlets (see also page 15 f)

(This system is particularly helpful in music with highly complex rhythms.)

Falsetto

Diamond-shaped note-heads should be used to indicate falsetto voice.

The word *falsetto* should be used at first occurrence; it should be spelled out, not abbreviated.

Flutter Tongue

It is generally more practical to write the sound of flutter tongue into the text than to use special notation. For an accented attack, *trrrr* should be used; for an unaccented entrance, *rrrrrr*. Certain text words are also suitable for flutter tongue, such as *grrreed, crrrrrawl, tarrrrr-get,* etc.

Trr - ue love, trr-trr-trr - trr~~ rrr~~

If the sound is not incorporated into the text, the notes should be written as tremolos and the words *flutter tongue* added on first occurrence (*fl.t.* in subsequent places if deemed necessary). This notation is most useful in passages of pure vocal sounds without text:

A   bi(rd)-rrr - d   ha

If an unvoiced sound (tongue only; no vocal cords) is wanted, x-shaped noteheads somewhat away from the staff should be used, and the *rrrrrr*-sounds written as text:

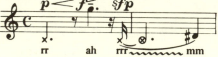

rr   ah   rrr~~~~~ mm

Highest Note/Lowest Note

Highest notes

Lowest notes

N.B.: The stems go to the center of the notes.

Quick slide to the highest note

Ordinary (measured) glissando to the highest note

Free notation (no staff-lines required)

Inhale/Exhale

A. Voiced (Pitched) Inhaling and Exhaling

The inhale and exhale signs should be placed above the music or, in spoken passages, above the text:

B. Unvoiced Inhaling and Exhaling (Air Sound)

The notation should be the same as for whispering (see Whispering, page 304 f).

C. Instrumental Notation

In certain situations, the use of instrumental air-sound notation may be a good solution (see Wind Instruments: General Topics, Air Sound or Breathy Sound, page 186 f):

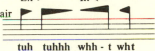

Interpretive Markings (Articulation, Dynamics, Expression Marks)

In vocal music, unlike all other music, dynamics, expression marks, and most articulation marks are placed above the music so as not to interfere with the text. Only staccato dots and tenuto lines, i.e., signs that take up very little space, are generally placed at the note-heads regardless of whether the heads point up or down:

Mouth Positions

The following symbols should be placed above the notes:

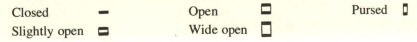

When no signs appear, normal mouth position is implied.

For the continuation of one specific mouth position, a broken extension line should be used. The line should end with a short down-stroke which obviates the use of *ord.* or *norm.:*

For gradual changes from one mouth position to another, an arrow should be used:

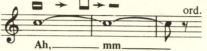

Nasal Voice

The symbol Δ should be placed above the notes.

Notations for continuation, cancellation, and gradual changes match those discussed under Mouth Positions: ord.⟶ Δ ⟶ ord.

Phonetics

Text-sounds without linguistic meaning, as well as transliterations, should be spelled by means of the International Phonetic Alphabet, or a footnote should indicate the language on which the spelling is based, for example: *Italian pronunciation; *English pronunciation; etc.

Portamento

The notation of a vocal portamento consists of the same thin line as used for a glissando. Consequently, the abbreviation *port.* must always accompany the line (not only at first occurrence):

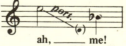

N.B.: In music in which both glissando and portamento are used, it is best to add abbreviations for both sound productions throughout. (No verbal identification is necessary if only glissandos occur.)

For short, quick portamento slides, see page 20, bottom.

Slurs

Although the slurring of notes sung on a single syllable is essentially superfluous if the text is positioned properly, the custom of doing so should be upheld. The slurs do convey at a glance how to group the notes, which is very helpful.

Most of the rules for the slurs are the same as the general ones given in General Conventions, Slurs and Ties, page 35 ff. The few exceptions concern accents and the numerals and brackets of irregular note divisions. These should generally be placed above the notes regardless of the stem directions, so that they will not interfere with the text. (Staccato dots and tenuto lines are not included in these exceptions.)

Ky - ri - e— e - lei - son, e - lei - son.

Occasional deviations are permissible if the notes lie so high that there will be enough space below them for accents, numerals, and even brackets without encroaching on the text. This is especially useful if, as in two of the triplets of the following example, the note-heads are slurred and the numerals can thus be gotten out of the way:

Ky - ri - e—— e - lei-, e - lei - son.

Sprechgesang, Sprechstimme, Spoken

The first two of these three types of voice production lie between singing and speaking:

Sprechgesang (German for speech-song), or Sprechton (speech-tone),* is closer to singing than to speaking;

Sprechstimme (German for speaking voice but actually meaning speechlike voice) is closer to speaking than to singing.

A. Sprechgesang or Sprechton

The notated pitches are adhered to, but only initially, after which the voice assumes speech timbre, and the pitch, which is now indefinite, may rise or fall.

Notation: traditional notes with an x through the stem:

Ky - ri - e

---

*The term used by Arnold Schoenberg in *Pierrot Lunaire* (1912).

B. Sprechstimme

The voice has speech timbre throughout, but rises and falls as notated.

Notation: x-shaped note-heads to indicate that the pitches are spoken and thus are largely approximate:

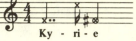

Ky - ri - e

C. Spoken or Speaking

Different from ordinary speech only in that voice inflections (usually only high, medium, and low) and/or rhythms are notated. (There are no precise pitch specifications.)

Notation:

1. WITH VOICE-INFLECTION GRID AND RHYTHMS (DURATIONS)

e - le - i-son

2. WITH RHYTHMIC INDICATIONS ONLY

Ky - ri- e   e - le-i - son

N.B.: If short, spoken interpolations appear in an otherwise staff-notated context, the ideal notation would be:

Fare -well, Miss   Nick-el-son,   Do___

The elimination of superfluous staff-lines for such brief phrases, however, is time consuming. If, therefore, the spoken phrases are notated without interrupting the full staff, the word *spoken* must be added to avoid misinterpretation of the x-shaped notes as speaking-voice pitches:

Fare - well, Miss   Nick-el - son,   Do_____

Text Placement under the Music

A. Centered or Flush-Left Alignment

A fine point of text placement—a tradition now frequently ignored—is to make a distinction between single-note words or syllables and those sung on more than one note:

single-note words and syllables are centered below the note;

multinote words and syllables are aligned flush left with the initial note.

(See the example below which incorporates these conventions: [1] = centered; [2] = flush left.)

B. Extenders

If a monosyllabic word or the last syllable of a multisyllabic word is to be sung on more than one note, an extension line or extender is drawn at period level from the end of the word or syllable (or from its punctuation mark, if any) to the last note. (Obviously, if the last of these notes is no farther to the right than the end of the word or syllable, no extender is necessary.) (See [3] for extenders.)

N.B.: Extenders stop at the last note; they are not drawn to the end of its sound:

Punctuation must appear in its normal position, i.e., not at the end of the extender.

C. Articulation of Final Consonants

If rhythmically precise articulation of certain final consonants is wanted, it is important to spell each syllable out completely at its initial location to prevent mispronunciations. The articulated consonant should then be repeated in parentheses at the point of its exact rhythmic occurrence, for example:

sake_____(k)

moon, _____(n)

Other methods of division can cause confusion:

Incorrect   sa - ke *or* sa_____ke

(Divided this way, the one-syllable *sake* turns into a two-syllable Japanese drink!)

In other words, splitting up a syllable renders vowel pronunciation ambiguous and must be avoided.

D. More than One Line of Text

If the two texts differ in the number of syllables and/or in syllabic placement, it is generally clearest to resort to double stemming in the passages in question, with upstems and up-slurs for the upper text line and downstems and down-slurs for the lower line:

glo - ri - fi - ca - - - mus
Let us sing Thy glo - - ry, Lord

If the differences in text placement, etc., are very great, such as in the following example:

1. Di - es i - rae, di - es il - la,
2. Quan - tus tre - mor est fu - tu - - ra

it is better to write out both verses separately, one after the other.

Text Presentation

A. Adherence to the Original Presentation of Poetry or Prose

Ideally, it should always be possible to restore the original form of a poem from the way it appears as text in a musical composition. For this reason, the original system of capitalization and punctuation should be reproduced exactly as it appears in the source. If different editions of the same poem show different styles of capitalization, a version in which each line begins with a capital letter should be used, so that the original structure of the poem remains recognizable even after the poem has been transferred into the music.

If the poet does not use capitals (for example, e. e. cummings), short, raised strokes may be used to mark the line breaks, and a footnote should be added to explain that the strokes are editorial additions to clarify the poem's structure.

B. Repeats or Partial Repeats of Text

If a complete line of a poem is repeated in the music, and the line begins with a capital letter, the repeat should also begin with a capital. A comma should be placed between the lines.

If only part of a line is repeated, and the repeat consists of the beginning of a capitalized line, the capital may or may not be retained in the repeat, depending on the sense of the passage in question. The same applies to the editorial strokes in uncapitalized poems.

C. Syllable Division

If at all possible (i.e., if space permits), multisyllabic words should be divided into all their syllables:

poor: Love - liest of trees, the cherry now ...
preferred: Love - li -est of trees, the cher-ry now ...

or

poor: Overwrought with grief; de - spairing,
preferred: O-ver-wrought with grief; de - spair-ing,

Multiple hyphens should be used sparingly and should be well spaced:

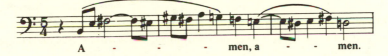

A - - - men, a - - men.

N.B.: Care should be taken that hyphens do not appear directly below a note, so that they will not be mistaken for tenuto lines.

D. Foreign Languages and Translations

If texts in foreign languages are used, accents and umlauts, etc., must be retained exactly as they appear in the original. Accents in Romance languages may be omitted from capital letters, but the umlauts of the Germanic languages must not. However, German capital letters with umlauts may be changed as follows: *Ä* to *Ae, Ö* to *Oe,* and *Ü* to *Ue.*

If foreign-language texts and their translations into singable English are combined under the music, the upper language should be in roman type and the language of the lower line in italic type (see pages 284–5).

Tremolos

In addition to the basic tremolos dealt with on pages 74 ff and 147 ff, there are a few forms peculiar to vocal music, as outlined below.

Three methods of producing vocal tremolos must be distinguished:

The guttural or repeat tremolo (the *repercussio gutturis* of ages past, which has made its reappearance in the music of our time). It consists of more or less rapid repetitions of a single tone.

The hand tremolo, which is akin to alternating muted and open sounds of brass instruments: moving the hand back and forth in front of the mouth, but without changing the pitch.

The trill tremolo, which is actually a wide vibrato (see Pitch, Trill/Tremolo/Vibrato, page 74).

A. Guttural Tremolo or Repeat Tremolo

It may be notated like a single-tone string tremolo (with a verbal explanation at first occurrence):

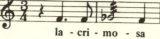

la - cri - mo - sa

It may also be notated like the *Bebung* (Ger. for tremor) in clavichord music (again with a verbal explanation at first occurrence):

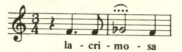

la - cri - mo - sa

If the rate of the tremolo-beats is to change (for example, increase or decrease gradually), the tremolo should be written out, but the abbreviation *trem.* should always be added to indicate the intended vocal technique:

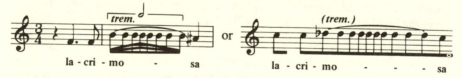

la - cri - mo - sa   or   la - cri - mo - sa

B. Hand Tremolo

Since this effect is similar to the brass effect of quickly alternating stopped and open tones, the notation should be the same also, with the verbal indication *hand trem.* at first occurrence:

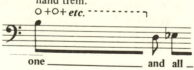

one ——————— and all —

C. Trill Tremolo

In general, wide, wavy vibrato lines should be used (suggesting approximate pitches):

Constant width

la - cri - mo - sa

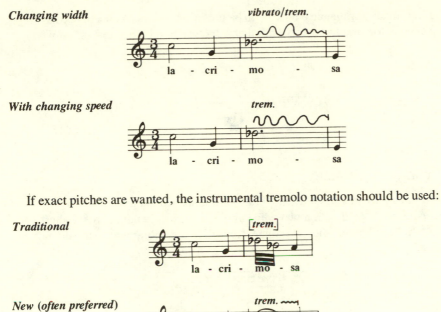

Changing width

With changing speed

If exact pitches are wanted, the instrumental tremolo notation should be used:

Traditional

New (often preferred)

For further details, see Pitch Notation, page 76, and Durational Notation, page 149 ff.

Unvoiced Vocal Effects

In accordance with analogous instrumental sounds, unvoiced vocal effects, such as tongue clicks and lip smacks, should be notated with x-shaped note-heads on a line outside the staff, on a single line, or on a register grid.

The effects should be labeled in full because of their relatively rare occurrence. Phonetic indications may be added where appropriate.

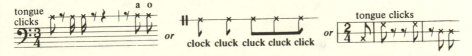

If specific pitches are desired for the tongue click, the x-shaped notes are placed inside the staff:

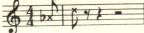

If lip smacks or tongue clicks are to be produced as grace notes to normal singing sounds, or simultaneously with them, they should be notated as follows:

Vibrato/Non Vibrato

All ordinary singing has a slight vibrato. If a more pronounced vibrato is wanted, it should be notated with a wavy line above the music, ending with a short vertical stroke. (Unlike the wavy line for trills, the vibrato line should not be shaded.)

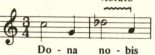

If more convenient, the wavy line may be replaced by the verbal instruction *vibrato,* which must be cancelled with the abbreviation *ord.* or *norm.:*

Non vibrato (which is not identical with "ordinary" singing) should be indicated with the abbreviation *n.v.* (This abbreviation is preferable to *s.v.—senza vibrato—*even though the latter is found quite often.)

If more than one note are to be sung non vibrato, the *n.v.* should be followed by a broken continuation line which must end in a down-stroke. There is then no need for *ord.* or *norm.:*   **n.v.** -----------¬

Whispering

The notation should be the same as that for Speaking (see *Sprechgesang,* etc., page 297 f), except that broken lines should be used for stems:

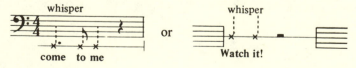

If pitch inflections are wanted, the notes may be placed on, above, and below the single line:

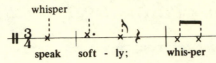

The instruction *whisper* should always be added at first occurrence.

Whispering should not be notated in the full staff, since specific pitches are virtually impossible to achieve.

XVI. *Bowed String Instruments*

Preliminary Note	306	*Fingernail Flick*	311
Abbreviations	307	*Harmonics*	311
		A. *In Scores*	311
Arpeggio		B. *In Parts*	312
see pages 3 and 309			
		Muffling	312
Body of Instruments	307		
A. *Tapping or Striking*	307	*Pizzicato*	312
B. *Tablature Notation*	307	A. *Bartók or Snap Pizzicato*	312
		B. *Buzz Pizzicato*	313
Bowing	308	C. *Fingernail Pizzicato*	313
on Tailpiece	315	D. *Left-Hand Pizzicato*	313
		E. *Pizz./Finger*	313
Bridge	308	F. *Pizzicato Glissando*	313
A. *Bowing behind the Bridge*	308	Scordatura (Abnormal	
B. *Bowing on Top of the Bridge*	309	Tuning), see page 246	
		Snap Pizzicato, see page 312	
Chords	309	G. *Strumming (Fast Arpeggio)*	314
		H. *Two-Finger Pizzicato*	314
Clusters			
see page 57		*Portamento*	
		see page 20	
Damping (Étouffer)	310		
		Slapping the Strings	315
Double Stops	310		
		Tailpiece	315
Fingering without Bowing	311		

Preliminary Note

The techniques and special playing modes needed to produce particular forms of articulation and other effects on bowed string instruments are so numerous that most of them are better expressed verbally than by means of new notational devices.

It is for this practical reason that signs meant to convey specific playing techniques have been kept to a minimum.*

*For an excellent, detailed discussion of such techniques and their notation, see *Orchestration* by Walter Piston (New York: W. W. Norton, 1955), Chapter I: Stringed Instruments.

Abbreviations

col legno battuto	clb	ordinario	ord.
col legno tratto	clt	pizzicato	pizz.
divisi	div.	sul ponticello	s.p.
non divisi	non div.	sul tasto	s.t.
normale	norm.		

Body of Instrument

A. Tapping or Striking

If occasional tappings, etc., are wanted, they should be notated with x-shaped note-heads on an extra line below the staff:

An indication should be added whether to use knuckles, fingertips, or finger-nails. (There are no abbreviations or pictograms in general use.)

If percussion beaters are to be employed, pictograms should be used (see Percussion, Pictograms, page 210 ff). Explanations of the pictograms must be added on first occurrence because string players are less familiar with them than percussion players.

If a specific location on the instrument is to be tapped, verbal instructions must be provided. If several places are to be tapped, it is advisable to notate such passages in tablature and add a drawing to show the desired locations, as explained below.

B. Tablature Notation

The number of lines of the tablature staff depends on the number of spots on the instrument that are to be struck, etc. The following example has a four-line staff, with the spots labeled A through D, and a drawing which shows where the spots are located on the instrument(s). Furthermore, the spots are divided between the left and the right hand. (If other media for sound production are wanted, such as the wood of the bow or a drumstick, they must of course be specified.)

Since all sounds produced in this fashion are short, only relatively short note-values should be used unless, as in the example, there is a tremolo.

Other tablatures are also possible, such as the following:

Strike with bow

Top of Bridge
Behind Bridge
Tail Piece

For further details, see Bowing behind the Bridge, below.

Bridge

A. Bowing behind the Bridge

The sign of a curved "bridge" should be used, regardless of the notational method employed (see below). The note-heads should be x-shaped.

1. ORDINARY FIVE-LINE-STAFF NOTATION

The stems must be fairly long, especially those with flags, to provide enough space outside the staff for the bridge symbol to be clearly visible:

If several consecutive notes are to be bowed behind the bridge, a broken continuation line may be used:

2. TABLATURE NOTATION

The lines of the tablature staff, to be used only for extended passages or entire movements, represent the strings of an instrument, rather than consecutive pitches as in the ordinary five-line staff. The top line represents the highest string. It is recommended to label the strings at the beginning of each staff.

Note that the lines of a tablature or string staff must be drawn farther apart than those of an ordinary staff, so that the two kinds of staves are clearly distinguishable, especially when alternating.

Violin

3. NONSTAFF NOTATION

Since pitches are unpredictable and, in a way, almost immaterial in behind-the-bridge bowing, the staff may be omitted. This notation has greater visual immediacy because the lines representing the strings can be run across the bridge symbol. The method is best suited for use in spatial notation, because it requires no note-heads; the durations are expressed by the length of the beams.

The strings may be labeled. If they are not, the choice is left to the performer.

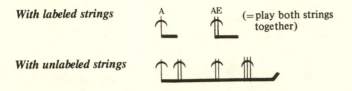

With labeled strings   (=play both strings together)

With unlabeled strings

B. Bowing on Top of the Bridge

For details, see Bowing behind the Bridge above.

Observe that the bridge symbol differs somewhat from that for bowing behind the bridge.

The pitch is indeterminate, although the sound changes from string to string. Fingering does not affect it.

N.B.: This notation must not be confused with *ponticello* playing, which actually means next to the bridge, rather than on top of it.

Chords

Solo players break a chord as they see fit. If, however, a specific break is wanted, square brackets should precede the chord to show which of the tones are to be played as double stops:

Individual orchestra players customarily do not play all the notes of a chord unless specifically instructed. Instead, the outside players of a desk play the upper note(s); the inside players the lower one(s).

It no double stops are wanted, the chord(s) must be marked *div. a 3* or *div. a 4,* respectively, followed by *non div.*

If the chords are to be broken, one tone after another without double stops, an arpeggio sign may be used (see Arpeggio, page 3 f), but it is best to write out such effects. Arpeggio chords occur chiefly in solo parts, but a continuous up and down arpeggio may also occur in a section, in which case it, too, is best written out. If such passages are fairly long, the initial written-out arpeggios may be followed by regularly notated arpeggio chords marked *etc. sim.:*

The double-arpeggio signs may also be omitted, since *etc. sim.* should be sufficiently explicit.

Damping (*Étouffer*)

Damping the string(s) after playing (unlike muffling while playing—see Muffling, page 312):

Double Stops

What was said in the section on Chords, above, also applies here: individual orchestra players usually play a double stop *divisi* (divided), the outside players of a section playing the upper note; the inside players, the lower one.

If double stops are wanted (i.e., all players playing both notes), a square bracket should precede each such double stop:

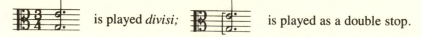

Prolonged passages should be marked *non div.* or *div.*, respectively:

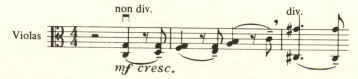

Unison double stops (playing the same pitch on two strings) are identified either with double stems or with double notes. Both notations are acceptable, but they should not be mixed in the same composition:

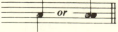

Fingering without Bowing

Specified pitches

Random or approximate pitches

Fingernail Flick

Flick the right-hand thumb from the second finger, or the second finger from the thumb, so that the nail will strike a string:

Vcl.

An explanatory note on first occurrence should be given.

Harmonics

A. In Scores

All harmonics, whether natural or artificial, should be notated at sounding pitch, topped by a small harmonics circle. (A zero should not be used, since it denotes an open string rather than a harmonic.)

To avoid confusion, it is advisable to mention at the beginning of a composition that all harmonics are notated at sounding pitch.

The notation of natural harmonics usually does not indicate the string on which to play the harmonic, nor where to touch it to produce the desired pitch. These details are generally left to the player. If a specific string is wanted, however, it should be indicated either by its roman numeral (counting from the highest string down) or by *sul D, sul A,* etc.

If it is found desirable to include the tablature notation for artificial harmonics (for example, as a guide for the copyist extracting parts, or if the score is to be used for playing), the tablature notes should be added; where applicable, with small note-heads and in parentheses:

Double-bass harmonics are occasionally notated at sounding pitch, in G-clef, even though the regular notes are notated one octave above actual sound. If this is done, the words *actual pitch* (or *suono reale* for international convenience) must be placed at each occurrence, or a general footnote put at the beginning of the score:

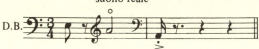

B. In Parts

Natural harmonics should be notated as in the score.

Artificial harmonics should be notated in tablature (full size) and the sounding pitches with small note-heads in parentheses, either above the tablature or immediately behind it, as space permits. (Note that the diamond-shaped note-heads of the tablature are *always* open.)

Double-bass harmonics must be notated at the same pitch as the regular notes. The sounding pitches of tablature notation are best omitted because they are usually too high for proper bass-clef notation and thus too cumbersome to accommodate.

Muffling

Bowing on one or two open strings while the left hand muffles them (without creating harmonics!):

(Compare the use of the same sign in Damping, page 310, where the strings are muffled after having been played.)

Pizzicato

A. Bartók or Snap Pizzicato

The string is plucked straight up from the fingerboard, between two fingers, so that it snaps back sharply:

B. Buzz Pizzicato

The string must rebound and vibrate against the fingernail.

To assure proper execution, verbal instructions should be added on first occurrence.

C. Fingernail Pizzicato

The string is plucked with a fingernail:

The fingernail symbol may also be drawn: ⌒

D. Left-Hand Pizzicato

In combination with bowed notes, the cross must appear at the note to be plucked:

N.B.: The plus sign (+) is so well established as the sign for left-hand pizzicato in string notation that it would be unwise to change it even though it is also used as the sign for muting, especially in horn notation.

E. Pizz./Finger

Pluck the first note; finger the second note without plucking:

(The second note is full size, unlike the second note in pizzicato glissando.)
An explanatory note must be provided on first occurrence.

F. Pizzicato Glissando

Pluck the first note; immediately begin to slide the left-hand finger to the indicated pitch (small note) or, in the second example, to a higher pitch ad lib.:

Specified final pitch and duration   *Free*

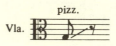

(The second note is small, unlike
the second note in pizz./finger.)

G. Strumming (Fast Arpeggio)

If a chord is marked *pizz.*, the player understands that the chord is to be strummed (arpeggiated) from the bottom up. If the chord is to be strummed downward, a small downward arrow should be placed above it.

If a fast succession of the same chord is to be strummed, the player will arpeggiate it up and down. Small arrows may, however, be placed above the chords to assure proper execution:

See also Arpeggio, page 3.

H. Two-Finger Pizzicato

If two strings are to be plucked simultaneously, precede the notes with a square bracket:

This playing mode is best suited for cellos and basses, as in the following example:

N.B.: It is advisable to add the verbal instruction *2 fingers* in orchestral parts. For solo players, the bracket should prove sufficient. (See also Double Stops, page 310.)

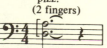

Slapping the Strings

A verbal instruction, such as *slap with palm of hand,* must be added on first occurrence:

With specified pitches   *With unspecified pitches*

This effect requires that the hand bounce off the strings immediately, or they will not reverberate.

Because of the need for very short slaps, no long note-values are involved, and thus no need for white "note-heads" to express half and whole notes. It is suggested that only flagged notes with rests be used.

If the hand is to remain on the strings after slapping them, no pitches need to be indicated, since different fingerings will not affect the sound. A verbal instruction (*strike strings with palm*) and notes with x-shaped note-heads, placed above the staff, should be used:

strike strings w.
palm of hand

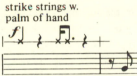

Tailpiece

To indicate bowing on the tailpiece, draw wedges through the stems. The note-heads should be x-shaped and placed either on a single line, or on a separate line below the staff, with the stems extending above the staff.

Single-line notation   *Staff notation*

XVII. *Taped (Prerecorded) Sound*

Electronic Notation   316   *Continuous versus Interrupted*
Cuing of Taped Sounds   317   *Tape*   320
A. *Notation of Sounds*   317
B. *Notation of Rhythm and Meter, etc.* 318

Electronic Notation

In the field of prerecorded or taped sound, notation serves four purposes:

1. As a composer's worksheet.

2. As a visual aid to the listener's understanding of the music. These "listeners' scores" may omit a great deal of secondary or background material in order to focus more effectively on important "themes" or other primary ingredients. In other words, such scores need not be (and in fact seldom are) *complete* records of *all* occurrences.

The notation of a listeners' score may range from very freely invented graphics (which reinterpret the taped sounds, with or without the aid of colors) all the way to highly controlled and detailed drawings, such as graphs, calibrations, curves and other lines and shapes, letters, numerals, and abbreviations, plus an arsenal of symbols which occasionally even includes conventional notation.

3. As entrance cues for performers (musicians, actors, dancers) of works in which taped sounds and performance actions have to be coordinated.

4. As permanent graphic documents for use by theorists and students who wish to reenact the process of producing a tape from a composer's notation.

The least frequent use of electronic notation, at least at the present state of development, is for instant, live performance, and since this guidebook deals exclusively with notation for live performance, electronic notation is covered rather briefly and selectively. The following chapter concentrates on the third of the categories above.

Cuing of Taped Sounds

The virtually unlimited possibilities for taped sounds preclude any universally appropriate system of notation. This, in turn, presents problems regarding entrance cues for the performer of any live music that has to be synchronized with the taped sounds. The choice of the notational method for such cues must always be decided from case to case, depending on the particular kinds of taped sounds involved and the kinds of interactions required for the performance.

A. Notation of Sounds

1. ORDINARY PITCHED SOUNDS
Cues are notated the same as cues for ordinary live music.

2. UNCONVENTIONALLY PITCHED SOUNDS (MICROTONES, SLIDES, ETC.)
See the section on Microtones, page 67 ff.

3. APPROXIMATE PITCHES OR PITCH LEVELS
X-shaped note-heads or headless stems are best suited (encircled x's for half and whole notes):

Symbolic notation

or

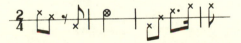

Spatial notation

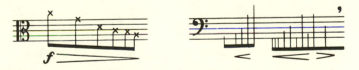

4. INDEFINABLY PITCHED SOUNDS
These are bands of sound, gradually rising or falling, growing wider or narrower, vacillating between definable and indefinable pitches, but without rhythmic impulses or patterns. Lines or bands suggesting expansions and contractions, as well as up and down movements, should be used. Degrees of density, pitch definition, and other characteristics, can be suggested by changing the bands' in-

side areas from blank, via hatching and cross hatching, or via different degrees of grey, to black. Dynamics should be placed below the staff. Verbal descriptions should be added. In short, visual analogues must be created which trace the changing sounds:

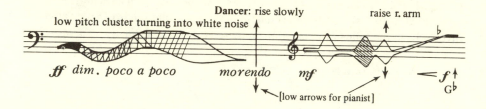

It is helpful to use arrows to indicate points at which live sounds or actions should enter, coincide, or drop out.

5. WHITE NOISE AND RELATED SOUNDS

White noise is a hissing sound consisting of an infinitely close, equidistant "cluster" of frequencies through the entire audible sound spectrum. White noise is best represented by a broad horizontal band, blank or hatched. (Solid black bands, such as are used for instrumental cluster notation, have been found to be less effective for instant recognition because their darkness contradicts the concept of "white" noise. The band should be labeled *White Noise,* and dynamics should be added below.

Abrupt or gradual modifications, such as norrowing the overall range, or stressing the higher, middle, or lower frequencies ("pink noise," "blue noise," etc.), or changes from discernible pitches or chords to white noise and vice versa, should be shown with changes in the width of the band and/or with changes in the density of the hatching, along with verbal indications.

6. OTHER SOUNDS

Most other electronic sounds are more elusive and do not even fit into the vague categories of shapes and "fillings" of bands mentioned so far. Appropriate analogues must be invented from case to case and supplied with verbal descriptions if at all possible, to help the performer recognize the sounds with which he must coordinate. As mentioned before, labeled arrows for proper coordination are always useful, too, unless the taped sounds are sufficiently obvious in character to make arrows unnecessary.

Concrète sounds, especially if not too distorted, present fewer cuing problems, if any. If distorted beyond recognition, they will automatically fall into the categories dealt with above.

B. Notation of Rhythm and Meter, etc.

1. ORDINARY METRIC/RHYTHMIC ORGANIZATION
Cues are notated as in ordinary live music.

2. SEPARATION OF RHYTHM AND SOUND
Because of the frequent difficulty of notating the sound of taped music efficiently and convincingly, metric/rhythmic notation often emerges as the most dependable means of cuing. In such cases, the sounds are notated separately from the rhythm: the sound notation usually consists of quite free visual analogues with or without descriptive matter, while the rhythmic notation is placed underneath or above (using x-shaped note-heads) and must be as explicit and precise as the sounds permit, whether in symbolic or spatial notation.

3. ARROWS
If the taped sounds do not lend themselves to any rhythmic interpretation, they must be examined for other clearly discernible phenomena. If such can be found, arrows should be drawn at suitable places in the score, pointing to the performer's (i.e., live) material and serving as guideposts.

4. "BEAT-STROKES" OR "BEAT-BARS"
These graphic devices (usually measured in half seconds or seconds) are most effective if used with a metronome or a click track, at least during practicing and rehearsals. Without the help of audible devices, beat-strokes naturally are less reliable, because the musicians are unlikely to count long periods of silent beats with sufficient accuracy to reach certain points in their music at exactly the same moment as the tape.

5. FERMATAS
If the music permits, fermatas are ideally suited to help coordinate entrances of either the tape or the live music or actions. (They can also help "lost" performers to find their places!)

C. Place of Tape Cues in Scores or Parts
It is best to place cues above the music. In piano music and other music notated on two staves, certain cues—especially rhythmic ones—may be placed between the staves as long as they do not interfere with dynamic markings, etc. In full scores, tape cues should be placed in the solo area above the strings.

If the tape sounds come from two or more speakers, cues are often separated, appearing above and below the music. This is not recommended for scores, where all cues, regardless of the number of speakers they represent, should always appear above the strings, on as many lines or staves as necessary.

In case of an unusually large number of speakers and cue lines, decisions will have to be made from case to case. No universally appropriate practices have been developed as yet.

Continuous versus Interrupted Tape

From a purely practical point of view, continuous tape is preferable to interrupted tape because it obviates the need for coordinating the tape operator(s) with the performer(s). Even so, certain tape events must be cued into the live music to assure proper synchronization.

If, on the other hand, the taped sound includes prolonged silences, one or more tape operators become necessary. In such cases, all tape entrances and stops must be cued carefully with identifying letters or numerals, on the tape leaders as well as in the score.

Appendix I: Neumatic Notation (Plainchant or Gregorian Chant) and Later Developments

The earliest music notation of the Christian era dates back to the ninth century and consists of neumes (from the Greek word meaning melody). Neumes are signs which, according to one hypothesis, derived from conductors' hand motions tracing the up and down movement of melody lines. Neumes generally were placed above the liturgical texts intended to be chanted.

Unlike modern notes, early neumes showed neither exact pitches nor durations. The imprecision of pitches was overcome when the neumes were placed on, above, or below horizontal lines which increased in number and eventually became standardized as the four-line staff still in use in modern publications of Roman Catholic plainchant (Gregorian chant).

While exact pitch notation was thus accomplished, no durational information was ordinarily conveyed. Whatever durational signs and interpretations are found in modern editions of Gregorian chant are usually recent additions.

The neume signs themselves became more and more stylized, until by the thirteenth century they had become the square- and diamond-shaped note-heads which to this day are found in publications of Gregorian chants, such as the *Liber Usualis* (*LU*). This collection, issued by the Benedictine monks of Solesmes, was first published in 1904 and represents the presently most widely accepted version of many chants.

Twentieth-century musicians must familiarize themselves with plainchant notation if they wish to deal with the music it represents, and especially if they wish to incorporate plainchant material in a composition.*

The following charts show the neumes as used in the Solesmes editions, and their modern equivalents.

---

* Even though the Roman Catholic church has moved away from using traditional plainchant in the service, chiefly because of the recent change from Latin to vernacular languages, the music itself continues of course to be of undiminished historical and musical value.

Clefs

The clefs indicate relative pitch only. There is no absolute pitch for plainchant. The choice of clefs is purely practical—to prevent the notes from going beyond one leger line at the top or bottom of the staff.

C clefs

F clefs

Neumes

SIMPLE NEUMES CONSISTING OF ONE, TWO, AND THREE NOTES AND HAVING INDIVIDUAL NAMES

Names of neumes	Early (St. Gall) neumes	Square (Roman) neumes	Modern notation
SINGLE NOTES			
Punctum			
Virga			

TWO-NOTE NEUMES

(Neumes consisting of two or more notes are also called ligatures.)

Ascending:
   Pes or **Podatus**

Descending:
   Clivis or **Flexa**

THREE-NOTE NEUMES

Ascending:
Scandicus

Descending:
Climacus

Observe that the
descending notes are
diamond-shaped.

Second note higher than the others:
Torculus

Second note lower than the others:
Porrectus

Note the oblique
two-note signs.

COMPOUND NEUMES (More than three notes)

Pes or
Podatus
subpunctis or
subbipunctis

Porrectus
flexus

Porrectus
subpunctis or
subbipunctis

Scandicus
flexus

Torculus
resupinus

There are many more compound neumes, but once the principle of such combinations is understood, all of them can be read easily.

DOUBLE AND TRIPLE NEUMES

There is no certainty concerning how these neumes were intended to be performed. Present-day custom is to sing them as long notes, equivalent to the total duration of the respective note-heads, possibly with a very slight stress at the outset and on each subsequent note:

Double notes also occur as part of a neume. Among such instances are:

LIQUESCENT NEUMES

There are two major categories: notes of small size, which are to be lightly touched only, and the *quilisma,* which may have been intended as a slight inflective tremolo or slide (it normally represents the middle tone of an ascending third).

Small-note Neumes

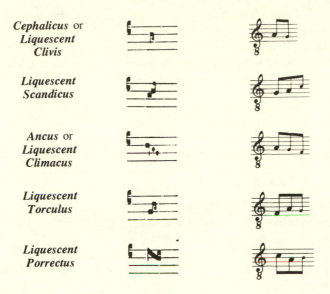

Cephalicus or ***Liquescent Clivis***	
Liquescent Scandicus	
Ancus or ***Liquescent Climacus***	
Liquescent Torculus	
Liquescent Porrectus	

Quilisma

Many transcriptions into modern notation indicate the *quilisma* with the common zigzag ornament known as trill, *tremblement, Schneller,* etc., but the sign is used merely to denote "ornament":

Accidentals

Flats and an occasional natural are the only accidentals used in plainchant notation.

The flat is placed before a neume or group of neumes that includes the note(s) to be lowered; i.e., the flat does not necessarily appear directly in front of the respective note(s). The flat must be repeated before subsequent groups of notes.

Wherever there is doubt concerning whether a flat is or is not still valid, another flat or a natural appears.

For examples see Compound Neumes above: the *Pes* or *Podatus subbipunctis* has a flat directly in front of the note to be lowered; the *Porrectus subpunctis* has a flat in front of a neume whose fourth note is to be lowered.

The Solesmes Editions (*Liber Usualis* or *LU*)

The most prominent additions found in the publications of the monks of Solesmes concern the *ictus,* and variations in the durations of the notes.

THE ICTUS

The ictus—a short, vertical stroke or *episema* above or below a note—is intended to assure the chant's subdivision into an irregular, ever-changing mixture of two-note and three-note grouplets, regardless of the syllable stresses of the text, and without actual accentuation or prolongation of the notes thus marked.* In general, the ictuses appear only sporadically. Those that are not indicated are considered self-evident.

The following example shows the ictuses as quite independent of the text, as well as of the neume groupings (see, for example, the ictus on the last note of *térra*):

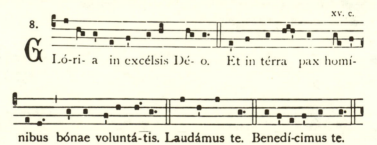

DURATIONS

A tenuto line or *horizontal episema* above or below a note calls for a very slight prolongation (but not an accent). If several successive notes are to be prolonged in this way, the tenuto lines are connected, forming one line, as at the end of the following example:

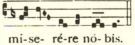

mi-se- ré-re nó- bis.

---

*The monks' invocation against stresses and prolongations—in opposition to the dictionary definition of an ictus—makes the proper interpretation seem somewhat mysterious, but the singers' mere awareness of the ictuses does seem to infuse the music with a fascinating rhythmic life.

A dot following a note doubles its duration. The example above (*Gloria*) shows several such dots. If both notes of a two-note neume are dotted, the dots are aligned vertically, as at the end of the following example:

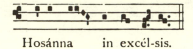

Hosánna   in excél-sis.

PAUSES

In general, a combination of a tenuto line and an ictus on the same note may act as a breath mark. A comma   is also found.

Longer pauses are indicated by a quarter barline   or a half bar   .

Sections are subdivided by a full bar   or a double bar   .

Transcription into Modern Notation

It has become customary to use eighth notes, so that neumatic groups can be indicated with beams, while individual notes are written with flags, as shown in the following examples. (The chant is taken from the *Liber Usualis* and the transcription from the *Saint Andrew Daily Missal* issued in 1962 by Dom Gaspar Lefebvre and the monks of St. Andrew's Abbey, and published by Biblica, Bruges, Belgium):

THE PLAINCHANT NOTATION (*Liber Usualis* version):

XI. c.

5.

S Anctus, * Sánctus, Sán-ctus Dóminus Dé- us

Sá- ba- oth. Plé-ni sunt caé- li et tér-ra gló-ri- a

tú- a. Ho- sánna in excél- sis. Bene-díctus qui vé-

nit in nómine Dómi-ni. Ho- sánna in excél- sis.

The *St. Andrew Transcription* into modern notation:

The numeral 5 at the beginning (of both versions) means that the chant is in the fifth mode (also called Lydian).

At the very end of each staff (except the last) in the *LU* version, a vestigial note-sign appears: the *custos*. It shows the first pitch of the next line and is intended to help the singer keep his pitch while going from line to line. This practice continued to be used in every kind of music, right into the Baroque era.

The accents (∧) are not found in the *Liber Usualis* version.

The slurs substitute for beams in combinations that cannot be beamed because they involve quarter notes.

Liquescent notes are rendered as small eighth notes.* (Note that they are *not* of shorter duration; they are merely different in character.)

---

*The liquescent note on *sán* of the first *Hosánna* is here full size—no doubt a misprint. The second time it is correct, but this time the slur begins too late—on B-flat instead of the preceding C.

Tenuto lines (horizontal episemas) have been added occasionally where the *LU* has none. The elongated tenuto line covering more than one note has been retained even though it is not "modern."

The quilisma appears as a zig-zag of a staff-line, rather than as a separate ornament.

An eighth rest has been added at each complete barline (placed rather inconsistently either before or after the barline). In the *LU* this rest is only implied.

NOTE-HEAD TRANSCRIPTION

Another approach to modern notation is to use black note-heads and no stems. Neumatic groupings are then indicated by slurs instead of beams. This method prevents the performers from being influenced, at least subconsciously, by the unintended metric rigidity implied by eighth and quarter notes.*

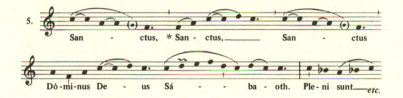

Text

Note that the *LU* version has accents on all stressed syllables, while the more recent St. Andrew version has accents only on words with more than two syllables. This latter method has also been followed in the note-head version. Both the *LU* and the St. Andrew versions have a single hyphen directly after the hyphenated syllable, while the note-head version follows the present-day practice of centering one or more hyphens between the syllables, and to use extenders on single or final syllables if sung on more than two notes.

Asterisks (*) in the text mean that the subsequent passages are to be sung by the full chorus. (By implication, the music preceding an asterisk is sung by one to four solo voices.)

---

*Note-head notation is also found with a four-line staff and with old clefs. Once one transcribes the neumatic notation, however, one might as well go all the way and not retain purely technical vestiges for the sake of lending "archaic flavor" to the renotation.

The Historic Development of Notation
(greatly simplified)
from Square Neumes to Modern Notes and Rests

SQUARE NEUMES (SINCE 12TH CENTURY)		BLACK MENSURAL NOTATION (c.1250 –c. 1450)	WHITE MENSURAL NOTATION (c.1400 –c.1600)			MODERN NOTATION (SINCE c.1600)	
			Notes	*Rests*		*Notes*	*Rests*
	Maxima						
	Longa				Longa		
						no longer in use	
	Brevis				Brevis		
						now rarely used	
	Semibrevis				Whole		
	Minima				Half		
	Semiminima				Quarter		
						*used till c.1900	
	Fusa				Eighth		
	Semifusa				Sixteenth etc.		

Tablature

During the fifteenth century, when instrumental music began to gain independence, notational systems (called tablatures) were invented which, instead of indicating pitches, showed how to manipulate the instrument to produce them. Particularly prevalent were several systems of lute and keyboard tablature.

With the exception of lute tablature, which persisted to the end of the eighteenth century, most tablature notation faded again in the seventeenth century, when composers began to use pitch notation for all music, vocal as well as instrumental.

In twentieth-century music, the only vestiges of tablature notation are the guitar and ukulele symbols used in popular music. In music for bowed strings, the notation of artificial harmonics is also a form of tablature in that the diamond-shaped notes indicate finger positions rather than the desired pitches.

While the twentieth-century musician may have to read and transcribe plainchant notation, he is not likely to be exposed to tablature, unless he specializes in the period in question. Most of the music originally notated in tablature is now available in modern notation.

Scordatura is also a form of tablature. For details, see pages 246 f (Harp) and 311 f (String Harmonics).

Appendix II: The History and Operation of the Index of New Musical Notation and the International Conference on New Musical Notation

In the late 1960s, the author, together with Richard F. French, then professor of music at Union Theological Seminary in New York (and presently at Yale University), applied to the Rockefeller Foundation for the funding of a research project to survey the notational scene and to find out if some form of standardization might be possible, at least for those new signs and procedures that permit standardization. (As mentioned elsewhere, intentionally ambiguous notation was not to be considered.)

Our application was endorsed by four American composers representative of the major stylistic trends of contemporary music at that time: Earle Brown, Elliott Carter, Bernhard Heiden, and Gunther Schuller. Furthermore, The Library of the Performing Arts at Lincoln Center, New York, in the persons of its chief, Thor Wood, and head of its music division, Frank C. Campbell, offered to house the project.

In 1970, the Rockefeller Foundation granted funds for a three-year operation (later expanded to four years), and the Index of New Musical Notation was established with the author as its director.

Before initiating the actual operation of the Index project, it was ascertained that no similar efforts toward notational standardization were underway elsewhere. Next, a full-time assistant was found—Gerald Warfield, then of Princeton University—and procedures were worked out for the notational analysis of scores and parts containing new devices and methods, etc. The "Notation Analysis Form," (see pages 334–5), was the outcome. It includes twenty-three categories, of which only the first six are actually spelled out (box in upper right of first sheet) because they pertain to all music, unlike the remaining seventeen (Nos. 7–23), which change from piece to piece. These seventeen items cover the following criteria:

7. Tempo and Time Signature(s)
8. Microtones

  9. Timbre
10. Articulation
11. Sound-Descriptive Notation
12. Manipulative Notation
13. Unconventional Sound Source(s)
14. With Tape or Electronics
15. Notational System
16. Multi-Media
17. Theatrics
18. Score Layout
19. Signs for Instruments or Equipment
20. Symbols Peculiar to Specific Instruments, Instrument Types, or Voice
21. Performed from Score
22. Ambiguities
23. Cross References

An x in the right-hand margin at a particular numeral shows that the score contains innovative material of that numeral's category. In this way it was possible to see at a glance the kinds of new notation contained in any one score.

The notational innovations were also incorporated in a card file arranged according to musical phenomena, instruments, and voice. Thus all new signs, etc., were recorded from two different vantage points:

  1. by context, as they appear in a given composition;
  2. isolated from the context of specific compositions, to show all symbols used for the same musical phenomena.

In addition to the above, a file of signs and symbols was set up to show which symbols were used for more than one musical phenomenon.

Realizing that all examinations up to this point had dealt only with scores and parts already in existence, i.e., with the past (be it ever so recent), an eight-page Notation Questionnaire was worked out to elicit opinions and suggestions concerning notational preferences for future compositions.

This questionnaire (in English, French, and German) was distributed worldwide (on request). Roughly 1,000 copies were sent out, and about 300 were returned. These were classified as exceptional, adequate, and insufficient (the last category gratifyingly small).

The answers in the first two categories were incorporated in the files and all findings processed statistically to determine which devices had already achieved sufficiently widespread acceptance to qualify as candidates for standardization. For example, signs such as the square fermata for long holds, or the Bartók piz-

TISHCHENKO, Boris (b. Leningrad, 1939). The Third Symphony (1970). MY3blKA

2 MICRO-FORM

Material for improvisatory sections is given in boxes as in the
brass and percussion parts below, or is drawn from the contents
of chord clusters as in the piano part:
(p.54)

Degrees of determinacy ➤	EXACT	APPROX	FREE	CHOICE	CHANCE	
1 MACRO-FORM	X					1
2 MICRO-FORM	X	X				2 X
3 DURATIONS	X					3 X
4 PITCHES	X	X				4 X
5 INTENSITIES	X					5 —
6 SYNCHRO.	X					6 —

7	X
8	—
9	X
10	X
11	—
12	—
13	—
14	—
15	—
16	—
17	—
18	—
19	—
20	X
21	—
22	X
23	—

Note that rhythmic configurations are sometimes given, as in the case of the horn
part above. The jagged lines apparently suggest the contour of the improvisa-
tions.

A similar indication for continuation is shown in #9b--first example.

3 DURATIONS

= ritardando and accelerando, respectively; the total duration
of the figure is at times explicitly indicated by the use of
a "time signature" (above or below the figure) and a bracket
which extends for the length of the notes in question:

e.g.,

(p.1, pno.)
the accelerando must take
place within the time of five sixteenth-notes, or

or:
(p.1, ob.)
the accelerando takes place within
the time of a quarter-note.

4 PITCHES

Clusters are notated as in the example for #2 and as on p.47:

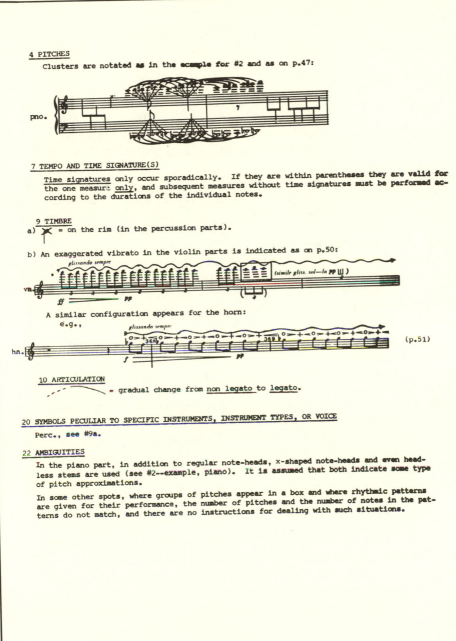

pno.

7 TEMPO AND TIME SIGNATURE(S)

Time signatures only occur sporadically. If they are within parentheses they are valid for the one measure only, and subsequent measures without time signatures must be performed according to the durations of the individual notes.

9 TIMBRE

a) ✗ = on the rim (in the percussion parts).

b) An exaggerated vibrato in the violin parts is indicated as on p.50:

vn.

A similar configuration appears for the horn:

e.g.,

hn.

(p.51)

10 ARTICULATION

⌣ = gradual change from non legato to legato.

20 SYMBOLS PECULIAR TO SPECIFIC INSTRUMENTS, INSTRUMENT TYPES, OR VOICE

Perc., see #9a.

22 AMBIGUITIES

In the piano part, in addition to regular note-heads, x-shaped note-heads and even headless stems are used (see #2--example, piano). It is assumed that both indicate some type of pitch approximations.

In some other spots, where groups of pitches appear in a box and where rhythmic patterns are given for their performance, the number of pitches and the number of notes in the patterns do not match, and there are no instructions for dealing with such situations.

zicato, are already in universal use, while the notations of microtones or even of percusion rolls have by no means achieved comparable uniformity.

In cases of insufficient data the members of the Index* exercised their own judgment.

The Ghent Conference

When Mr. Jan Kestelyn of the music division of the Belgian Ministry of Culture came to New York, he visited the Index project. Through his good offices, contact was initiated with Professor Jan L. Broeckx, director of the Seminar for Musicology at the State University of Ghent, Belgium, and his principal assistant, Dr. Herman Sabbe.

The outcome was the International Conference on New Musical Notation, which was held in Ghent, October 22–25, 1974, as a joint undertaking of the Ghent University and the Index project. The Conference was sponsored by the [American] Music Library Association and the Belgian Ministry of Culture, as well as the State University of Ghent, assisted by the staff of the Centre Belge de Documentation Musicale (CeBeDeM) in Brussels, and especially by the untiring efforts of CeBeDeM's scientific advisor, Dr. Diana von Volborth-Danis, who had been interested in the Index project almost from its inception.

American financial assistance was derived from the extension of the Rockefeller grant mentioned earlier and a Ford Foundation grant which enabled the Index to hire additional help for the preparation of the Conference and, later, for summing up its results.

The Conference was attended by over eighty active participants from seventeen countries (see list on page 337 ff).

Prior to the Conference, the Index had prepared close to 400 proposals for new signs and procedures to be considered for endorsement by the Conference. All participants, regardless of their musical specialties, received copies of all proposals. They also received copies of the Criteria for the Selection of New Notational Signs and Procedures. These had been worked out and used by the Index and were subsequently adopted by the Conference:

NOTATION SUITED FOR STANDARDIZATION

1. Proposals for standardization of new notational devices should be made only in cases where a sufficient need is anticipated.

2. Given a choice, the preferable notation is the one that is an extension of traditional notation.

3. The notation should lend itself to immediate recognition. This means it should be as self-evident as possible.

---

* By this time three part-time research assistants had been added to the staff—Frances Barulich, John Epperson, and Bruce J. Taub—and Gerald Warfield was promoted to associate director.

4. The notation should be sufficiently distinct graphically to permit a reasonable amount of distortion due to variations in handwriting and different writing implements.

5. Given a choice, the preferable notation is the one that is spatially economical.

6. Given a choice, the preferable notation is the one that has already received relatively wide acceptance.

7. Analogous procedures in different instrumental families should, if possible, be notated similarly.

8. The notation used should be the most efficient for the organizational principles that underlie the respective composition.

NOTATION UNSUITED FOR STANDARDIZATION

1. Graphic notation which is unique to the composition in which it appears, i.e., notation which is an integral part of the creative effort.

2. Notation specifically designed for nonstandard situations.

3. Notation of procedures or effects so rarely used that verbal instructions would be more efficient.

The participants were divided into groups, each charged with a special subject. On the last day of the Conference, the spokesmen of each group reported their findings and proposals to the full assembly for general acceptance or further deliberation.

All accepted signs, etc., are contained in the complete Conference Report published in *Interface* (see Bibliography).

Participants in the International Conference on New Musical Notation Ghent, Belgium, October 22–25, 1974 (Affiliations, etc., as of the time of the conference)

Ammann, Benno (Composer, Basel, Switzerland)
Anderson, Ronald (Trumpeter, New York, U.S.A.)
Bartholomée, Pierre (Conductor, Pianist, Composer, Brussels, Belgium)
Beckwith, John (Dean, Faculty of Music, University of Toronto, Canada)
Bengtsson, Ingmar (Prof. of Musicology, Uppsala University, Sweden)
Bernstein, Giora (Prof., Pomona College, Claremont, Calif., U.S.A.)
Blatter, Alfred (Horn Player, Composer, Editor Media Press, Urbana, Ill., U.S.A.)
Blauvelt, Frances (Singer, U.S.A.)

Bosseur, Jean-Yves (Composer, Musicologist, Paris, France)

Broeckx, Jan-Lea (Prof. of Musicology, State University, Ghent, Belgium)

Brown, Earle (Composer, Conductor, New York, U.S.A.)

Bruzdowicz, Joanna (Composer, Paris, France)

Bukspan, Yael (Musicologist, Tel Aviv, Israel)

Campbell, Charles (University of Miami, Coral Gables, Fla., U.S.A.)

Caskel, Christoph (Percussionist, Cologne, Germany [F.R.])

Castaldi, Paolo (Composer, Milan, Italy)

Coppens, Claude (Composer, Pianist, Ghent, Belgium)

Crumb, George (Composer, University of Pennsylvania, Philadelphia, U.S.A.)

De Meester, Louis (Composer, Ghent, Belgium)

Dempewolf, Jürgen (Musicologist, Berlin, Germany [F.R.])

De Smet, Raoul (Composer, Antwerp, Belgium)

Dianda, Hilda (Composer, Düsseldorf, Argentina/Germany [F.R.])

Elias, William (Editor, Composer, Managing Dir. Israel Music Institute, Tel Aviv, Israel)

Epperson, John (Staff Member, Index of New Musical Notation, New York, U.S.A.)

Fleming, Larry (St. Paul, Minn., U.S.A.)

French, Richard F. (Editor, Prof. of Musicology, Yale University, U.S.A.)

Godjevatz, Velizar (Author, New York, U.S.A.)

Goethals, Lucien (Composer, Institute of Psycho-Acoustics and Electronic Music, Ghent, Belgium)

Gottwald, Clytus (Choral Conductor, Musicologist, Stuttgart, Germany [F.R.])

Hambraeus, Bengt (Composer, Musicologist, McGill University, Montreal, Canada/Sweden)

Harris, Russell G. (Prof., Hamline University, St. Paul, Minn., U.S.A.)

Haubenstock-Ramati, Roman (Composer, Editor, Musikhochschule, Vienna, Austria)

Jenni, Donald M. (Composer, University of Iowa, U.S.A.)

Kabalewski, Wladislaw (Vice-Pres. Polish Authors' Society, Poland)

Kalish, Gilbert (Pianist, New York, U.S.A.)

Karkoschka, Erhard (Author, Conductor, Composer, Stuttgart, Germany [F.R.])

Kimbell, Michael A. (Clarinettist, Johnson State College, Vermont, U.S.A.)

Koenig, Wolfgang (Trombonist, Buir, Germany [F.R.])

Lehmann, Hans Ulrich (Composer, Zurich, Switzerland)

Lobaugh, Bruce (Chairman Dept. of Music, University of Regina, Canada)

Malec, Ivo (Composer, Delegate SACEM, France)

de Marez Oyens-Wansink, Tera (Composer, Genootschap van Nederlandse Componisten, Holland)

Makedonski, Kiril (Musicologist, Skopje, Yugoslavia)

McCarty, Frank L. (Percussionist, Composer, Electronicist, University of Pittsburgh, Pa., U.S.A.)

Meier, Gustav (Opera and Symphony Conductor, Eastman School of Music, Rochester, N.Y., U.S.A.)

Mutsaers, Henry (Canadian Music Centre, Toronto, Canada)

Nørgaard, Per (Composer, Copenhagen, Denmark)

Papineau-Couture, Jean (Composer, Pres. Canadian Music Centre, Canada)

Parent, Nils (Composer, Université Laval, Québec, Canada)

Pépin, Clermont (Composer, Delegate Ministère des Affaires Culturelles du Québec, Canada)

Raes, Godfried (Composer, Ghent, Belgium)

Read, Gardner (Composer, Author, Boston University, U.S.A.)

Reeder, Krystyna (Editor Universal Edition, London, England)

Reynolds, Roger (Composer, Dir. Center for Music Experimentation, University of California at San Diego, U.S.A.)

Rosseau, Norbert (Composer, Ghent, Belgium)

Rudzinski, Zbigniew (Composer, Delegate Polish Authors' Society, Poland)

Sabbe, Herman (Musicologist, State University, Ghent, Belgium)

Sandresky, Margaret (Prof., Salem College, North Carolina, U.S.A.)

Schernus, Herbert (Choral Conductor at WDR, Cologne, Germany [F.R.])

Schmidt, A. Warren (Waverly, Iowa, U.S.A.)

Schudel, Thomas (Dept. of Music, University of Regina, Canada)

Schuyt, Nico (Composer, Delegate Stichting Donemus, Amsterdam, Holland)

Schwartz, Elliott (Composer, Bowdoin College, Brunswick, Maine, U.S.A.)

Schwartz, Francis (Composer, Dir. Music Dept. University of Puerto Rico, Puerto Rico)

Sommer, Jürgen (Editor Bärenreiter-Verlag, Kassel, Germany [F.R.])

Souffriau, Arsène (Composer, Electronicist, Brussels, Belgium)

Steuermann, Clara (Pres. [American] Music Library Association; Archivist Arnold Schoenberg Institute, California, U.S.A.)

Stone, Kurt (Editor, Author, Musicologist, Dir. Index of New Musical Notation, New York, U.S.A.)

Stricz, Erich (Editor Universal Edition Vienna, Austria)

Szentkiralyi, Andräs (Composer, Fleckeby, Germany [F.R.])

Taub, Bruce L. (Composer, Staff Member, Index of New Musical Notation, New York, U.S.A.)

Tomaszewski, Mieczyslaw (Editor, Dir. Polish Music Editions, Cracow, Poland)

von Volborth-Danys, Diana (Editor, Delegate CeBeDeM (Centre Belge de Documentation Musicale), Brussels, Belgium)

Vouillemin, Sylvain (Composer, Dir. Conservatoire Liège, Delegate, SABAM, Brussels, Belgium)

Warfield, Gerald (Composer, Author, Assoc. Dir. Index of New Musical Notation, New York, U.S.A.)

Weisberg, Arthur (Conductor, Bassoonist, New York, U.S.A.)

Wood, Joseph (Composer, Oberlin College, Ohio, U.S.A.)
Wuorinen, Charles (Composer, Pianist, Conductor, New York, U.S.A.)
Wyner, Susan Davenny (Singer, New Haven, Conn., U.S.A.)
Zukofsky, Paul (Violinist, New York State University at Stony Brook, U.S.A.)

A fair number of additional people attended the plenary sessions as observers.

Appendix III: Facsimile Reproductions

A growing practice in the field of music publishing is to issue new music in facsimile reproductions. Although these have value as examples of the composer's own handwriting, such reproductions are almost always inferior in legibility to engraved or otherwise professionally produced editions.

Facsimile reproductions have become necessary for two reasons peculiar to our era:

1. The difficulty, if not impossibility, of reproducing most new notational signs and symbols with existing mechanical means, such as engravers' tools, music typewriters, transfer type, stamping, or electronic devices. Only autography is capable of dealing with new notation because it is independent of "prefabricated" dies, type, labels, etc.;

2. The negligible earnings from serious contemporary music, which make it almost impossible to retrieve the considerable cost of autography or any other method (typewriting, engraving, etc.), regardless of the notational system used.

In view of this double dilemma, the composer is well advised to strive toward meeting as many of the external requirements for a publishable manuscript as possible. Among the most important of these are the following:

1. Legibility, consistency, and uniformity in the sizes of the notes and the various signs and verbal instructions. To arrive at the proper proportions of the various sizes one should consult good engraved editions of standard music. At the same time one must remember that manuscripts are usually larger in format than the printed editions made from them, so that verbal instructions and vocal texts must be drawn or typed fairly large in order not to become illegible after reduction.

2. Uniformity of the format of the image area, i.e., the proportions of width versus height throughout a given score or set of parts. If the musical substance makes it unavoidable to produce an oversized page—usually necessitated by a temporary increase in staff-lines—great care should be taken to retain the format by way of increasing the width in proportion to the height of the oversized pages. This is usually accomplished with the help of a proportion wheel (available in larger stationery or art-supply stores), so that photographic reductions will result in an image area equal

to that of the regular pages. (Beware of first pages! The music must be condensed in height to make room for the title and the copyright notice, etc., because both must fit into the same image area.)

3. The horizontal spacing (width) of each line or brace of music should be sketched out first with light-blue pencil (which will not reproduce in photo-offset) to assure a good, proportionate distribution of the notes, etc., and to make sure that all lines end flush right. No music or verbal instructions should ever extend into the margins. (See also Spacings, page 44 ff).

4. In all music except conductors' scores and choral music, the planning must aim at practical page turns. Pages should be numbered properly: even numbers for left-hand pages, odd numbers for right-hand pages. If this is not done, right-hand pages spaced out for easy page turns may turn into left-hand pages because the printer was unaware of the significance of the intended layout.

5. If deshon paper ("transparencies") is used for music intended for facsimile publication, rather than for Ozalid reproduction only, the notes must be written on the staff-line side of the paper. It is advisable to use paper with staff-lines printed on both sides, because erasures can be made without having to restore erased staff-lines. The lines on the other side of the paper will be sufficient for reproduction by the Ozalid method. For photo-offset, however, the staff-lines must be restored, or the publisher notified that some of the surface lines are damaged, and special processes must be employed for making offset negatives or plates.

6. India ink or equivalent should be used, as well as a ruler and other graphic aids wherever possible. For typewritten texts and instructions, the use of a carbon ribbon is preferable to ordinary ribbons. (Electrographic pencils on transparent music paper are useful for Ozalid reproduction, but their imprecise outlines are not satisfactory for offset reproductions.)

Bibliography

This bibliography is highly selective and contains only a very small number of books and articles. It does not, for example, include collections, such as those by Erhard Karkoschka or Howard Risatti, nor any of the more personal guidebooks, such as David Cope's or Reginald Smith Brindle's. For these, and for related material, the reader should consult the comprehensive annotated bibliography (452 titles) which was produced by the Index of New Musical Notation under the direction of its associate director, Gerald Warfield (see below under Warfield).

Cole, Hugo. *Sounds and Signs: Aspects of Musical Notation*. London: Oxford University Press, 1974.

Hindemith, Paul. *Elementary Training for Musicians*. New York: Associated Music Publishers, 1946.

International Conference on New Musical Notation: Proceedings. Ed. Herman Sabbe, Kurt Stone, and Gerald Warfield. *Interface—Journal of New Music Research*, IV/1 (November 1975). Amsterdam, Holland: Swets & Zeitlinger.

Read, Gardner. *Music Notation—a Manual of Modern Practice*. Boston: Allyn and Bacon, 1964.

Rosenthal, Carl A. *Practical Guide to Music Notation for Composers, Arrangers and Editors*. New York: MCA Music, 1967.

Ross, Ted. *The Art of Music Engraving and Processing*. New York: Hansen Books, 1970.

Vinton, John, ed. *Dictionary of Contemporary Music*. New York: E. P. Dutton, 1974.

Warfield, Gerald. *Writings on Contemporary Music Notation—an Annotated Bibliography*. Prepared under Gerald Warfield's direction by the Index of New Musical Notation, Kurt Stone, director. Music Library Association Index and Bibliography Series, No. 16. Ann Arbor, Michigan, 1976.

Stone, Kurt. "New Music Notation—Why?" *Musical America* (in *High Fidelity*), XXIV/7 (July 1974), pp. MA16–20.

———. "New Notation for New Music" (Parts I and II), *Music Educators Journal*, LXIII/2 (October 1976), pp. 48–56, and LXIII/3 (November 1976), pp. 54–61.

———. "The Piano and the Avant-Garde," *The Piano Quarterly* LII (1965), pp. 14–28.

———. "Problems and Methods of Notation," *Perspectives of New Music*, I/2 (1963), pp. 9–31.

———. "Symposium on New Musical Notation," *Contemporary Music Newsletter*, VII/1 (January 1973), pp. 1–2.

Index

a2, a3, etc., 175–176
abbreviations, 3
   Perc., 205–213
   Strgs., 307
abnormal tuning (scordatura), harp, 246–247
accelerando beams, *see* feathered beams
accents, 4–6, 42–44
accidentals, 44–47, 53–56
   cancellations, *see* naturals
   cautionary, 55
   at clef changes, 54–55
   double sharps and double flats, 54
   microtonal, 67–71
   note-for-note, 55–56
   in scores, 55
   tied, 54–55
accidentals and cancellations in divisi parts, 166
aeolian tremolo, harp, 250
afterbeats, 77
air pressure, woodwinds, 191
air sound, winds, 186
aperiodic durations, 92
appoggiatura, 22
approximate pitches, 66, 70–71
arithmetrical progression, iii, 120
arpeggio, 3–4
arpeggio/non arpeggio, harp, 228
arrowheads, 122
arrows, 24–25, 99, 142–145, 161–162
   for durational equivalents, 127
   for dynamics, 17
   for microtones, 67, 70
arrow-shaped note-heads, 31
articulation, 4, 6, 27
   repeated, 33
   signs in context, 42–44
   syllables, 186–187

Babbitt, Milton, 112, 181
Bach, Johann Sebastian, 35

band score, standard setup, 173–174, 176
barlines, 6–9
  dotted, 8, 115
  double, 8–9
  vertical alignment, 8
Baroque music, 22
Bartók, Béla, 82, 84f, 86
Bartók pizzicato, strings, 312
beaming, 27–30, 109–110, 113–114
  by beat-units, 14, 85, 109–110, 120, 124
  compound meters, 110
  cross rhythms, 115
  irregular metric divisions within a measure, 114
  irregular note divisions, 26–30, 111–112
  polymetric music, 116–119
  rhythmic versus metric, 114
  by rhythms and phrases, 82
  simple binary measures, 110–113
  simple meters, 110
  simple ternary measures, 113
  syncopated entrances, 15
  in two-staff notation, 12–14
beams, 48, 50
  bridging, 15–16
  corners, 13–14
  extended, 15–16, 28–30; *see also* duration beams
  fractional, 12
  graphic aspects, 9
  metric divisions, 14
  slanted, 10–12
  versus flags in vocal music, 293
  with different time-values, 13–14
  with stemlets, 15–16
beater indications, percussion, 220
beaters, pictograms, *see* mallet pictograms
beat-units, 14, 85, 109–110, 127, 178
Beethoven, Ludwig van, 261
bending the pitch
  harp, 229
  winds, 187
Berio, Luciano, iv, 99–100
bipartite progressions, 129–132
bisbigliando, harp, 229–231
bocca chiusa, voice, 25
Boulez, Pierre, iv, 95–96, 109
bowing, 35, 308, 315
boxed pitches, 142
brackets, 23–24
  versus slurs in irregular note divisions, 26–29
Brahms, Johannes, 129

Brant, Henry, 172
brass, notation, 197–204
breathing, winds, 35
breathy sound, winds, 186–187
broken lines, 25
    slurs, 122
Brown, Earle, iv, 104, 332
brush swishes, percussion, 221
Bussotti, Sylvano, iv, 105

Cage, John, iv
Carter, Elliott, 35, 86f, 90ff, 109, 112, 120, 172, 180, 332
chance, 154
choice, iii
choices, 152–153
Chopin, Frédéric, 261
choral music, 55
    divisi parts, 165–166
choral scores, dynamics, 32
clef changes, 46, 57
clefs, 44–45, 56–57
    in horn notation, 57, 199–200
    in scores and parts, 72–73
    transposing, 71–73
clusters, 57–63
    ensemble music, 58–63
    fast, rhythmic, 62–63
    harp, 231
    organ, 274
    piano, 259–260
    woodwinds, 195
Cole, Hugo, 122
commas, 128–129
common denominator, 120
composite meters, rests, 135
compound meters, 121, 181
compromise meters, 118–119
conductor's signs, 158–160
conventional notation, *see* traditional notation
Cowell, Henry, 259, 274
cracked tone, brass, 197
cross rhythms, 82, 115
C-scores, 71–73
cue lines for glissando, 21
cues, 49, 71
    for missing instruments, 161
    in parts, 160–162
    for reinforcement, 161
cuing taped sounds, 317–318

da capo, 34–35
dal segno, 34–35
damping, harp, 231–235
dead stick, percussion, 221
decibel levels, 16
diamond-shaped note-heads, 30–31, 219
divisi (div.), 175–176
divisi parts
    accidentals and cancellations, 166
    choral, 165–166
    instrumental, 164–167
    slurs and ties, 167
dotted barlines, 8, 115
dotted lines, 25
dotted notes, dot positions, 125–126
double barlines, 8–9
double sharps and flats, *see* accidentals
double stems, 49
double strokes, 128–129
double trills, 25
drag, percussion, 221
duplets, 129–132
durational equivalents, 127
duration beams, 96, 99
durations, 81–110, 124–147
    nonmetric, 92
dynamics, ii, 16–19
    absolute, 16
    by note-sizes, 18–19
    placement, 31–32

editions of old music, 129, 327–331
electronic music, *see* taped sound
embouchure, woodwinds, 192
equiton, 108
étouffer, harp, 231
expression marks, 32–33

facsimile reproductions, vi, 341–342
falsetto voice, 293
feathered beams, 23, 124
fermatas, 43, 128–129
    cornered, 99
fifteenth transpositions, 25
final barlines, 9
fingering
    brass, 198
    strings, 311
    woodwinds, 193–194
fingernail

buzz, harp, 235
    glissando, harp, 236–237
    plucking, harp, 235
fingernails, brass, 198
flags, 49
flam, percussion, 221
flat (non arpeggio), harp, 228, 235
flutter lips, 25
flutter tongue, 25, 188
    voice, 293–294
foreign languages, 3
    in vocal music, 301
four-hand piano music, 258–259
fragmentation in contemporary music, 94
French, Richard F., 332

Gabrieli, Giovanni, 288
geometric progression, iii, 120
Gesualdo, Carlo, 283ff
Ghent Conference, i, iv–v, 336–340
    participants, 337–340
gli altri, 176
glissando effects, brass, 199–200
glissandos, 19–21, 63–64
    dynamics and timbres, 64
    harp, 236–238
gong/tam-tam, 220
grace notes, 21–22, 42, 49–51
graphic notation, 103–107, 109
Gregorian Chant notation, *see* neumatic notation
grids, 23, 215
group stems, 162–163
growl, brass, 199
gushing chords, harp, 237

half pedal, harp, 239–240
half valve, brass, 25, 199
hand pop, brass, 200
hand stopping, horn, 201–202
hand tremolo, voice, 25
harmonics, 65
    harp, 239–240
    piano, 261–262
    strings, 311–312
    woodwinds, 192
harp
    notation, 226–256
    pedals, 244–245
    range, 246
Haubenstock-Ramati, Roman, iv

Hauptstimme/Nebenstimme, 18
Heiden, Bernhard, 332
hemiola, 129
Henze, Hans Werner, 179
highest note, 65
Hindemith, Paul, 281, 283
historical survey of new rhythmic notation, 82–108
history of notation, 321–331
    table, 330
horizontal lines, 22–26
horn
    stopped, 201
    transpositions, 199–200
humming while playing, winds, 188

ictus, 326
implicit graphics, iii, 26, 103–107
improvisation, iii
indeterminacy, iii, 152–157
indeterminate pitches, 66
    clusters, 61–63
    repeats, 154–155
Index of New Musical Notation, i, iii–v, 332–340
instructions, 32f
    placement, 26
International Conference on New Musical Notation, *see* Ghent Conference
irregular note divisions, 41–42, 129–133
    duplets, 129–132
    positions of numerals, etc., 26–30
    septuplets, 129–130
    specifications, 132–133

Karkoschka, Erhard, iii, 108
keyboard reductions, 281–291
key signatures, 44–45
key slap, winds, 187, 192–193
Kilar, Wojciech, 60
Kirchner, Leon, 119
kiss
    brass, 203
    woodwinds, 195
Krenek, Ernst, 289

laisser vibrer (l.v.), harp, 240
languages, 3
legato, 27
leger lines, 30
Liber Usualis (Solesmes Edition), 321–329
    see also neumatic notation
lip positions, woodwinds, 192

listeners' scores (electronic music), 316
l'istesso tempo, 128
lowest note, 65
Lutosławski, Witold, 172

Mahler, Gustav, 36
mallet pictograms, percussion, 211–213
manuscript, requirements for facsimile reproduction, 341–342
marimba, 221
measure numbers, 168–169
Mendel, Arthur, 35
mensural notation, ii, 330
meter
   changes, 8, 46, 146–147
   common denominator, 120
   composite, 135
   compound, 110
   irregular, 82
   reference, 90f
   simple, 110
   simultaneous speeds, etc., 108–109
metric divisions, 14
metric modulation, 92, 120
metronome, 120, 128, 159
microtones, ii, 67–71, 70–71, 76
mixed notation (old and new), 99, 142
mouthpiece pop, brass, 200
mouth positions, voice, 24
muffling, harp, 231–235
multiphonics, woodwinds, 193–195
mute positions, brass, 24
mutes, brass, 200–201
muting
   harp, 240–242
   woodwinds, 195

nasal tone, voice, 25, 296
naturals, 53–66
neumatic notation (neumes), ii, 321–329
   transcription into modern notation, 327–329
niente, 18
non arpeggio, 4
non div., 175–176
non legato, 5–6, 27
Nono, Luigi, 92–93, 288
non vibrato, 25, 80
notation
   suited for standardization (Index criteria), 336–337
   unsuited for standardization (Index criteria), 337
Notation Analysis Sheet (Index), 332–335

Notation Questionnaire (Index), 333
note-head extenders, 96
notes and rests, rhythmic alignment, 46–47
note-shapes, other than normal, 30–31, 219, 248

octave sign, 44
   in woodwind notation, 195
octave transpositions, 25
orchestra score, standard setup, 170–171
organ, notation, 274–280

page turns, 46, 163, 182
   in spatial notation, 142–143
partbooks, ii
parts, 183
   divisi, *see* divisi parts
   mute indications, 162
   page turns, 163
   in spatial notation, 145
   tempo indications, 164
   transpositions, 71–73
p.d.l.t., *see près de la table*
pedal
   effects, harp, 242–243
   indications, harp, 244–245
   indications, piano, 25, 269–272
   tones, brass, 65
Peinkofer, Karl, 216
percussion
   abbreviations, 206–209
   beater indications, 220
   effects and techniques, 221
   instrument specifications, 219
   locations on instruments, 222–224
   long-decay instruments, 220
   notation, 205–225
   note-shapes, 219
   pitched, ranges of, 213–215
   score order, 215–219
   short-decay instruments, 220
   slurs, 35
performance scores, 71, 182–183
phrasing, 26–27, 35–36
piano
   clusters, 259–260
   harmonics, 261–262
   notation, 257–273
   pedaling, 269–272
   playing inside, 262–269
   reductions, *see* keyboard reductions

pictograms, percussion, 206–213
Piston, Walter, 306
pitch, 52–80
    inflections, ii
pitches
    indeterminate or approximate, 66
    notated on a grid, 66
pizzicato, 312–314
plainchant notation, *see* neumatic notation
playing cues, 161
playing instructions, 32–33
playing scores, *see* performance scores
polymetric textures, general, 82, 116–120
    common denominator, 117
    compromise meter(s), 118–119
    rhythmic or metric cue lines, 118
polyrhythmic textures, 118
pop, brass, 200
portamento, general, 20
    voice, 296
precedente (in durational equivalents), 127
près de la table (p.d.l.t.), harp, 229, 236
proportional or proportionate notation, *see* spatial notation

quarter-tone accidentals, 67–72
    Tartini system of quarter-tone sharps, 68–69

ranges of pitched percussion, 213–215
Read, Gardner, iii
reductions (keyboard)
    choral music, 281–291
    orchestral music, 289ff
reference meters, 86–87, 90, 116ff, 120, 147
rehearsal letters/numbers, 168–169
Reimann, Aribert, 96–98
repeat bars, 34
repeated chords, measures, sections, 33–35
repeats, general, 154–155
repeat signs, 33–35
rests
    full measure, 135–136
    one or more measures in parts, 135–136
    positions in the measure, 46–47, 133–134
rhythm, 81ff, 123–151
    aperiodic, 108–109
    cues, 120, 161
rhythmic trends in 20th-century music, *see* historical survey of new rhythmic notation
ride cymbal, percussion, 224
rim shot, percussion, 224
rip, brass, 202–203

Risatti, Howard, iii
ritardando beams, *see* feathered beams
rolls, percussion, 225
Ross, Ted, 10, 44
ruff, percussion, 221
running-heads, 35
rustling glissando, harp, 238

Salzedo, Carlos, 228, 248–249
Schoenberg, Arnold, 4, 18, 297
Schuller, Gunther, 335
Schumann, Robert, 129
Schwartz, Elliott, 99, 101, 109
scordatura, harp, 246–247
score notation, details
    accidentals, 55
    conductor's signs, 158–162
    spatial notation, accel./rit., 122
    spatial notation, general, 136–145
    time signatures, placement, 177–183
score notation, succession of instruments
    band, 173–174, 176
    chamber ensembles, 172
    orchestra, 170–172, 175–176
    percussion ensemble or section, 215–219
    special setups, 172
septuplets, 129–130
Serocki, Kazimierz, 99
shaded lines (trills), 25–26
signals from player to player and to or from the conductor, 161–162
simile, 33
simple meters, 121
slapping the strings, string instruments, 315
slap pizzicato, harp, 247–248
slides, 19–21
    into a note, 64
slurred chords, 39–41
slurs, 35–44
    dotted, 35–36
    versus brackets in irregular note divisions, 26–27
    versus ties, 35–41
    in vocal music, 296–297
smacking sound
    brass, 203
    woodwinds, 195
snare-drum effect, harp, 242
solo, 175–176
spacing, 44–47, 341–342
spatial notation, 24, 61, 66, 96, 99, 109, 122, 136–145
    arrows, 142–145

beam extensions, *see* duration beams
beat indications, 159–160
black and white note-heads, 142
changes from spatial to traditional notation and vice versa, 141–142
cut-offs, 140
duration beams, 96, 99, 137–142
feathered beams (accel./rit.), 124, 141
grace notes, 140–141
note-head extenders, 96, 139–140
notes held over from line to line, 140
page turns, 143–144
performance materials, 142–145
scores, 142–145
tempo, 143
tempo changes, 143
tremolo, 141
versus traditional notation, 137–138
Sprechstimme, Sprechgesang, etc., 297–298
staccatissimo, 4–5
staccato, 6–7, 43–44
staff-lines, 22–23
standardization of new notation (Index criteria), 336–337
stem directions, 49–51
stemlets, 15–16
stems, 47–51
stick pictograms, percussion, 210–213
Stockhausen, Karlheinz, iv
Stone, Kurt, xiii, xviff, 284, 332ff
Stravinsky, Igor, 82–83, 87, 88ff, 109
striking the strings, harp, 249
string noise, harp, 238–239
strings, bowed, notation, 306–315
subito dynamic changes, 19
sub tone, clarinet, 195
syllable division in vocal music, 301
symbolic notation, 66, 99, 136–138, 141
syncopated entrance (beaming), 15
syncopation, 12, 82, 95

tablature, 330–331
    strings, 307–308
tailpiece, strings, 315
tam-tam/gong, 220
tam-tam sound, harp, 249
Tannigel, Fritz, 216
taped sound, 316–320
Tartini, Giuseppe, 68–69
tempo
    changes, 9
    different simultaneous speeds, 119–120

tempo (*continued*)
  glissando, 122
  indications, 32, 145–146, 164
  in spatial notation, 143
tenuto, 4–6, 43–44
text in vocal music, 24, 299–301
thunder effect, harp, 238–239
ties, 35–41, 43, 146
  in chords, 39–41
  in notes with accidentals, 54–55
timbral changes
  brass, 204
  indications, 24–25
  trills—brass, 77–78, 203
  trills—woodwinds, 196
timbre, ii
time signatures, 44–45, 146–147
  changes, 46, 82; *see also* meter changes
  conflicting, simultaneous, 85f
  with half beats, 183
  placement in scores and parts, 177–183
  with specified subdivisions, 158–159
  0 (''zero'' time signature), 141–142
Tishchenko, Boris, 335–336
tongued air sounds, 187
tongue positions, brass, 204
tonguing, winds, 188
traditional notation, i, iii–vi
  in new music, 108–110
  see also symbolic notation
transcription from neumatic to modern notation, 327–329
transposition
  clefs, 71–73
  in C-scores, 71–73
  horn, 199
  in parts, 71–73
  in performance scores, 71
tremolo, 74–76, 147–151
  accel./rit., 124
  hand, voice, 25
  lines, 26
  measured durationally, 148–150
  rhythmic alignment, 151
  two-staff notation, 151
triangular note-heads, 31, 219
trills, 25, 74–79
  afterbeats, 77
  endings, 77
  from line to line, 77
  with lower note, 76

    microtonal, 76
    nonroutine, 77
    timbral, 77–78, 196
    wide, 76
    woodwinds, 196
trill tremolo, 75–76, 149
    percussion, *see* rolls
tripartite progressions, 129–132
triplets, etc., *see* beaming, irregular note divisions
tuning key, harp, 229, 242, 253
tutti, 175–176
typefaces, 176

unpitched notes, 79
unpitched sounds, wind instruments, 190

valve click, brass, 204
vibrato, 26, 74, 80
vocal music
    irregular note divisions, 27, 42
    notation, 44, 55, 292–305
    slurs, 35–36
    texts, 24, 300–301
    unpitched sounds, 79
voice crossings in single-staff notation, 164–165

Wagner, Richard, 36
Walaciński, Adam, 106–107
wavy lines, 25–26
wa-wa effects, brass, 201
Webern, Anton, 36, 85f, 171
whispering
    harp, 229–231
    through an instrument, 187
whistling sounds, harp, 253–254
wind instruments, general notation, 186–190
woodwinds, notation, 191–196

x-shaped note-heads, 30–31, 219
xylophonic sound, harp, 240

"zero" (0) time signature, 141–142

DATE DUE